The Visitor's Guide
to
TURKEY

THE VISITOR'S GUIDE TO TURKEY

MPC
HUNTER
PUBLISHING INC

British Library Cataloguing in Publication Data:

Radel, Hartmut
The Visitor's guide to Turkey.—
(MPC Visitor's guides).
1. Turkey — Description and travel
— 1960 — Guide-books
I. Title II. Türkei. *English*
915.61'0438 DR416

Author: Hartmut Radel
Translator: A. J. Shackleton

Published by:
Moorland Publishing Co Ltd,
Moor Farm Road,
Airfield Estate,
Ashbourne,
Derbyshire
DE6 1HD, England

ISBN 0 86190 198 3 (paperback)
ISBN 0 86190 199 1 (hardback)

Published in the USA by
Hunter Publishing Inc,
300 Raritan Centre Parkway
CN94, Edison, NJ 08818

ISBN 1 55650 006 8

Printed in the UK by Butler and Tanner Ltd, Frome, Somerset.

Cover photograph: The Blue Mosque (Adrian Baker, International Photobank).

Black and white photographs and colour pictures of the Blue Mosque and Uçhisar were supplied by the Turkish Tourist Office.

Colour photographs of Edirne Mosque and Çanakkale were provided by Ron Scholes and the remainder of the colour photographs were supplied by Stephen Greenwood.

CONTENTS

	Introduction	7
1	Istanbul — Gateway to the Orient	28
	Touring Routes	
2	Route One: European Turkey	62
3	Route Two: Istanbul to Central Anatolia	65
4	Route Three: The Black Sea Coast Road	75
5	Route Four: The Aegean Coast	83
6	Route Five: Ancient Cities of Western Turkey	91
7	Route Six: The Mediterranean Coast	100
8	Route Seven: Southern Turkey and the Anatolian Plateaux	110
9	Route Eight: The Eastern Provinces	119
10	Cities, Towns and Places to Visit	125
11	Advice to Tourists	203
	Further Information	220
	Index	231

Key to Symbols

⌘ Items of cultural or historical interest.

A beautiful view or interesting natural phenomenon.

Touring Routes

The choice of route will depend in the first place on the amount of time available, and in the second place on what there is to see. Each of the tours described will require at least a week to do justice to it. Flying between Istanbul and Ankara will help to save travel time between the various centres. So the time available will also affect the choice of transport.

The suggested tours include all the most interesting places that are reasonably accessible by road. But travellers should not be limited by the routes given. They are designed so that they either meet or overlap each other, and travellers can combine whole routes or parts of them to create the tour of their choice.

The Touring Routes section concentrates mainly on the actual routes. Larger or more important places are dealt with in more detail in Cities, Towns and Places to Visit, where they are placed in alphabetical order. Such places are marked with an asterisk (*). The distances given below the heading to each route are cumulative, and refer to the distance from the beginning of that route.

INTRODUCTION

1. Turkey — Land of Adventure

Turkey is only a few hours by plane from London or New York, but in those few hours one is transported into another world — the Orient.

It is an often primitive world, with dripping taps, cupboard doors that jam and harsh penalties for wrong-doers. But Turkey is nonetheless a marvellous country for visitors with individual tastes.

Istanbul, for example, is a city full of wonder and mystery, with its thousands of minarets, bazaars and palaces. The Hagia Sophia and the Blue Mosque, the Golden Horn and the Bosporus, are each worth a trip for their own sake alone. The coasts are often beautiful, bordering on at least four different seas. Picturesque little ports alternate with majestic cliffs and lovely sandy beaches. The mountainous interior of Anatolia is equally fascinating and is steeped in history. It is remarkable for its wide expanses of dry steppe, the old caravanserais, the ruins of the ancient Urartu and Hittite empires, the bizarre landscape of Göreme, and the strange limestone terraces of Pamukkale — while the classical Greek and Roman sites of Ephesus, Miletus, Troy and Priene have an atmosphere all of their own.

Asia Minor might almost be called the cradle of human civilisation, ever since Noah's Ark is supposed to have rested finally on Mount Ararat. It is the meeting point for the Christian and Moslem religions, and no other country is so rich in history. A melting pot for countless warring races and cultures, it has formed the bridge between east and west since time immemorial.

The physical discomforts such as the strange diet and the extremes of climate and geography are amply compensated by the wonder and mystery of the Orient — the bartering in the market place, the women in veils, the caravan processions, the nomads in tents, and especially the marvellous Turkish hospitality. No trouble is spared to make the visitor feel welcome, creating a sense of warmth that is rarely found elsewhere.

Turkey is a land of adventure and discovery, though a visit requires a certain amount of courage and enterprise. '*Güle güle*!' as the Turks say. *Bon voyage*!

2. The Geography of Turkey

Asia Minor is bordered on all sides by seas and mountain ranges. Most of the north coast looks out across the Black Sea, while the west coast is divided from Europe by the Bosporus, the Sea of Marmara, the Dardanelles and the Aegean. The south coast is bordered by the Mediterranean, with the broad sweep of the Taurus Mountains only a few kilometres inland. The mountain ranges in the east bordering Iran and Armenia rise to heights of between 4,000m (13,120ft) and 5,000m (16,400ft). The mighty Pontic Mountains run parallel to the north coast, reaching their highest point (3,937m (12,913ft)) in the Kaçkar Daglari to the east.

If one looks at a physical map of the world, it is clear that the Turkish mountains are part of the Alpine fold mountain range that runs through southern Europe and Turkey to the Caucasus and into central Asia. They form a girdle around the central plateau of Anatolia.

At one time Anatolia (Anadolu in Turkish) referred to the whole of Asia Minor, but the name is nowadays restricted to the central plateau. In the Quaternary Period (about 12,000 years ago), this plateau rose by an average of 1,100m (3,600ft). It is an inhospitable region of arid steppes, salt wastes and bare uncharted mountains. But in the course of time the Turks have been able to reclaim some of the steppes for agricultural purposes. Thus the hot plains of Konya Ovasi are now covered in wheat, while rivers such as the Tigris and Euphrates are bordered by green fields and pastures. Even the area around Erzurum (1,950m (6,396ft)) is planted with wheat and sugar beet.

The land area of Turkey is given as 767,000sq km or 782,000sq km, (about 300,000 sq miles) depending on whether or not the European portion is included. Its land borders amount to 2,631km altogether, including 590km with the Soviet Union, 451km with Iran, 380km with Iraq, and as many as 790km with Syria. The European borders with Greece and Bulgaria are each

Amasra, on the north coast, looks out across the Black Sea

just over 200km long. The coastline reaches a total length of 6,600km. Asia Minor, which forms the majority of modern Turkey, is 1,600km from east to west and 650km from north to south.

The earth's crust is relatively thin in this part of the world. The country suffers from frequent earthquakes, some of which have been known to destroy towns. But the most destructive earthquakes occur mainly in regions not frequented by tourists. The worst-affected area is that bordering Lake Van in the far east of the country.

3. A Short History

The history of Turkey is so long and eventful that one could fill several volumes with it and still leave things out. It is a history that goes back several millennia.

At first Asia Minor was a region through which nomadic tribes passed on their way between Europe and Asia. These migrations often lasted several decades, and the people encamped on the way to help them survive periods of cold or famine. Sometimes a tribe would grow tired of wandering and settle down permanently.

The earliest signs of civilisation here go back to the sixth millennium BC, when Anatolia, Egypt and Mesopotamia appear to have formed a single cultural unit. Not without reason has it been claimed that Asia Minor was the cradle of human civilisation.

It is generally accepted that the coasts of Asia Minor were fully settled by 2500 BC, when an Indo-European people called the Hittites came south across the Caucasus from Russia. They came in several waves, and colonised the central plateau of Anatolia. A Hittite empire was founded under Labarnas, which first began to flourish in about 1500 BC. The Hittite capital of Hattusa was about 200km east of Ankara on the site known today as Bogazkale.

A number of Hittite tablets were discovered both at Bogazkale and at Kültepe near Kayseri. But it was not until relatively recently that experts first managed to read them, having at last found a means of deciphering the hieroglyphic script. Thus they were able to explain some of the secrets that surround this mysterious civilisation.

The Hittites reached their greatest period of expansion during the thirteenth century BC, when they overcame the Achaeans in the west and even managed to subjugate the Egyptians under Rameses II. For 80 years they were the undisputed rulers of the whole of the Near East.

It is difficult to appreciate the suddenness of their demise in about 1200 BC, when Asia Minor was overrun by Asiatic tribes. They conquered the Hittite capital at Hattusa, and went on to take Troy, which by now had become an important city-state.

There are no records of the period that followed these wars until the eighth century BC, when an empire was created in eastern Anatolia in the area around Lake Van. The Assyrians to the south called it Urartu, while in the Bible it is known as Ararat. By 600 BC it too had disappeared from the scene, though it left a valuable archaeological legacy, including fortifications and cave remains, strange stone statues and a number of written records.

Asia Minor was soon carved up into a patchwork of different peoples and races. Power was divided among the Phrygians, the Cimmerians, the Scythians, the Lydians, the Assyrians, the Persians and the Greeks. It was the period when the Greeks flourished in Asia Minor, founding great cities such as Miletus and Ephesus.

However, nothing could stop the inexorable advance of the Persians. Under Cyrus II they overthrew Croesus, the rich king of the Lydians, and in 513 BC Darius I crossed the Bosporus into Europe. The Greek cities along the coast of Asia Minor resisted fiercely, and for decades fought the Persians in the bitterest of struggles. But the war came to an end with the fall of Miletus in 494 BC.

The outcome in Europe was different: in 490 BC the Greeks beat the Persians in the battle of Marathon, and in 480 BC achieved an even greater victory by wiping out the Persian fleet in the bay of Salamis. But in spite of these defeats the Persians retained power in Asia Minor.

The situation remained much the same until 334 BC, when Alexander the Great crossed into Asia Minor with 35,000 soldiers, re-conquered Ephesus and Miletus, and went on to capture all the great cities of the Persian empire. It was Alexander who began the Hellenisation of Asia Minor. He first cut the famous Gordian knot at Gordium, and in 333 BC beat Darius III at Issus near the present-day town of Antakya in southern Turkey. He was eventually able to make Babylon the capital of his empire.

After Alexander's death his empire was divided among his successors. In 278 BC the Celts crossed the Bosporus and settled in Anatolia. They called themselves the Galatians — the name which is given to them in the Bible. But the wars did not end there. Rulers came and went, and one race after another gained ascendancy, so that by the time of Christ, Asia Minor was a melting pot of different peoples and races.

For a while Pergamum expanded its influence. But in 201 BC the Romans arrived. They began to conquer Asia Minor, creating the Roman province of Asia. These new masters showed no mercy towards the Greeks and other inhabitants, and there was a series of bloody rebellions; in 88 BC 80,000 Romans were killed. Almost all the important Roman generals achieved their first victories in Asia Minor, including Pompey, Lucullus, Crassus and Julius Caesar.

In AD 47 the apostle Paul began his missionary journeys through Asia Minor. In Ephesus he waged a war of words against the cult of Diana; he preached fiery sermons in the temple, which stands to this day. He is also supposed to have founded a small Christian community in the valley of Göreme. At Ephesus he was imprisoned on a pointed rock which is still to be seen between the city ruins and the sea.

During the first century AD, Asia Minor became increasingly important as the breadbasket of the Roman empire. Then on 11

The head of a statue of Alexander the Great, Istanbul Archaeological Museum

May AD 330, Emperor Constantine moved his capital from Rome to Byzantium (on the site of present-day Istanbul), which was renamed Constantinople.

Peace did not, however, last for much longer. The Visigoths were moving down into the Balkans from the north, while to the east the Persians were advancing across the plateau of Anatolia. In AD 476, while the Romans were fully occupied in warding off the Persians and the Huns on the eastern front, the city of Rome was captured by Germanic invaders. Thus ended the history of the western Roman empire.

Meanwhile the Byzantine empire continued to flourish, reaching a climax under Justinian I (AD 527-65). It was during this period that Hagia Sophia was built. But the Persians continued to make war, and took over Antioch (Antakya) in the south. In 548 the Slavs advanced towards Constantinople, and had to be bought off by Justinian at considerable cost.

In 622 the Persians were beaten back from Constantinople, and were finally routed near Nineveh. The Byzantine empire flourished again. The advancing Arabs were kept at bay, and around AD 800 Constantinople went through a period of cultural and economic expansion.

The Arabs made repeated attacks on Constantinople, which at the time was the best-fortified city in the known world. It repelled all these attacks and remained a bulwark of Christendom against the Moslem invasion of Europe. The Arabs did, however, conquer large areas of Anatolia. And it was during this period that a number of Armenian Christians fled into the strange mountains around Göreme and Ürgüp to escape the ravages of fanatical Moslems.

The first Turks had begun to move into Asia Minor about 200 years earlier. These were a group known as the Seljuks who originally came from central Asia. From AD 400-600 they remained in the area of Turkestan and Afghanistan. But then they began a great westward migration, the reason for which has yet to be explained. The Seljuks were a bloodthirsty race and were well known as outstanding warriors. It is no coincidence that Arab princes recruited their bodyguards from among their Turkish prisoners of war.

In 1071 the Seljuks under Alp Arslan routed the Byzantine army in the trackless wilderness around Manzikert (present-day Malarzgirt), not far from Lake Van. This opened up the route to the west, and the Seljuks advanced across Anatolia. They conquered Erzurum, Sebastea (Sivas), Iconium (Konya) and Trebizond (Trabzon). They even captured the former Greek (now Byzantine) cities along the Aegean coast, and built a fortification near Chalcedon (now Kadiköy) opposite Constantinople. Throughout Asia Minor Christianity gave way to Islam.

While the Seljuks prepared to attack Constantinople, the Mongols began to invade Anatolia from the east. In 1243 they routed the Seljuks at Konya, and took over what had by now become a centre of Islam. The Seljuk empire fell apart into thirty petty principalities under general Mongol domination. It was also during this period that a famous singer and religious philosopher called Jelâl ed-Dîn Rûmî founded the order of the 'whirling dervishes'.

One of these petty principalities was centred around Bursa and was ruled by the Ottoman dynasty. The Ottomans gradually increased their sphere of influence until Osman I (1290-1326) gained sovereignty over the whole of western Asia Minor. The Ottomans captured one Byzantine fort after another, and what they could not get by force they established a claim to by clever marriages of convenience.

In 1354, Süleyman crossed the Dardanelles near Troy, and began to advance into Europe. Constantinople was soon surrounded, and the Ottomans moved their capital from Bursa to Edirne (Adrianople). They were now fighting on two fronts. In Europe they overcame the Serbs at Kosovo, where their leader Sultan Murad I fell on the battlefield together with thousands of Christians and Moslems. In the east the Ottomans advanced on Ankara, capturing it from the Mongols in 1402.

For decades they continued to batter Constantinople. One only has to look at the city's massive walls today to understand why the Turks took so long to capture this eastern bulwark of Christendom. It was another 50 years before they finally succeeded. In the meantime Constantinople was gradually sapped of its strength, lacking a hinterland from which it could renew its forces. On 29 May 1453 it finally fell to the Turks.

The ruler at the time was Sultan Mehmed II 'The Conqueror'. He brought all his forces together and besieged the city for 2 months. Emperor Constantine XI stood on the battlements himself and wielded his sword to defend them. But he was felled by a poisoned arrow from the Turkish lines. His death weakened the morale of his troops. The Turks climbed up over the walls, opened the gates from inside, and butchered everyone in sight with their scimitars. They ransacked and plundered the city, destroying many priceless treasures. After a few days Mehmed II gathered his troops and began to rebuild the city.

The fall of Constantinople marked the end of the Byzantine empire. The city was renamed Istanbul, and soon became the capital of the Ottoman empire. To this day it remains the religious centre of Islam in Turkey. As a visible sign of the victory of Islam over Christianity, Hagia Sophia was turned from a church into a mosque. All the Christian paintings were whitewashed over, and four great tablets were hung in the inner chamber bearing the names of the prophet Mohammed and his successors.

The Turks finally managed to free Asia Minor from Mongol control. Selim I (1512-20) drove them right out of the Near East, and also forced the Arabs to retreat. Egypt, Syria and Mesopotamia came under Turkish domination. Süleyman II 'The Great' (1520-66) extended the empire north-westwards. He overran Belgrade, advanced through Hungary and by 1529 was encamped near Vienna. He was the most powerful Ottoman ruler, with an empire stretching from Vienna to Baghdad and from the Adriatic to the Black Sea.

All this was achieved at the cost of many thousands of lives. Thousands more languished in Turkish dungeons; and even the rulers themselves paid with their lives, for none of them died natural deaths. If they did not die in battle, they were poisoned, strangled or stabbed. These crimes were instigated by close colleagues, often by the rulers' own favourite concubines. Even the rulers' sons were often secretly killed to make way for more favoured heirs. No wonder the sultans later hid their crown princes in a monastery on the so-called Princes' Islands in the Sea of Marmara, to protect them from potential assassins until the time came for them to take over the reins of power.

All this political intrigue in the Topkapi (sultan's palace) weakened the empire from the inside. Quite apart from that, the peoples they had conquered allied themselves with the French, the English, the Hapsburgs in Austria and the powerful city-state of Venice.

In 1683 the Turks made a final sweep through Europe, and for 2 months laid siege to Vienna. The Viennese were about to capitulate when relief forces arrived led by Charles of Lorraine and John Sobieski of Poland. The Turks put up a fierce struggle, but the anger of the Christian cavalry proved too much for them. In the terrible carnage which followed the imperial armies held their ground and the Turks were quickly dispersed. They fled in haste, leaving behind hundreds of sacks of coffee. This is supposed to have been what started coffee drinking in Europe!

In 1697 Prince Eugene's troops inflicted a severe blow on the Turks at Zenta. After that the Balkan peoples rose up against their Turkish oppressors, who were being gradually squeezed out of south-eastern Europe. In 1787 the Russians declared war on them, and in 1792 forced them to sign the Treaty of Jassy. In 1798 the young Napoléon Bonaparte attacked the Turks in Egypt.

In the meantime murder and intrigue continued in the Topkapi. The sultans and their rivals spared no one, least of all each other, in their struggles for power. Patricide and fratricide were the order of the day. In 1807 Chief Sultan Selim III was hanged on the orders of Mustafa IV, which sparked off rebellions throughout the empire. Only a year later Mustafa himself was overthrown.

Under Mahmud II there was a brief period of internal reform in which the army was reorganised under the leadership of German officers such as Helmut von Moltke. But the carnage continued. In 1811 Sultan Mehmed Ali got rid of the rebellious Mameluke princes at a party in Cairo. Rulers who avoided drinking poison risked being stabbed to death. The sultans also had problems controlling the janizaries — the Ottomans' elite troops — so much so that they abolished them in 1826.

In the meantime the empire was falling apart. Enemies stood ready to attack on all borders — the Russians in the north, the Serbs and Greeks in the west. The Turkish Mediterranean fleet was wiped out by the combined forces of Britain, France and Russia. The Syrians invaded from the south and captured Konya. The British reached the Dardanelles and the Russians cut off Istanbul. In 1895 there was a plan to divide up Turkey, which was only prevented by German intervention.

1900 saw the rise of the so-called Young Turk reformers, who opposed the regime of the sultans. Their intention was to create a new Turkish state free of corruption and despotism. Some bloody conflicts ensued; the Young Turks suffered vigorous persecution, but retaliated with a concerted guerrilla campaign. In Adana, for example, they beheaded a whole series of government officials. People in Europe talked of the 'sick man of the Bosporus'.

In 1914 the outbreak of World War I put an end to the Young Turk reforms. Turkey fought on the side of Germany, and at first enjoyed considerable success. The British and the French suffered crushing defeats in the Dardanelles and around Gallipoli (Gelibolu). But the Russians proved more successful; they came in through Armenia and captured Trabzon (Trebizond), Erzurum and Bitlis in the east.

The turning point came in 1916, when the Arabs declared their independence and prepared to attack Turkey. In 1917, with the help of the British, they captured Baghdad and began to advance northwards through Mesopotamia. Colonel T. E. Lawrence joined the Arab nomads and led them in fighting the Turks in the desert.

1918 saw the death of the Turkish leader Mehmed V. He was succeeded by his brother Mehmed VI, who reigned 4 years and was the last of the Turkish sultans. By autumn the Palestinian front had collapsed; on 30 October the sultan requested a ceasefire and opened up the Dardanelles and the Bosporus. The Allied warships advanced on Istanbul and anchored in the Golden Horn, as if to set the seal on their victory.

But this was not the end of the war. Istanbul remained under Allied control; the Arab territories were occupied by the British and French; the Italians landed at Antalya and took over south-west Anatolia; the Greeks occupied Bursa and Izmir (Smyrna).

Rebels in Anatolia began a nationalist campaign against the foreign occupying forces and the Turkish government in Istanbul. The Grand Vizier sent out General Mustafa Kemal to quell this resistance, but the general changed sides and proclaimed himself the nationalist leader. He convened conferences at Erzurum and Sivas to discuss Turkish sovereignty. Then in 1920 an alternative government was elected by a nationalist assembly at Ankara, which rejected the humiliating conditions imposed on the Turks by the Treaty of Sèvres.

The sultan in Istanbul condemned Kemal to death as a traitor, but Kemal began his own negotiations with the occupying forces. In 1921 the Italians withdrew from Anatolia, the French from Cicilia and the Russians from Batumi.

Only the Greeks refused to negotiate, having plans for a new Hellenistic empire. This resulted in war. The Greeks advanced into Anatolia, but in 1922 were repulsed by the nationalists at the River Sakarya. The nationalists pushed them back towards the coast and eventually captured Bursa and Izmir, driving the Greeks out of Asia Minor altogether.

In November 1922 the Turkish nationalists delivered the decisive blow to the sultan's regime, and Mustafa Kemal announced the end of the sultanate. The nationalists surrounded the Topkapi; Mehmed VI fled to the harbour through a secret subterranean passage, and managed to escape on a British ship.

Kemal made Ankara his capital and negotiated with the Allies for peace; the Treaty of Lausanne reversed the harsh requirements imposed by the Treaty of Sèvres. In 1923 Turkey was declared a republic and the Allies withdrew altogether. In 1924 all the remaining members of the Ottoman dynasty were forced into exile. Mustafa Kemal-Pasa became the country's first president and adopted the name Atatürk or 'Father of the Turks'. His comrade-at-arms Imet Inönü became the first prime minister.

In 1927 Atatürk was re-elected president, and embarked on a programme of sweeping reforms designed to bring Turkey into line with twentieth-century Europe. He introduced the Gregorian calendar and the 7-day week, with Sunday as the statutory rest day. He banned polygamy, granting women the vote and professional equality with men. He reformed the legal system, modelling it on the Italian, Swiss and German codes of law. The fez was replaced by the more practical European hat. Since 1928 Turkish has been written in Roman instead of in Arabic characters. All Turks are now obliged to adopt a surname and to send their

Istanbul: the morning rush hour

children to school.

The Turkish capital of Ankara was previously only a small town on the arid steppes of central Anatolia. But thanks to Atatürk it has now become a large modern city full of skyscrapers and parks laid out with lakes and fountains.

Islam is no longer the state religion — a reform that understandably met with much opposition all over the country. The religious leaders have never forgiven Atatürk for disestablishing Islam. Istanbul was the main centre of Moslem resistance; the 'whirling dervishes' also tried to prevent reform by committing acts of terrorism and stirring up discontent among the people. But Atatürk was not to be deterred.

In 1925 and 1930 the Kurds in the eastern mountains staged a rebellion. On each occasion Atatürk retaliated with a bloody purge — a vicious act of revenge, designed to deter any further opposition to his regime.

From 1930 onwards Atatürk entered into pacts of friendship with other countries, including Greece, Rumania, Bulgaria, Persia, Iraq and Afghanistan. His successor Imet Inönü continued this policy by making pacts with Britain (1939), France (1941) and Germany.

Atatürk died on 10 November 1938 aged 57. Turkey had lost a national hero. Mustafa Kemal-Pasa had had a mausoleum built for himself on a hill overlooking Ankara, and this became the scene of some considerable drama. For weeks men and women filed past him in tears to pay their last respects. Nomads came from all over the country — from the Black Sea coast and the saltmarshes of Konya to the lonely eastern fastnesses around Lake Van. They revered him like a god, and yet few understood the reforms he had made. Turkey is still full of reminders of Atatürk, the most important figure in modern Turkish history. He is represented in massive portraits, statues and illuminated pictures in cities all over Turkey.

Turkey remained neutral during most of World War II, and did not declare war on Germany until 25 February 1945. By this time it was of little significance, since both Germany and Japan were well on the road to defeat. Turkey's reason for declaring war was to make its position stronger in relation to Russia, which was trying to gain a foothold in the Turkish straits. Turkey sought the protection of the western powers, and was one of the first countries to join the NATO pact.

In 1950 President Imet Inönü was replaced by Celal Bayar, who was re-elected for a third term in 1957. 1960 was a year of internal political crisis. On 28 April students demonstrated in the streets, and there were some bloody clashes with the police. Martial law was declared in the two university cities of Ankara and Istanbul.

On 27 May 1960 the army took over. They ousted the civilian government and placed their commander-in-chief General Cemal Gürsel in charge. Over 6,000 officers were arrested, together with the President Celal Bayar, Prime Minister Menderes and his Cabinet.

At a mass trial in 1961, fifteen people were condemned to death and thirty-one to life imprisonment. Celal Bayar, the once-celebrated president, was committed to gaol for life, but was pardoned a year later. Prime Minister Menderes was hanged together with his foreign minister Zorlu and his finance minister Polatkan. The other twelve death sentences were commuted to life imprisonment.

In 1961 a new constitution was declared, and Turkey became a parliamentary republic. The internal political situation improved for some years.

In 1971 things became difficult again when some American soldiers were abducted by terrorists and the Israeli ambassador was kidnapped and murdered. In 1972 the army placed guards on all public buildings such as post offices, ministries, banks, airports, stations etc. Regimes came and went in close succession. The country has since returned to parliamentary democracy, albeit with the support of the military.

But tourists will notice little of the country's present political unrest, except perhaps the army presence in the streets. The army has become extremely vigilant in its eagerness to nip any rebellion in the bud.

4. Climate and Travel

Turkey is divided into three main climatic zones: the central plateau, the north coast and the west and south coasts. Of these the central plateau has a continental climate, with hot summers and cold winters in which temperatures may drop as low as –35°C (–1°F).

The Black Sea coast also has rather cold winters, with temperatures dropping to –20°C (14°F). The summers there are hot, but also have plenty of rain.

The coasts of the Mediterranean, the Aegean and the Sea of Marmara enjoy a Mediterranean climate, with mild winters and hot dry summers. Most of the tourist centres along the west and south coasts come within this more favoured climatic region. In July and August, however, temperatures can sometimes climb as high as 40°C (104°F).

The best time to travel is between May and October. Travellers who prefer to avoid the heat should note that September can also be very hot, especially inland. Spring is the best time for seeing the Mediterranean flowers in all their glory. Only the central plateau remains obstinately bare of vegetation. Autumn provides a rich harvest of fruit.

Average temperatures in Anatolia are somewhat distorted by the climatic extremes. Diyarbakir has a yearly average of only 15.8°C (60°F), while Ankara has 11.7°C (53°F) and Erzurum only 5.9°C (42°F).This hides the fact that all three cities can still be

Ayvalik on the Aegean coast enjoys a warm climate

unpleasantly hot in September. In Diyarbakir the extremes are 46°C (115°F) and –24°C (10°F); in Ankara 38°C (100°F) and –25°C (9°F); in Erzurum 34°C (93°F) and –30°C (4°F). Istanbul benefits somewhat from Mediterranean influence, but still has extremes of 39°C (102°F) in summer and –16°C (18°F) in winter.

All regions apart from the north coast receive most of their rain between the months of October and February. The rest of the year is normally dry, and travellers can count on blue skies for the majority of their trip.

However, the climatic variation provides an additional excitement of its own. It is only a day's trip from the heat of the coast around Antalya to the eternal snows of the nearby Taurus Mountains. Visitors can run around in the snow and return the same day to bathe in the warm waters of the Mediterranean.

5. The People of Turkey

Asia Minor forms a bridge between Asia and Europe, and throughout history the land had been settled by numerous different races and cultures — Phrygians, Hittites, Celts, Huns,

Greeks, Arabs, Romans, Persians and Turks, to name only a few. They took over the land, and either preserved their own culture or mingled with the people around them. The result was a melting pot of different peoples and cultures, and the racial differences are still apparent as one travels through Turkey from west to east.

Of the present population of 51 million, 91 per cent are Turks, 7 per cent Kurds, 1.3 per cent Arabs and 0.3 per cent Greeks. The remainder is made up of small pockets of Circassians, Armenians, Jews and Georgians. The majority religion is Islam; 1 per cent of the population are Christians and 0.2 per cent are Jews.

The Armenians

The majority of Armenians are Christians. They suffered considerable persecution from the Seljuks and the Ottomans, who attempted to exterminate them. But since the founding of a Turkish republic, the Armenians have remained unmolested. Of the 4,700 Armenians remaining, the majority live in Istanbul, while the rest live in and around Adana and Iskenderun.

The Greeks

The Greeks are no longer as powerful in Turkey as they once were. At the end of World War I, when the Turks were in considerable disarray, the Greeks attempted to take over the country. But the Turkish nationalists gathered under the leadership of Kemal Atatürk and drove the Greeks out of Asia Minor. Ever since then relations between the two countries have been dogged by a simmering hostility that has occasionally flared up into war over the disputed territory of Cyprus. There are Greeks still living in Istanbul and along the Aegean coast, constituting a small national minority.

The Kurds

The large Kurdish minority live in the far east of Turkey. Their villages are to be found on the undulating steppes of eastern Anatolia, in the basin around Lake Van and in the mountains along the Russian, Iranian and Iraqi borders. Some of the Kurds live out beyond these borders.

The Kurds have managed to hold on to their traditional way of life. They strongly resisted numerous attempts by Kemal Atatürk to assimilate them into Turkish society. The Turkish government troops had enormous problems trying to break their resistance in the trackless wastes of the east. There were a number of bloody skirmishes, and some horrific acts of retribution.

Atatürk in desperation banished them from their homeland. Hundreds of thousands of Kurds were uprooted and forced to resettle in western Anatolia. But even this did not break their resolve. The rebellious Kurds sought the support of the Soviet Union in their attempts to turn their homeland into an autonomous Kurdish state outside the Turkish republic.

This move was blocked in 1961 by a further resettlement programme. Nowadays the Kurds are being accused of underground terrorist activities including bomb attacks and kidnappings, which they are allegedly using to undermine the Turkish state.

Visitors usually find the Kurds a rather sombre people, who are somewhat shy of strangers and they react very strongly against impoliteness. Stabbings are still fairly frequent because the vendetta is still part of their way of life. The Kurds are very poor. Many still pursue a nomadic existence. It happens sometimes that tourists camping or caravanning in the uninhabited region around Lake Van are robbed by a band of Kurds.

But visitors who are received by the Kurds are treated with enormous hospitality. A handshake or an invitation to *çay* (tea) is a sure sign of their willingness to be friendly. This is usually followed by an invitation to a yogurt meal in which everyone eats out of the same pot. Visitors must overcome any squeamishness, since refusal to eat is a terrible insult to the host.

In the winter, many of the nomadic Kurds move with their herds of sheep, cattle and camels to winter quarters on the coast or on the plateau. Then in the spring they take down their black tents and simple wooden huts, and wander off into the mountains again. Their routes take them past salt lakes such as the Tuz Gölü where they collect salt to sell in the towns.

The Turks

Several million Turks are still semi-nomadic. In the summer whole families move up into the mountains where they live in primitive tents. Even city dwellers think it important to have a summer residence in the country. The government makes strenuous efforts to settle the nomads and semi-nomads. They have built permanent settlements for them around Ankara, in the Taurus Mountains and along the Black Sea coast. These consist of whole villages of small concrete huts.

National costume from the Erzurum province

The Muhacirs

This interesting minority originally consisted of Moslem refugees from the Balkans, who in the eighteenth century sought refuge in Asia Minor as the Ottoman empire disintegrated. In the nineteenth century they were joined by Tartars expelled by the Russians from the Crimean peninsula and the steppes between the Black Sea and the Caspian Sea. These in turn were joined by Circassians and Cossacks, who similarly sought refuge in Turkey.

The Turks resettled them mostly in areas that were largely uninhabited, such as the steppes of Anatolia, the plains of Pamphylia and Cicilia, and the European province of Thrace. The Muhacirs have proved to be skilful farmers and have thus benefitted the Turkish economy.

Education

The general level of education is improving. Out of 51 million inhabitants, the literacy rate is moving towards 86 per cent.

Of the foreign languages spoken, English and German are the

most frequent. English is taught as the first foreign language, while German is spoken by many Turks who have worked in Germany as *Gastarbeiter* ('guest workers'). French is the third foreign language.

The Main Centres of Population
The biggest city is Istanbul, with a population of 5½ million. This is followed by Ankara, with 2,880,000 inhabitants. Other centres of population include Izmir (1,800,000), Adana (1,200,000), Kayseri (500,000), Bursa (850,000), Eskisehir (400,000), and Konya (900,000).

6. Fauna and Flora

Wild Animals
Turkey has a large number of carnivorous species that are not found in Europe. There is, for example, the so-called Turkish leopard, which lives mostly in the area around Antalya known as the Turkish Riviera. It can also be found around the towns of Burdur, Erzurum, Bodrum, Bursa and Siirt.

There are jackals and hyenas in the salt wastes around Konya, in eastern Anatolia and along the Syrian border. They are shy of human beings and are not often seen, but can frequently be heard howling at night. Other unusual animals to be found are the sable and the lynx. The lynx is rare these days, but can still be found in the Pontic and Taurus Mountains and around Bolu and Kastamonu.

Bears are still common in the Taurus Mountains, and like foxes in Britain are hunted by the Turkish upper classes. Bears normally avoid human company, but can be dangerous if one actually meets them. If bears block the way on some lonely mountain pass, then one should keep calm, turn off the engine and wait patiently until they leave. Under no circumstances should one leave the vehicle!

Wolves are still common, especially north and south of Van. They also hunt in packs across the central steppes. In harsh winters they come close to human habitations. The nomads either shoot at them or use their dogs to scare them away. One sometimes reads of packs of wolves that have killed flocks of sheep or have attacked children.

Apart from the wild boar and the wild goat, many of the other animals are similar to those in Britain and the United States including roe and fallow deer, rabbits and hares, squirrels, foxes and badgers, martens, weasels and stoats. They live all over Turkey, but especially in the forests along the Aegean and Black Sea coasts.

One speciality is the mountain goat or ibex, which ranges between Izmir and the Dardanelles in the west, and around Kars, Van and Siirt in the east. The chameleon is most at home in the rocky steppes from Balikesir as far as Malatya. Gazelles prefer steppes and open woodland, but have been decimated by the local population. The so-called red sheep is a kind of mouflon that lives around Diyarbakir and on the northern flanks of the Taurus Mountains towards Konya.

Domestic Animals

Dogs and cats are the two main pets. The long-haired Angora cat originated in the area around Kayseri, though its name comes from an old name for Ankara.

The mule is still the chief means of transport in Turkey, closely followed by the donkey. Camels are uncommon, though caravans can be seen near Denizli and Elâzig, in the salt wastes around Konya, south of Izmir and in the area around Antakya. Most people in the countryside live from livestock such as sheep, cattle and goats.

Birds

Common birds of prey include eagles, hawks and falcons. There are numerous wild geese and ducks along the banks of the rivers. Wild swans are less common, and are mostly found around Lake Van, near Edirne and along rivers such as the Maritsa and the Meriç. Some birds have become pests, such as snipe, partridges, quails, starlings and pigeons. But the rock doves that live in the karst landscape of Göreme and Ürgüp are now a protected species.

Marine Life

The coastal waters are full of fish, the most interesting of which are the swordfish and tuna that are caught in the Mediterranean and Aegean. Dolphins can often be seen leaping around boats on the Black Sea.

Vegetation

Central Turkey consists mostly of steppes, which make up 24 per cent of the land surface. The commonest plants include dry grasses, thistles, wormwoods and spurges. Oases can be recognised by the presence of trees and green grass.

Forests are less common, making up only 13 per cent of the land surface, so wood is in short supply. Most of the forests are in regions near the coast. In the Pontic Mountains they consist mostly of beech and fir, while in the Taurus Mountains they are of pine, juniper and cedar; the Aegean coast is characterised by fig, pine and chestnut. There are mulberry trees in Thrace and in southern Anatolia, while the date palm grows along the Turkish Riviera. The Mediterranean coast is lined with cotton plantations, and vast areas along the coast and in the Taurus Mountains are being taken over for forestry. This could easily bring about a change in the climate, with increased rainfall.

At harvest time the markets are inundated with all kinds of fruit, including oranges, mandarins, lemons, grapes, peaches, apricots, bananas, figs, apples, pears, pomegranates, walnuts, chestnuts and olives.

The vegetation generally is typical of the Mediterranean, including cacti, agaves, orchids, oleander, rosemary, lavender, myrtle, broom, and sage. Thyme and evergreen buckthorn also thrive on the dry soils. The laburnum and strawberry trees create a marvellous display of colour in the spring.

Forests like this one at Lake Abant, Bolu, are rare in Turkey

1 ISTANBUL — GATEWAY TO THE ORIENT

Istanbul is not only the largest city in Turkey, but is also the most beautiful and the most colourful. It has a style all of its own that compares with that of no other metropolis on the European continent.

It is full of eastern promise, with its markets crowded with bustling humanity. The noise, the dust, the smoke and the traffic are amply compensated for by the oriental music, the prayers of the Imams from the minarets, the beautiful forest of domes, minarets, towers and walls, and the Golden Horn with its harbour full of ships. All this combines to make Istanbul one of the most exotic places in the world. Arab scholars have called it the 'mother of the world', while Alexander von Humboldt describes it as one of the world's three most beautiful cities.

The city is divided into three main parts. The first is the old city of **Stambul** on the site of the former imperial city of Byzantium, sandwiched between the Golden Horn and the Sea of Marmara. On the opposite side of the Golden Horn is the newer area of **Beyoglu**, which incorporates the former suburbs of Galata and Pera. It is now mostly occupied by office buildings and diplomatic headquarters. The third part is **Üsküdar**, the old city of Scutari, which is situated on the Asian side of the Bosporus.

Old Istanbul, like Rome, is situated on seven hills, each of which is crowned by a mosque. Beyoglu has also been built according to a well-ordered plan, the main traffic routes being the Istiklâl Caddesi and the Pera Road.

The City's Early History

The beginnings of the Greek city of Byzantion lie shrouded in mystery, though it is traditionally supposed to have been founded in 658 BC. The founders were Greeks from Megara, who are supposed to have begun a colony here on the instructions of the oracle at Delphi.

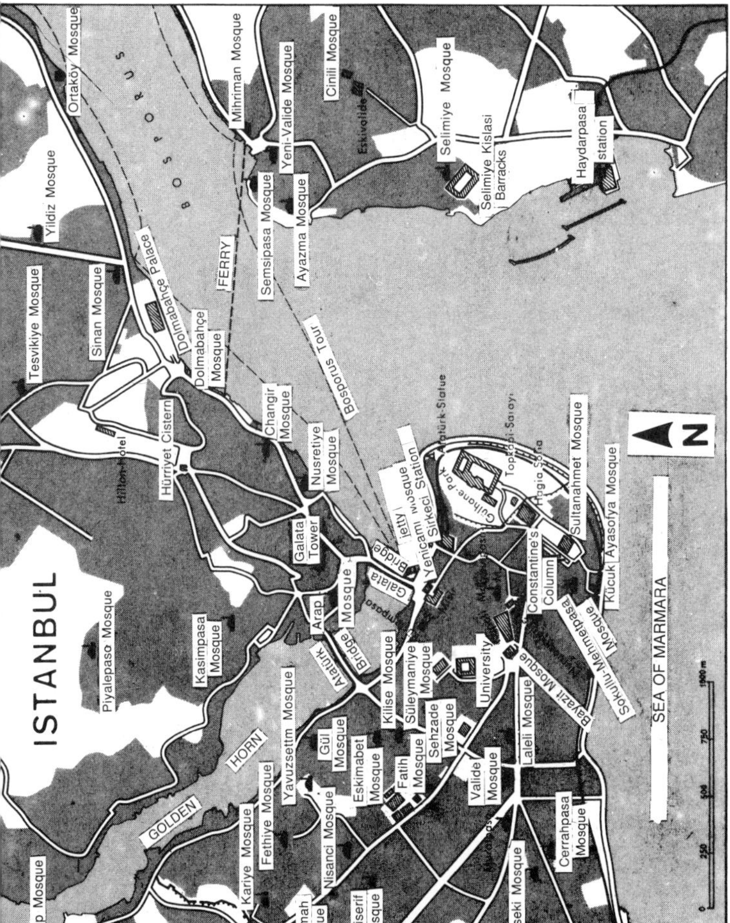
ISTANBUL
Eyüp Mosque
GOLDEN
HORN
Piyalepasa Mosque
Kasimpasa Mosque
Tesvikiye Mosque
Sinan Mosque
Yildiz Mosque
Ortaköy Mosque
BOSPORUS
Dolmabahçe Palace
Dolmabahçe Mosque
FERRY
Mihriman Mosque
Semsipasa Mosque
Yeni-Valide Mosque
Ayazma Mosque
Cinili Mosque
Selimiye Mosque
Selimiye Kislasi Barracks
Haydarpasa station
Hürriyet Cistern
Hilton Hotel
Changir Mosque
Bosporus Tour
Nusretiye Mosque
Galata Tower
Galata Bridge
Jetty
Yenicami Mosque
Sirkeci Station
Atatürk Statue
Topkapi Sarayi
Gülhane Park
Hagia Sofia
Sultanahmet Mosque
Kücük Ayasofya Mosque
Constantine's Column
Sokullu-Mehmetpasa Mosque
Bayazit Mosque
University
Laleli Mosque
Süleymaniye Mosque
Kilise Mosque
Arap Mosque
Atatürk Bridge
Yavuzsettm Mosque
Gül Mosque
Sehzade Mosque
Fatih Mosque
Eskimabet Mosque
Valide Mosque
Fethiye Mosque
Kariye Mosque
Nisanci Mosque
Mihrimah Mosque
Hirkaiserif Mosque
Haseki Mosque
Cerrahpasa Mosque
Hekimoglu Alipasa Mosque
Kocomustafapasa Mosque
Imrahor Mosque
SEA OF MARMARA
N
0 250 500 750 1000 m

According to legend the fortified city was attacked by Philip of Macedon in 340 BC. The moon is said to have appeared from behind the clouds, allowing the inhabitants to pre-empt the attack and save the city. This is supposed to be the reason why the crescent was adopted as the symbol of the city.

When the Romans extended their empire eastwards, the city was conquered and destroyed by Septimius Severus. But his son Bassianus had it rebuilt and reinstated as a city. The Roman city of Byzantium was protected by a new wall, and included a forum, a hippodrome and a large number of temples and palaces.

In the fourth century AD Emperor Constantine recognised the city's strategic importance, and was so struck by its beautiful setting that he moved his imperial palace from Rome. He called the city New Rome, and it became the new capital of the Roman empire. It was during this period that the city was rebuilt according to a plan that can still be seen to this day. A new fortification was built nearly 3km further to the west, and the city was divided into thirteen districts.

The city was renamed Constantinople. In the following century it was further extended under Theodosius (AD 408-50), though this effectively only completed the work begun by Constantine. Indeed, the walls remained substantially unchanged until the ninth century. In 439 a sea wall was built, creating a girdle around the whole city, and in 447 a ditch and a second wall were constructed outside the existing land fortifications. These reinforcements were designed to repel the attacks of the Huns and the Goths who were sweeping across Europe. They are still the first part of the old city that the visitor encounters when approaching by land from the west.

During the centuries which followed, different parts of the Empire were overrun by invaders, and the city was besieged by many enemies, including the Arabs, the Persians and the Avars. But it survived every onslaught, thanks to its impenetrable defences.

Then between 817 and 1057 the city flourished again under the emperors of the Macedonian dynasty, reaching the pinnacle of its development. The Bulgars and Moravians became Byzantine subjects and were converted to Christianity. Meanwhile the city's influence spread through both Asia and Europe, far beyond the boundaries of the Byzantine empire. The cathedral of Hagia Sophia became the model for churches as far afield as Italy, France and Russia, many of which look exactly like it.

Rumeli Hisari, Istanbul — Rumelian fortress built by Fatih Sultan Mehmet in 1452 prior to the city's conquest

In the eleventh century a crisis occurred, and the city went into a decline. It was eventually captured by crusaders in the Fourth Crusade. The Byzantine empire was reinstated under Michael Palaeologus, but it was only a shadow of its former self. It was impoverished by the ravages of war, and the population had dropped to 100,000. The trade routes had meanwhile been taken over by the Venetians and Genoans.

1453 saw the decisive battle between the 45-year-old emperor Constantine XI and the 19-year-old Turkish ruler Mehmed II. The Turks had an army of 200,000, while Constantine had no more than 20,000 Greek troops. Not only did the Turks have a massive numerical advantage, but they also had a new form of weapon called a cannon. The Greeks had drawn an iron chain across the Bosporus to prevent ships using it. But the Turks bypassed it by dragging their ships overland on rollers and relaunching them on the Golden Horn. They captured Constantinople at last, setting the seal on the end of the Byzantine empire.

The city of Istanbul became the capital of the mighty Ottoman empire, which was to last until 1918.

Tours of the City

Istanbul makes a wonderful starting point for a Turkish holiday. But the city can be confusing at first. The noise of the traffic and the maze of narrow streets can be difficult to cope with for the first few days. And on top of that there are problems with the language.

So it is essential to prepare for the visit well in advance. This includes making a hotel booking and consulting maps and guides to work out what to visit in the city. Before leaving the hotel, it is important to work out where it is on the map so that it is possible to find it again in the evening!

Day One

Galata Bridge • Topkapi • Hagia Sophia • Yerebatan Cistern • Hippodrome • Blue Mosque

Wherever the hotel is located, the best place to start is the **Galata Bridge**, which spans the Golden Horn, linking the old city of Stambul with Galata and the modern suburbs. This historic bridge is crossed by an endless stream of cars and pedestrians, and at one time was the only bridge over the Golden Horn. This is no longer the case, but the Galata Bridge is still thought of as the centre of the city.

The bridge is 468m (1,535ft) long and 26m (85ft) wide. It is made of steel and rests on floating pontoons. It was built in 3 years (1909-12) by a German firm of manufacturers. The central section can be swung aside to let ships in and out. The part of the Golden Horn adjoining the Bosporus is known as the outer harbour, while the area between the Galata Bridge and the Atatürk Bridge is called the inner harbour. The innermost section is reserved for the Turkish navy.

The piers at either end of the bridge are for boats to Üsküdar on the Asian shore, to other places along the Bosporus, to the Princes' Islands and to ports across the Sea of Marmara. The piers are covered with a colourful cross-section of humanity, including old fishermen, and women in veils. The milling crowds around the invitingly decorated fruit and fish stalls provide a rich field of subjects for photographers. There are cafés under the arches of the bridge, where the people withdraw to smoke their hookahs and sip *çay* (sweet tea) in the shade.

From the middle of the bridge there is a comprehensive view of

The Blue Mosque, Istanbul

Edirne Mosque

Traditional basket-making, near Manisa

View from the fortress at Alanya

the old city of **Stambul**. In a large park to the left is the **Topkapi**. Straight ahead at the end of the bridge is the **Yeni Valide Mosque**, and behind it the **Egyptian Bazaar**. The **Grand Bazaar** is further up. The scene is dominated by the **Süleymaniye Mosque** to the right. The famous Blue Mosque is not visible from here, as it looks out across the Bosporus, welcoming ships approaching from the south. The end of the Golden Horn is overlooked by **Eyüp Cemetery**.

The view of **Galata** on the opposite bank is equally as interesting. It is dominated by the **Galata Tower**, a relic of the former Genoese fortifications. To the right is Galata Quay, where all the overseas ships dock. The bridge leads directly into Karaköy Square, at the opposite end of which is the Galata Road leading to the Üsküdar ferry.

The suggested route starts at the Stambul end of the Galata Bridge by the **Yeni Valide Mosque**. It is best to visit this on the way back during evening prayer. The route goes round the back of the mosque along the Hamidiye Caddesi, which goes straight on up to the Topkapi. The route turns right below the palace wall and comes out into the Ayasofya Meydani or Hagia Sophia Square.

One can spend a whole day visiting the buildings around this square. The old city of Istanbul has as many as 247 large mosques and 664 small ones, plus three enormous shopping areas. Each bazaar consists of a maze of passages, with over 4,000 stalls altogether, selling all kinds of oriental goods. However, the goods are much cheaper in the bazaars off the Istiklâl Caddesi in Beyoglu and in the Cumhuriyet Caddesi beyond the Taksim Square.

The history of the many-chambered **Topkapi** is shrouded in mystery and romance. Also known as the Sultan's Palace or Seraglio, it has been the inspiration for countless stories and tales in which elements of fact, fantasy and tradition are gloriously woven together. These include works such as Mozart's opera *Die Entführung aus dem Serail* ('*The Abduction from the Seraglio*') and Ambler's detective thriller *Topkapi*.

The route goes left round the Hagia Sophia, and eventually arrives at the Babihumayun or Sultan's Gate — the entrance to the park that surrounds the Topkapi. A small building in front of the gate contains the city's best-preserved covered well. It is known as **Ahmed III's Well**, and was constructed in 1728. Visitors should note that the Sultan's Palace is closed on

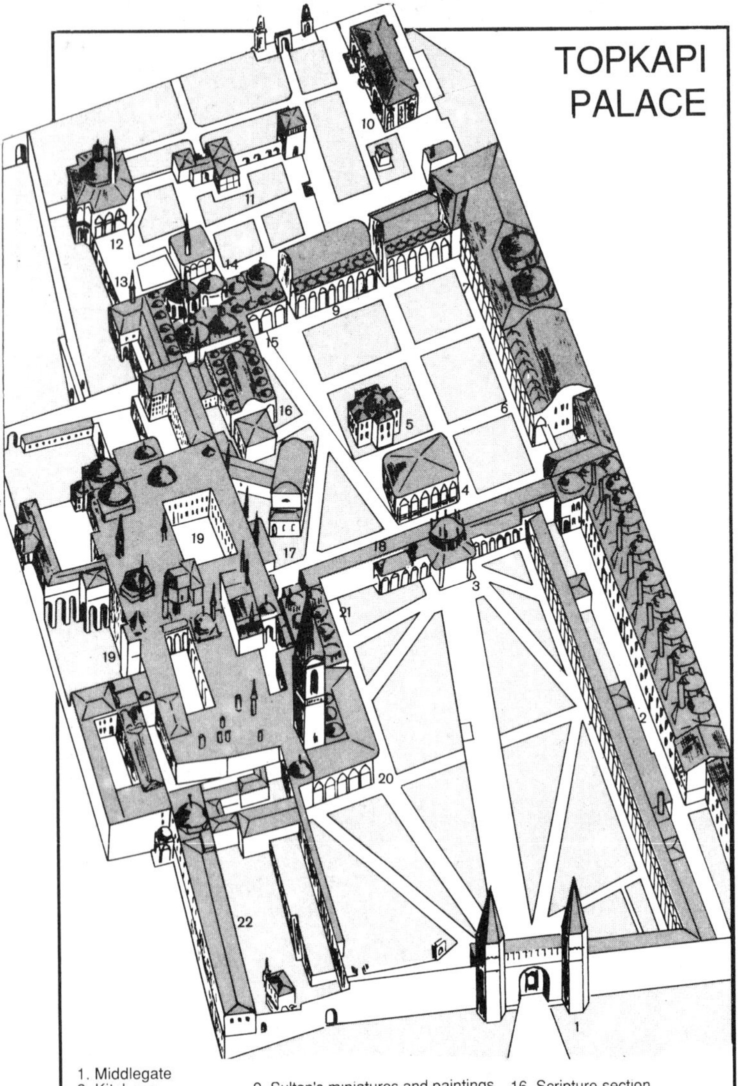

1. Middlegate
2. Kitchens
3. Gate of Felicity
4. Throne room
5. Palace library
6. Sultan's robes
7. Treasury
8. Management office
9. Sultan's miniatures and paintings
10. Mecidiye pavilion
11. Safa Mosque
12. Baghdad pavilion
13. Circumcision room
14. Revan pavilion
15. Hall of the Prophet
16. Scripture section
17. Library
18. Turkish Embroideries
19. Harem
20. Reception hall
21. Armoury collection
22. Private stable of the Seraglio

Pavilion of the Sacred Mantle, Topkapi

Tuesdays. Entrance tickets can be obtained from the booth just in front of the gate.

It is a further 300m walk from the gate to the main palace entrance. To the left is the famous **Executioner's Well**, where the sultan had all traitors beheaded. The present main entrance is known as the middle gate, because at one time it divided the inner from the outer seraglio. It now forms the entrance to the first of three courtyards.

To the left of the courtyard is a 42m (138ft) high tower that goes back to the sixteenth century. The building in front of it is the **Divan**, where the Grand Viziers held their councils of state. If one goes into the inner chamber, one can see a large grille high up in one of the walls. The sultan could hide behind here and eavesdrop on what was being said in the chamber. The next room is the reception hall, where ambassadors presented their formal requests. The other rooms are also open to the public, and contain collections of porcelain and weaponry.

The building next to the Divan is the famous **Harem**, for which a second entrance fee is charged. The Harem has become a place of pilgrimage for tourists lured by colourful tales of kidnapped princesses, eunuchs and tragic love affairs. It contains some beautiful porcelain collections, but is chiefly remembered as the place where the sultan kept his wives, sometimes voluntarily and sometimes against their will. The first-ever foreign visitor to the Harem was Queen Elizabeth II on a state visit to Turkey in 1971. The Turkish government granted her a special favour by allowing her to explore the labyrinthine passages of the former women's quarters.

On the opposite side of the courtyard are the many-domed palace kitchens, where twenty-four ovens were used to make meals for about 20,000 beggars in the city.

The second courtyard is smaller, and is entered via the so-called **Gate of Felicity**. A pavilion in the centre contains the throne room, where Süleyman the Great used to hold audiences. He sat on a magnificent throne covered by a canopy. Foreign suppliants were unable to see him as he used to hide behind a grille. A second pavilion used to house the palace library (1719). Neither pavilion is open to the public.

But the rooms around the courtyard are very much worth seeing. They contain a massive collection of oriental treasures — carpets, porcelain, uniforms, ceremonial robes, weapons, gold, precious stones, ornaments, holy relics, calligraphy and beautiful editions of the Koran.

The most costly items are kept in the **Treasury** on the right. The most priceless of these include the throne of Ahmed I (1604-17), richly encrusted with gold and precious stones, and the throne of Murad IV (1632-40). Of particular interest is the throne of the Persian Shah Ismail, which contains 25,000 pearls. It was captured from the Persians by Selim I, and was placed in the palace in 1514. There is a reliquary containing what is supposed to be the hand of John the Baptist, together with a cradle of pure gold and other priceless treasures.

There is a heavy guard around the **Spoonmaker's Diamond**, the largest finished diamond in the world. It can be viewed behind a thick pane of reinforced glass. It weighs 86 carats, and is framed by 49 smaller diamonds.

The third and final courtyard is very extensive. There are several pavilions scattered around the courtyard and the small park that adjoins it. To the right is the **Safa Mosque** (1809). One pavilion, the **Mecidiye Kösk**, is noticeably Baroque in style, though it was built in 1840. Three of the pavilions were used to house guests, these being the **Arzt Kösk**, the **Mustafa**

Pasa Kösk and the **Revan Kösk**. Also of interest is the tulip garden, created under Ahmed III, who was fond of flowers.

The most impressive pavilion is the **Bagdad Kösk**, which stands close to a fountain and is easily recognisable from its dome. It is beautifully decorated with porcelain tiles, stained-glass windows, and wood carvings inlaid with gold; the doors are also fascinating. It was built by Murad IV as a memorial to the triumphant Turkish conquest of Constantinople.

Also near the fountain is a small pavilion called the **Sünnet Odasi**, which is where the sultan's princes were circumcised. Just across from this building is a balcony with a golden canopy running along the palace wall. It is a popular subject for photographers as it can be combined with a magnificent view of Istanbul.

Returning to the second courtyard, it is important to visit the **Hall of the Prophet**, which is to the right opposite the treasury. This room contains supposed relics of the prophet Mohammed. His bow and sabre are kept in a golden cask, which can be seen behind glass from a suitably respectful distance. Behind the cask is the prophet's cloak. Photographs are strictly forbidden. The room is decorated with beautifully glazed porcelain tiles.

Returning through the other courtyards, one leaves the palace grounds via the **Gate of Salvation**, in front of which is a 1,000 year-old oak tree with a trunk measuring 3m (10ft) in diameter.

The adjacent building is **St Irene's Church**. This was ⌘ originally built under Constantine the Great in the fourth century AD, making it one of the oldest of all Byzantine churches. It was also the meeting place of the famous Council of Constantinople in AD 381. Until recently it was used as a museum of Turkish weaponry — hence the cannons that still stand in front of it. According to archaeologists, it was built over the foundations of a Greek temple to Aphrodite. The church was destroyed several times by fire or earthquake, and the present structure was built in the years 750-75.

One of Istanbul's main attractions is the **Hagia Sophia**, ⌘ which stands just outside the precincts of the Topkapi. After the Blue Mosque it is the most important religious building in Istanbul. The original church was built in 360 under Constantine the Great, and was modelled on the Church of the Holy Sepulchre in Jerusalem. This building was several times destroyed by fire, earthquake or war.

In 532 it was completely destroyed during the Nika rebellion.

Emperor Justinian had 30,000 rebel prisoners executed at the hippodrome, and immediately set about rebuilding it. But this time the structure was much larger and more beautiful. 10,000 workmen were employed over a period of 5 years on a building that was to be one of the great architectural wonders of antiquity. It was dedicated on 27 December 537. Justinian strode in through the narthex (western porch), took his seat on the throne and officially opened it to the people of the Byzantine empire.

The vast dome collapsed on several occasions as a result of Istanbul's many earthquakes. In the sixteenth century the Turkish conquerors resolved this problem by building four extra supporting columns around the outside. They also turned the Hagia Sophia into a mosque, placing a minaret on each of the four corners.

The area in front of the building is scattered with columns and capitals left over from previous buildings. The visitor enters through the magnificent west door, which is made of bronze. Immediately to the right of the entrance is the clock room, with four burial chambers beyond it; to the left are the old kitchens, and there is a seventeenth-century washing fountain on the way to the narthex.

Above the door into the **Narthex** is a beautiful mosaic of the Virgin Mary receiving gifts from emperors Constantine and Justinian. Constantine offers her the city, while Justinian makes a symbolic offering of the church. The narthex itself is 60m (197ft) long and 10m (33ft) wide. There are nine great doors leading to the interior of the building. The largest door was reserved for the emperor alone. Above it is a mosaic showing Emperor Leo VI kneeling before Jesus Christ.

The building's two architects were Isidor of Miletus and Anthemius of Talles. Their purpose in building the enormous dome was to create an impression of the greatness of the almighty. The dome measures 55m (180ft) from the ground to the topmost point, and has a diameter of 33m (108ft). This makes it the fifth-largest dome in the world. The main interior chamber is very nearly square, being 77m (252ft) long and 72m (236ft) wide. In order to make the dome structure light, a special kind of tile was used, which had to be shipped in from the island of Rhodes. The base of the dome contains forty windows. The light coming through them makes the construction seem less heavy. Every hour the sun shines through a different window, lighting up a different mosaic. The dome rests on four mighty columns, each of which has a history of its own.

The smaller green columns leading into the side chambers were brought here from Ephesus, though the green marble came originally from Elba. The yellow marble columns are from North Africa, and the white marble was quarried on nearby islands in the Sea of Marmara.

One column on the right-hand side opposite the entrance is clearly marked with a handprint, which according to legend is that of Mary the mother of Jesus. A column nearby bears a slash that is reputed to have been made by the sword of the Turkish conqueror Mehmed II. There appears to be a hoof print at the foot of this column, where his horse is supposed to have reared up against it. A more likely explanation is that an icon was placed where the slash is now to be seen, and that people used to pray below it, placing their hands on the pedestal. This would have worn away with time, creating a depression resembling a hoof print.

The third interesting column is to the left of the entrance. It is known as the **Sweating Column** because it feels wet to the touch. Merely touching this column is supposed to cure eye disorders and to enable barren women to conceive children. The authoities have tried to get rid of this superstition by placing a metal cover around the base of the column. Visitors, however, have managed to make a hole in the metal just big enough to let a finger through. Anyone who can get his finger in is allowed to make a wish. There is even a legend to the effect that Mehmed II placed his finger in the hole when he conquered the city in 1453, turning the church round towards Mecca so as to make it into a mosque. There is a scientific explanation for the 'sweating' of the column. Marble, being porous, tends to absorb water from the ground below.

The two enormous vases either side of the entrance were brought here from Pergamum. They are made of alabaster, and each has a capacity of 1,250 litres (275 gallons). The great iron chandelier is fitted with oil lamps, which are lit up on special occasions. Above the entrances to the side chambers are four enormous green tablets bearing the Arabic symbols for Allah, Mohammed and the great caliphs. They were hung up there by the Turks to symbolise the fact that the Hagia Sophia had been turned into a Moslem mosque.

Next to the small **Prayer Temple** (a later Moslem addition) is the place where the Byzantine emperors were crowned. There is a

Kariye Museum, Istanbul

cross on the ground showing where the dome ended. This was used to measure the actual size of the dome. The pulpit has a beautifully-decorated staircase leading up to it. Next to the main apse is the so-called 'cold window', where the air remains cool on the hottest of days.

Visitors who wish to see the valuable mosaics in the **Women's Gallery** must do so in the company of a guide. The southern section used to be reserved for members of the emperor's family, and so contains one of the finest of the mosaics. Alas, only fragments remain of the mosaic of the Deisis — a twelfth-century work depicting Jesus Christ, Mary and John the Baptist. A stone slab in the gallery bears the name Henricus Dandalo — a Venetian doge who died in Constantinople in 1205 and was buried in the Hagia Sophia.

Professor Underwood has uncovered two more beautiful mosaics. One is of Mary with the child Jesus conferring a blessing. The other depicts Emperor John II Komnenos, and to the right of him Empress Irene, daughter of St Ladislaus of Hungary. Yet another mosaic shows Christ throned in glory, flanked by Emperor Constantine IX and Empress Zoë.

The grave towers in the courtyard of the Hagia Sophia form the last resting places of Turkish sultans Murad III, Selim II and Mehmed III.

The next item on the route is the **Yerebatan Cistern**. This is reached by turning right out of the Hagia Sophia and crossing the first road out of the Hagia Sophia Square. The building is behind a postcard kiosk to the left. The cistern was built during the sixth century AD, when Emperor Justinian constructed a series of reservoirs around the city for providing water at times of great need. The Yerebatan Cistern is the best-preserved of those that remain. It consists of a vast underground chamber 141m (462ft) long and 73m (239ft) wide, and supported by 336 thick columns. Thousands of Christians hid in these cisterns at the time of the Turkish conquest. The atmosphere in the vault is very creepy, but it is perfectly safe, and the water dripping from the walls keeps it pleasantly cool.

There is plenty more to see around the Hagia Sophia Square. Crossing it in the direction of the Blue Mosque, one passes **Kaiser Wilhelm's Well** on the right, which the German monarch gave to the city on the occasion of a state visit.

The Blue Mosque stands next to the **hippodrome** (**Atmeydani**), which now forms a long rectangular park area adjoining the Hagia Sophia Square. The hippodrome was once the focal point of the Byzantine capital of Constantinople. It was the place where political parties met, festivals were celebrated, prisoners were executed and chariot races were held. It was built in the reign of Septimius Severus in AD 124. It originally had long grandstands either side, seating up to 150,000 people.

In the middle of the hippodrome is a group of three interesting columns. The one in the middle, known as the **Snake Column**, is one of Istanbul's oldest monuments. It goes back to 479 BC, and was originally erected in the sanctuary at Delphi to celebrate the Greek victory over the Persians at Salamis and Plataea. It was commissioned by thirty-one Greek cities, the names of which are engraved on it. It now measures only 5$\frac{1}{2}$m (18ft), but was originally at least 8m (26ft) high. It bears three carved snakes, which originally drank from a gold basin.

Immediately next to this is an **Egyptian Obelisk**. It is 25m (82ft) high, and was brought over from Egypt by Emperor Theodosius in AD 390. The hieroglyphics indicate that it was originally carved in 1547 BC during the reign of Pharaoh Tuthmosis III. It is made of porphyry and rests on four bronze supports. The marble pediment is 6m (19$\frac{1}{2}$ft) high, and carries reliefs depicting Theodosius and his family.

The third column is known as the **Walled Column**, and is

remarkable for its height of 30m (98ft). It was erected in the tenth century AD, and was originally covered with bronze plates. But the crusaders removed them and melted them down.

⌘ It is only a few paces from the hippodrome to the **Blue Mosque**, known in Turkish as the **Sultan Ahmed Camii**. The Blue Mosque with its six minarets is the second-largest mosque in the Moslem world, the largest being in Mecca itself. In order to build it, Sultan Ahmed I was obliged to have a seventh minaret added to the most holy mosque of all at Mecca so as to preserve the religious priorities of Islam.

The domed structure is vast, but is nonetheless graceful in its architecture. It stands on the foundations of the former imperial palace. When Ahmed I built the Blue Mosque, his intention was to create something greater and more magnificent than the nearby Hagia Sophia, which had been built by Christians. The Blue Mosque is still the city's main mosque.

The whole mosque complex is surrounded by a wall, and also includes a school and several other buildings. A courtyard opens up to the left of the mosque. An open staircase leads up through a beautiful doorway into the vestibule, which has thirty domes supported by twenty-six granite columns with stalactite capitals. In the middle of the vestibule is a hexagonal washing fountain supported on six columns with a pointed arch above it.

The dome itself is 43m (141ft) high and has a diameter of 22m (72ft). It is decorated with a variety of mostly blue porcelain tiles, which together create one of the most beautiful porcelain designs in the whole of Turkey. The effect is heightened by the light coming in through the 260 round windows. The white marble pulpit is modelled on the one at Mecca. Opposite the entrance is a small niche (*mihrab*) showing the exact orientation of Mecca. It is inlaid with precious stones, and below it is a piece of the black stone of the Kaaba in Mecca.

The prayer chamber on the left contains the sultan's lodge. (The sultan used to ride into the mosque on horseback.) On special Moslem festivals, the people of Istanbul stream into the prayer chamber and light their oil lamps. The glow of the lamps is reflected on the tiles, and mingles with the red of the luxurious carpet that covers all the floors of the mosque. A service here is an experience not to be missed. In other mosques visitors are often sent out when the Moslem services begin, but in the Blue Mosque they are allowed to stay and listen.

⌘ In front of the Blue Mosque is the tomb of its builder, Sultan

View of the Bosporus

Ahmed I (1609–16). The same mausoleum contains the tombs of Osman II, murdered in 1622, and Murad IV. The mosque in the summer is the subject of a *son et lumière* performance, in which its history is retold in music, commentary and lights.

The places described so far are enough for one day's sightseeing. But there are plenty of interesting things to do in the evening. One might, for example, treat oneself to a meal at the prestigious *Renommier Restaurant* in the Galata Tower.

A twilight boat trip is also to be recommended. Every few minutes a passenger boat leaves the Galata Bridge for a trip up the Bosporus. There is a marvellous panorama of the city from out on the water. The city's more prosperous suburbs spread out along both sides of the Bosporus. They include millionaires' villas and the city's diplomatic quarters. The boat goes under the impressive Europa Bridge, which links Europe with Asia. It stops at piers on alternate sides of the channel, which means that one can alight on the European side and return by bus to the city centre (there is an all-night bus service). Visitors who are unsure of where to get off are recommended to do so at Yeniköy. Yeniköy is about two hours from the centre by boat, and provides a variety of pleasant restaurants.

Day Two

Nuruosmaniye Mosque • Grand Bazaar • Egyptian Bazaar

The recommended route for the second day begins at the Hagia Sophia, and runs along a wide avenue called the Divan Yolu. The road rises gently, and after a quarter of an hour arrives at **Constantine's Column**, known in Turkish as the **Çemberli Tas** or **Burnt Column**.

It was erected by Constantine in AD 324 to commemorate the fact that Byzantium had become the capital of the Roman empire. The 35m (115ft) high column was brought here from the Temple of Apollo in Rome. In order to symbolise the religious freedom that Constantine wished to encourage, it is supposed to contain relics from all over the empire. These are said to include pieces from the paladium at Troy which had reputedly been taken by Aeneas to the Temple of Vesta in Rome. Even more far-fetched are Noah's axe, the rock that gushed with water when struck by Moses, and twelve baskets filled with crumbs from Christ's 'feeding of the five thousand'. No evidence has been found to support this claim.

In 1105 it collapsed in an earthquake, and the statue on the top, which presumably showed Constantine on horseback, was completely destroyed. The column was rebuilt and reinforced with iron rings. It was given its Turkish name in 1779 when the city was destroyed by fire.

To the right of the column is the city's oldest Baroque mosque — the **Nuruosmaniye Camii**. It was built in 1748 according to the plans of an architect called Sinan. It has two minarets and is contained within an enclosing wall. Of particular interest are the sultan's lodge and the choir gallery. It is one of several so-called merchants' mosques to be built near bazaars, where pious merchants can come in during business hours to pray to Allah. They leave their stalls in the dark passages of the bazaar, and spend a few minutes here, either asking Allah to grant them favourable trade, or else thanking him for having already done so. Those with only small businesses bring their goods in with them, and are loaded down with items such as furs, cloths and spices.

The **Grand Bazaar** (**Büyük Çarsi**) is the most fascinating of all the sights in Istanbul. The bazaar quarter extends from the Nuruosmaniye Mosque to the Yeni Valide Mosque by the Golden Horn, and is enclosed by a wall. There are eleven entrances to this vast labyrinth of narrow passages. Some are enclosed, while others lead to small hidden courtyards, gloomy storehouses and smoky little cafés. The bazaar contains a total of between 4,000 and 6,000 little shops, selling everything from a bottle opener to a suite of furniture. The tradespeople are particularly keen on selling to tourists. Loud flattery is often used to cajole people into buying goods that are sometimes almost pressed into their hands. One need only stand still for someone to open up his stall and spread out everything he has to sell.

The origins of the Grand Bazaar go back to the Byzantine period, when this area was the city's main trading and commercial quarter. Then in the fifteenth century Mehemmed the Conqueror had the area extended, creating an enormous covered market. The bazaar was burnt down on repeated occasions, and in the seventeenth century the wooden structure was replaced by a stone one. In 1894 the bazaar was flattened by a severe earthquake.

In 1954 a great fire raged through the narrow passages, destroying whole sections of the bazaar. One can still recognise the parts that were affected, as they are noticeably more modern than the rest. With their shop windows and neon lighting, they have none of the oriental atmosphere that can still be found elsewhere.

By contrast the old *bedesten* or cloth market is full of the old eastern promise. It is a rectangular building with two small domes, and stands on the exact site of the former Byzantine market. It is heavily guarded at night because of the large number of valuable goods that are sold, including ornaments, jewellery, antiques and copperwear.

Visitors can orientate themselves from the two main thoroughfares that run from the top to the bottom of the bazaar. One should note the small mosques and the observation windows once used by the sultan's guards to detect fires or other disturbances. The few old fountains that remain are usually besieged by Turks. Trading, and oriental trading especially, is a decidedly thirsty occupation. The entrances to the bazaar are also particularly impressive.

The bazaar is divided into several different sections, each selling goods of a particular kind. One street, for example, is devoted to skins and furs, while another sells only shoes, and so on. The open passages in the area around the old cloth market are so narrow as to be scarcely distinguishable from the covered passages of the bazaar proper. Again there are hundreds of little shops, with yet more tradespeople and fruit sellers out in the

Hand-made Turkish musical instruments

street. In the high summer large awnings are stretched over these passages to keep the sun off.

The fringes of the bazaar are the domain of the craftsmen, who also have their workshops here. This is also where the most interesting khans and caravanserais are to be found. They include the ⌘ **Zincirli Han**, the **Çuhaci Han**, the **Valide Han**, and opposite them the **Büyük Yeni Han**. Of particular interest is the **Balkanpa Han** in the Rüstem Pasa quarter down towards the Golden Horn. This old storehouse goes back to the Byzantine period, and was once also a meeting place for merchants. Two more khans nearby are the **Hurmali Han** and the **Rüstem Pasa Han**. The main difference between a khan (*han* in Turkish) and a caravanserai was that a khan was usually no more than a storage depot, while a caravanserai was used for the direct exchange of goods between the visiting caravans and the tradesmen of the city. Caravanserais, unlike khans, were usually fortified with a surrounding wall.

Bolder visitors may care to venture into some of the darker passages, and will be sure to find themselves in some old khan or caravanserai where goods are stored or exchanged. If they are lucky they will find an old craft workshop where work is still going on. It is fascinating to watch dyers or smiths or carpet-weavers at work. Visitors are always welcome in such places. The more the bazaar is modernised, the more necessary it is to go to the rather down-at-heel khans and caravanserais in order to find the oriental atmosphere that one might expect from Istanbul.

The route from the Grand Bazaar to the Galata Bridge goes right past the **Egyptian Bazaar** — a spice market that goes back to 1660. Nowadays it sells food and drugstore items as well as spices. But the air is still full of the many and varied fragrances of the Orient.

When shopping in the bazaar, one should never accept the first price that the vendor names. Even if the item seems cheap by one's own standards, its actual value will be only half that price at the very most. Bargaining is a serious matter in the bazaar, and haggling over the price is an important part of the etiquette. The vendor and the customer are expected to negotiate the price between them. If the customer makes no attempt to knock the price down, this is taken as a sign of indifference towards both the vendor and the goods he is selling. He is insulted, and the customer pays for this with a grossly inflated price.

The bazaars are closed an hour before sunset. This is announced well in advance, though a foreigner can easily miss the announcement. One should allow at least four hours for shopping around the bazaar. And if one finds a suitable souvenir, one should buy it on the spot, as it will be virtually impossible to find the same shop again later on.

Day Three

Beyazit Mosque • University • Süleymaniye Mosque • Prince's Mosque • Valens Aqueduct • City Museum

The route for day three starts in the Beyazit Square near the top end of the Grand Bazaar. Next to the square is the **Beyazit Mosque**, which was built under Beyazit in the fifteenth century. It is popularly known as the 'Pigeon Mosque', as it is always swarming with pigeons. The interior is similar to that of the Hagia Sophia. One should particularly note the doors to the washing fountain.

The northern door of the mosque leads out into a park, on the opposite side of which is the **Serasker Tower**. This tower provides a panorama of the whole city, and until recently was manned by a lookout, who would warn the fire brigade of any suspicious-looking plumes of smoke. Nowadays it is just used as a viewing point. The magnificent view makes it well worth the climb.

Immediately to the north-west is the main university building. **Istanbul University** is the most important university in the whole of Turkey. Originally founded in 1845, it is housed in the former war ministry premises, which were converted in 1934 by a Swiss architect called Malche.

Not far from here is the **Süleymaniye Camii**. This mosque is surrounded by a complex of domed buildings containing schools, libraries, hospitals, baths and kitchens. The Süleymaniye Mosque is in a dominant position overlooking the old city. It is easily recognisable from its massive dome and its four minarets, two large and two small. The architect was Sinan, who designed so many of the city's medieval mosques. It took 7 years to build between 1550 and 1557. Artists and materials were brought in from all over the empire, and the mosque could scarcely be more beautiful. It stands in a wide courtyard, and its dome is 53m (174ft) high. The interior is lit up by 138 windows, and is lined with magnificent tile decorations.

The Süleymaniye Mosque complex stands over the foundations of a former imperial palace, whose great stones were used to build the mosque. All the columns, including those that support the ante-chamber, were brought over from the hippodrome.

In a cemetery to the east of the mosque are the mausoleums of several of the sultans. The largest and most beautiful is that of Süleyman the Great. Smaller but equally tasteful is that of his favourite wife Roxelane. Other members of the dynasty to be buried here are Süleyman II, Ahmed II, Mehmed, Mirihmah, Aliye, Saliha Dilasub and several crown princes and princesses. Also buried here is Sinan, the most important architect in medieval Turkey. His white marble tomb is distinctive, being triangular in shape with a domed fountain also made of marble.

From the mosque one should take a taxi or a *dolmus* down the Bozdogan Kemer, turning right along the Sehzade Basi Caddesi. The next port of call is the **Prince's Mosque**, built between 1544 and 1548 by Süleyman I in memory of his favourite son Mehmed, who had died in 1543. This mosque was again designed by Sinan.

It is only a few minutes' walk to the **Valens Aqueduct**. This is to the right of the Prince's Mosque, and crosses above the Atatürk Boulevard, the city's main north–south thoroughfare. Although the aqueduct goes back to between AD 364 and 378, a 900m (2,952ft) section of it is still substantially intact. One can

Süleymaniye Camii

climb up onto it at either end.

Close to the aqueduct is the **City Museum** (**Belediye Müzesi**) on the Atatürk Boulevard. The building was originally a Moslem school run by the white eunuchs. It contains innumerable historic items from ancient Constantinople, including weaponry, puppets and gowns. Its fifteen rooms are well worth a visit. ⌘

The Atatürk Boulevard leads down to the **Atatürk Bridge**, which crosses the Golden Horn to the more modern parts of the city. Like the Galata Bridge, it has a swing bridge in the middle to let ships through.

Day Four

Boat Excursions

There are two possible boat trips from Istanbul. One is along the **Bosporus** to the bathing beaches of the **Black Sea**. The other is to the **Princes' Islands** in the **Sea of Marmara**. This exotic group of islands is only an hour's voyage from the Galata Bridge. Of the nine islands only four are inhabited, and the southernmost island of **Büyük Ada** is the largest and most prosperous. There is a monastery on each of the island's two hills, where crown princes were once banished by the sultans to safeguard them from being murdered. The main town, also called Büyük Ada, provides varied if modest hotel or guesthouse accommodation. There is plenty to amuse the visitor, including bathing and water sports, folk festivals, discos, boats for hire and donkey rides all over the island.

Day Five

Sultan Mehmed Mosque • Mollazeyrek Mosque • Sultan Selim Mosque • Fethiye Mosque • Mihrimah Mosque • Kahriye Mosque • Tekfur Saray • land fortifications • Eyüp Mosque • Eyüp Cemetery

The city's fourth hill is crowned by the **Sultan Mehmed Mosque**, also known as the **Conqueror's Mosque** or **Fatih Camii**. It was built between 1463 and 1470 on the site of a former Byzantine church. The vestibule has twenty domes, supported on eigheen columns. It is unusual in having two balconies. This is where the muezzin once stood and repeated the prayers of the imam for the benefit of those outside for whom there was no room left inside. In front of the mosque are the tombs of Mehmed II and Sultana Gülbahar. The mosque is surrounded by a complex of buildings including schools, baths, kitchens, hospitals and even a caravanserai.

Two mosques to the east of the Fatih Camii were originally Byzantine churches, which the Moslems simply adapted for their own purposes. The first of these is the **Mollazeyrek Camii**, which is north of the city centre along the Atatürk Boulevard. It was actually made up of three churches, the first being that of St Saviour Pantocrator, which was linked to a monastery. The church at the southern end was dedicated to the Holy Virgin (Theotocos Eleusa). Both churches were built in the early twelfth century. They once contained valuable relics such as those of St Blasius and St Demetrius, but no one knows what became of these. The third church is a burial chapel linking the two larger buildings.

Not far away is the **Rose Mosque** (**Gül Camii**). The original church was built in the eighth century, and was dedicated to St Theodisia.

The **Sultan Selim Mosque** stands on the city's fifth hill next to the Yavuz Selim Caddesi, and commands a magnificent view of the Bosporus. At the southern end of the mosque is a former open cistern, which has been drained and converted into a

No cars are allowed on one of the Princes' Islands

garden. The grounds contain remains of a former imperial palace, which has been attributed to Emperor Bonus.

Also worth visiting is the **Fethiye Camii**, which is further out towards the land fortifications. This was once the Byzantine church of the Pammakaristos or Most Blessed Virgin. The ground plan of the basilica is in the form of a Greek cross. It was probably built in the twelfth century. The mosaics inside are from the fourteenth century.

The **Mihrimah Mosque** stands just inside the land fortifications and to the left of the Fevzipasa Caddesi. It was built in 1550, and was designed by Sinan for Sultana Mihrimah, daughter of Süleyman the Great. It has unfortunately been badly damaged by earthquakes, and has been heavily restored on several occasions.

Not far away near the banks of the Golden Horn is the **Kahriye Mosque** or church of **St Saviour in Chora**. This is one of the few Byzantine churches to have been fully preserved. The central prayer chamber is entered via the narthex, and the adjoining side chapel has some beautiful frescos. The original fifth-century building was part of the monastery of Chora. But it fell into disrepair when the monastery was dissolved. It was rebuilt in 1057 by Mary Ducas, niece of Emperor Isaac of the Comnenes dynasty. The frescos and mosaics were added in the thirteenth century. The church was converted into a mosque in the fifteenth century following the Turkish conquest. It has now been turned into a museum. It is famous for having the largest-known collection of Byzantine mosaics, with up to forty-eight designs.

⌘ Linked to the land fortifications are the remains of the **Tekfur Saray** or former imperial palace. This once luxurious palace was built in the tenth century by Emperor Constantine VII. During the thousand years leading up to the Turkish conquest of 1453, it was customary for each emperor to build a palace of his own to live in. The foundations of these palaces are scattered all over the city. The Turks tried to wipe out all memories of the Byzantine empire by replacing all the palaces with mosques. But the Tekfur Saray was an exception: it formed part of the city's fortifications, so it was in their interests to keep it.

The ornamental façade is still beautifully preserved. It is built of a whole variety of different stones such as marble, sandstone and granite, creating a rich and decorative pattern. This is a typical feature of the buildings of the Palaeologues — the last of the Byzantine dynasties. The last important person to live in the Tekfur Saray was Empress Eugénie of France in 1869.

The ruins can be visited in return for a small entrance fee. If one gives the warder an extra 3TL or so, he will explain everything he knows about the palace. He will also show the way to the ⌘ lookout point from which the best view can be had of the **land fortifications**.

For a thousand years these massive walls repelled countless invaders, including Arabs, Seljuks, Russians, Huns and Magyars. Only 6½km remain of the original land fortification. When it was originally built under Theodosius II (AD 413–69), it was 65km long, and extended from the Sea of Marmara to the Black Sea coast. Such a wall has never been matched in Europe. It was subsequently further strengthened by a second wall and a moat. The moat was later filled in and a road built along it. The main wall is up to 13m (43ft) high and 5m (16ft) thick. There are square towers at intervals of 55m (180ft) with an average height of 18m (59ft).

The walls run through one of the poorer parts of the city. The wooden shacks on either side are typical of old Istanbul, and are in stark contrast to these magnificent remnants of the city's glorious past.

⌘ The southern end of the wall is at the **Yediküle Palace** by the Sea of Marmara, where the land and sea fortifications meet. Yediküle is not so much a palace as a fortified castle built for purely military purposes. For strategic reasons it was placed by the **Golden Gate**, where a wide street led into the city. This was the gate through which the Byzantine emperors rode in triumph on their return from a successful campaign. When Sultan Mehmed II conquered the city, he also recognised the vulnerability of a position that could be attacked from sea and land simultaneously. So he had the fortress extended and further reinforced.

The Yediküle later became the state prison, where all executions were carried out. The Ottoman sultans hid the imperial treasure in the castle. From the fifteenth century onwards, the Yediküle became a notorious place of carnage. Many people fell victim to the brutal struggles that went on between the pretenders to the throne. Hundreds were beheaded or hanged, including Grand Vizier Mahmud, Sultan Osman II, and Davud Pasa. Many foreign diplomats were incarcerated in the east tower, including the French and Russian ambassadors and an envoy from the republic of Venice. Many of these prisoners inscribed the reasons for their imprisonment on the walls of their cells. These inscriptions remain to this day — a witness to the ruthless and bloodthirsty methods of the Turkish rulers of the time.

Visitors can climb up onto the battlements of the east tower and enjoy a wonderful view of Istanbul and the sea. The southern tower of the Golden Gate contains a room with a well where executions were carried out. The victims' heads were simply thrown into the well. A small staircase leads up to two cells, the smaller of which is where Sultan Osman II was hanged.

The northern end of the present-day wall is by the site of the fifth-century **Blachernae Palace**. It was destroyed by the Turks in 1453, but its cellar vaults can still be seen. This area near the Golden Horn was where the Byzantine emperors resided from the twelfth century onwards. Thus it was full of palaces, including the Tekfur Saray (see above). There is a place marked by the shore as the site of the famous Ayvansaray Pier. This is where the emperors and their retinue disembarked on their return from a voyage.

An irregular paved road runs along the shore of the Golden Horn through the rather down-at-heel suburb of Ortakalar. It eventually comes to the **Eyüp Camii**, which is Istanbul's holiest mosque. The mosque is 20 minutes by bus from the Atatürk Bridge. It can also be reached by a motorboat taxi service from a

Traditional wooden houses, originally built for the wealthy, now inhabited by Istanbul's poor

pier to the left of the Galata Bridge (approaching from the bazaar). Visitors by motorboat should agree on a price with the pilot beforehand, and should also fix a time for the return trip (allowing 2 hours for sightseeing).

Relatively few tourists come out as far as this. There are some lovely subjects for photographs, but visitors are advised to be careful, as photography is greatly frowned on by the locals. The courtyard in front of the mosque is full of old people, and there are plenty of beggars around. It is also teeming with pigeons. The general effect is both strange and picturesque.

The mosque was built in 1458 following the Turkish conquest in 1458. It was extended in 1591. It then fell into disrepair for the next 200 years. It is not known why this happened. In 1798 it was rebuilt under Selim III.

A small burial chamber next to the main building contains the tomb of Eyub Ansare, companion and standard-bearer of the great prophet Mohammed. He fell in AD 670 during a Moslem attack on the land fortifications. The burial chamber is to the left of the inner courtyard. Entry is forbidden to 'unbelievers', but one can look in through a small window. The walls are richly decorated with tiles.

The tomb is visited by many thousands of Moslem pilgrims each year. And at one time all the sultans came to the Eyüp Camii to be given a sword as a token of their power. Even today, the holiness of the site is sufficient reason for many Moslems to wish to be buried as near to the mosque as possible.

Consequently, the nearby **Eyüp Cemetery** is the largest in Istanbul. The graves are piled on top of one another on the hillside above the mosque, creating a forest of column-shaped tombstones. The Moslems never tend their graves, many of which have been dug up. The result is wild and chaotic, and strange to western eyes. Visitors should take a walk up the hill to the famous *Café Piyerloti*. It is named after the French author Pierre Loti, who described the wonderful panorama it afforded of the city and the Golden Horn. The view is indeed unparalleled.

Day Six

Galata Tower • Taksim Square • Dolmabahçe Palace • Rumeli Hisari • Europa Bridge

A whole day is needed to visit the area north of the Golden Horn, especially Galata and the more modern parts of the city around the Taksim Square.

In the twelfth century the city state of Genoa built a fortress on the site of present-day **Galata** as a bridgehead to secure its oriental trade routes. The Byzantine emperor of the time banished all the city's foreign communities to the north side of the Golden Horn, because their frequent bloody feuds had an adverse effect on the native inhabitants. The Genoese granted permission for Jews, Asians and Europeans to live within their walls. Many centuries later, at the request of the sultanate, all the foreign embassies were built on the northern shore of the Golden Horn. The one notable exception was the German embassy, which was granted a privileged position not far from the sultan's palace. Galata was originally limited to the area between the Atatürk Bridge and the Bosporus. But the city's modern suburbs have spread northwards along the shore of the Bosporus.

Galata's chief attraction is the **Galata Tower**. This 70m (230ft) high tower is in a dominating position on the hill top above a sea of houses. It goes back to the Byzantine period, and was incorporated into the Genoese fortifications. It was heavily restored in 1875, and now contains a restaurant, a nightclub and a coffee bar. The viewing gallery provides a marvellous view of the

Golden Horn and the old city of Istanbul. There are several steep alleyways leading down to the Karaköy Square and the Galata Bridge. The tower is surrounded by an area of old houses with narrow winding streets. Visitors should keep away from here and from the old city of Stambul after dark.

In order to get from the Galata Tower to the Taksim Square (Taksim Meydani), one first follows the Yüksek Caddesi as far as the Tünel Square, and then continues along the Istiklâl Caddesi. Taksim Square is the hub of modern Istanbul, with broad avenues radiating from it in all directions. The square itself forms a single enormous taxi rank and bus station. On the west side is the Monument of the Republic, in the middle a statue and on the east side the Opera House.

Immediately to the north are the **Taksim Gardens**, now known as the **Cumhuriyet Meydani**. The Cumhuriyet Caddesi runs alongside these gardens, and continues through Beyoglu in the direction of Sisli and Kilyos. This is the city's most prestigious shopping boulevard, and contains all the important banks, department stores, tourist offices, surgeries, etc.

One road to the right off Taksim Square is the Gümüssuyu Caddesi, which goes down towards the Bosporus. A tall building on the right provides visitors with a view of the Dolmabahçe Palace and Mosque, and across the Bosporus to the Asian shore. To the left is the Mithat Pasa Stadium.

⌘ The **Dolmabahçe Palace** stands in the middle of a park next to the Bosporus, in front of the populous suburb of **Besiktas**. This magnificent Renaissance palace was the Turkish sultan's residence until 1918. It now forms the Turkish president's summer residence. It is nevertheless open to the public (except on Mondays and Saturdays). Next to the shore by the Besiktas ⌘ pier is the **Maritime Museum**. There is a clock tower in the large square in front of the palace. The main square inside the palace contains the mausoleum of the notorious Admiral Hayreddin Barbarossa, whose fleet was the terror of the western Mediterranean in the fifteenth and sixteenth centuries.

One place along the Bosporus which is particularly worth ⌘ visiting is the **Rumeli Hisari** or **European Castle**. This is 10km north of the city at the narrowest point of the Bosporus. The strait here is only 650m (2,132ft) wide. The castle was built by Mehmed II as part of his preparations for the siege of Constantinople. He wanted to be sure of a safe route both for supplies and in the event of a possible retreat. The sultan also wanted to

Dolmabahçe Mosque

prevent the Greeks in Constantinople from being helped by reinforcements from the Black Sea.

Emperor Constantine XI conducted a fierce campaign to prevent the castle from being built, but his efforts were in vain. According to legend, the emperor allowed the sultan to build a pavilion only big enough to cover an ox skin. Mehmed then cut up the ox skin into strips so thin that when placed end-to-end they were long enough to encompass the whole area required for the fortress. The castle was finished 9 months before the fall of Constantinople. Afterwards the sultans used it as the state prison.

The best view of the whole site is from the **Saganos Pasa Tower**. The walls are up to 5m (16ft) thick. It is also possible to make out the foundations of a mosque. On the opposite side of the Bosporus is the smaller **Anadolu Hisari** or **Asian Castle**, which the Turks built even earlier than the European Castle. Together they were intended to guard the narrowest point of the strait.

⌘ The road to Rumeli Hisari runs past the **Europa Bridge**, which was opened to traffic on 29 October 1973, the fiftieth anniversary of the Turkish Republic. At the time it was the longest and most up-to-date suspension bridge in both Europe and Asia, though it has since been surpassed by the Humber Bridge in England. It spans the Bosporus about 5km north of the Galata Bridge, from **Ortaköy** on the European side to **Beylerbeyi** on the Asian side. It is about $1\frac{1}{2}$km long altogether. The two towers carry between them a span of a just over a kilometre of road. The main supporting wires are 23in thick and weigh 6,000 tonnes. It took a British firm $3\frac{1}{2}$ years to build it at a cost of about 45 million pounds.

This bridge is the fulfilment of a dream that goes back nearly 3,000 years. Back in the sixth century BC, Darius I of Persia constructed a floating bridge of wood across the Bosporus. Since then, architects have repeatedly attempted to design a bridge that would survive both earthquakes and storms. The most advanced plans were those made by French engineers in 1860. But the sultan at the time saw no urgent need for such an expensive project, and these plans were never actually implemented.

It was over a hundred years before the idea finally came to fruition. In the meantime, the ferries between Istanbul and its eastern suburb of Üsküdar had become completely overloaded, with associated congestion of the approach roads. The enormous increase in traffic made a solution even more urgent, and the bridge was at last constructed. Now not only does it relieve the ferries, but the motorway links either side enable through traffic to bypass the city, relieving congestion still further. The costs of construction are offset by tolls.

Visitors are recommended to take the ferry one way and return via the road bridge. It is a fantastic journey across one of the longest suspension bridges in the world, 68m (223ft) above the historic Bosporus Straits. The new bridge provides the Bosporus with yet another claim to fame.

Day Seven

Üsküdar

The Asian part of Istanbul, called **Üsküdar**, is really a town in its own right, though it has none of the splendour and bustle of the European metropolis. Üsküdar can be reached via the Europa Bridge (see above) or by a 15-minute ferry journey.

Waterside home on the Bosporus

The ferry goes from the pier at Kabatas, which is on the west bank of the Bosporus, 2km from the Galata Bridge. The boat runs close to the **Leander Tower**. This is where Leander is supposed to have drowned when he tried to swim the Bosporus to get to his beloved Hero, who was a priestess of Aphrodite. The legend has inspired poets down the ages, including Ovid, Marlowe and Schiller. The Turks associate the tower with a different story. A sultan's daughter is supposed to have been hidden here when an oracle prophesied that she would die young as a result of a snake bite. But her enemies managed to kill her by hiding a poisonous snake in a basket of fruit.

Üsküdar today still has a more primitive feel to it than the metropolis on the European side. It has also undergone considerably less change over the years, though it too has had its share of wars and earthquakes. Üsküdar has always stood in the shadow of its neighbour across the Bosporus. The area between the pier and the Great Cemetery is full of old mosques and weathered wooden houses. There has been a settlement here since time immemorial. For thousands of years it was at the end of a caravan route that came through Asia Minor from Persia and Afghanistan. The town was a prosperous one. Then the Greeks built fortifications and founded a colony here.

One of the most interesting mosques is the **Büyük Camii**, which is to the left of the pier. It was built in 1547 during the reign of Süleyman II. To the south of it is the **Yeni Valide Camii**, built in 1710. In the nearby Toptasi quarter is the **Atik Valide Camii** or **Mosque of the Sultan's Mother**. This is supposed to have been designed by the architect Sinan for Sultana Naru Banu, mother of Murad III. A stone above the main entrance gives its foundation date as 1583. The most notable feature of this great mosque is the rich ornamental tiling. The same can be said of the blue tiling in the **Çinili Camii**, which was built in 1640. The harmony of the colours and the beauty of the ornamentation make it a jewel among mosques in Istanbul.

The **Great Cemetery** is on higher land to the south-east of Üsküdar. It is in fact the largest cemetery in the whole of the Orient. The eastern section is particularly impressive, and is where all the oldest graves are to be found. In the centre of the site is a monument to the favourite horse of Sultan Mahmud I. The jumble of gravestones is interspersed with many ancient cypress trees that cast a beautiful pattern of shadows.

Also to the east of the Bosporus is the more well-to-do suburb of **Kadiköy**. Once the Greek city of Chalcedon, it now forms the modern part of Üsküdar. In spite of the factories around its fringes, it still remains a popular seaside resort on account of its marvellous bathing beach.

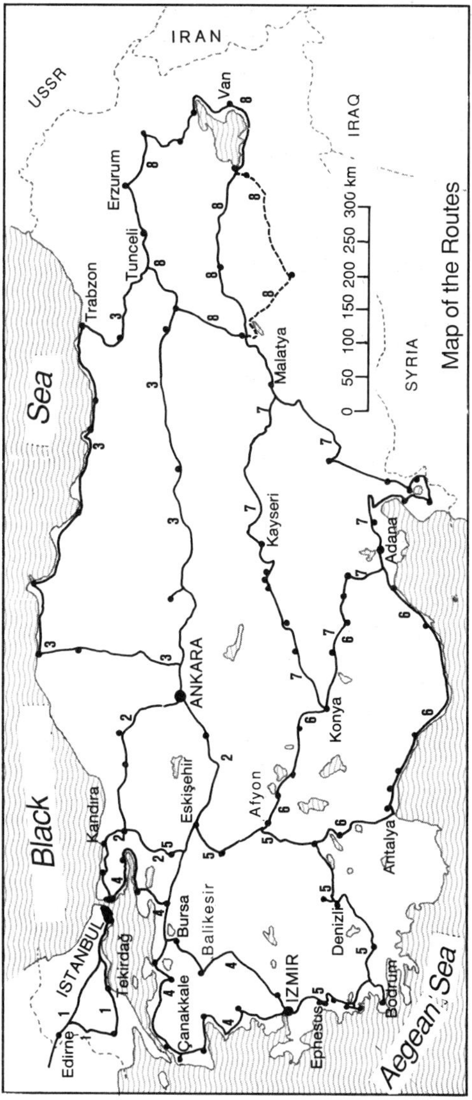

Map of the Routes

2 ROUTE ONE: EUROPEAN TURKEY

Edirne • Çorlu • Istanbul (235km) • Tekirdag (375km) • Malkara • Kesan • Uzunköprü • Havsa • Edirne (580km)

Edirne* is the nearest Turkish town to the Bulgarian border post of Svilengrad, and is also close to a border post with Greece. Its most impressive building by far is the Selimiye Camii, which is a masterpiece of Ottoman architecture.

The route across Thrace goes past nothing of particular interest. The landscape is flat and almost treeless. For those travelling on into Asia Minor, it provides a foretaste of what is to come. About half-way to Istanbul, the road passes through the small country town of Lüleburgaz, which again contains little of special interest.

The route continues via **Çorlu**, and meets the Sea of Marmara just before **Silivri**. The landscape now becomes greener and

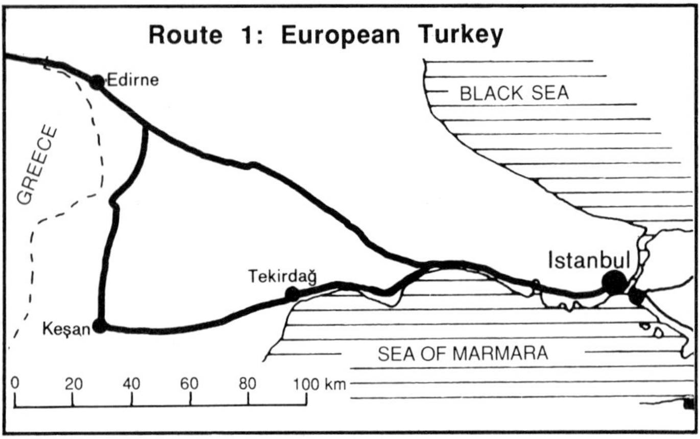

The Selimiye Camii, Edirne

more friendly. Near **Büyükçekmece** the road passes several bays and small lakes. Just before **Yesilköy** there is a long bathing beach to the right. Yesilköy is also the site of Istanbul's civilian airport.

The road enters **Istanbul*** via the grand avenue along which the Byzantine emperors used to process in triumph on their return from a successful campaign. Travellers are recommended to spend a few days at least in Istanbul, in order to gain a full appreciation of its beauty and magic.

The route leaves Istanbul via the same route. Just after Silivri it goes left, and continues along the coast to **Tekirdag**. which is 140km from Istanbul. This pretty little port is picturesquely situated in a bay. Its name means 'slate hill', and comes from the range of slate hills to the south-west of the town. Tekirdag has a mosque built by the famous architect Sinan, and affords some marvellous views across the sea.

The E5 (south) turns inland, and continues through an undulating region to the hill town of **Malkara**. In the next town of **Kesan** the route turns north along the N6. The E5 (south) meanwhile continues west towards the Greek border and beyond. 60km north of Kesan is the border town of **Uzunköprü**, from which one can make a short excursion into Greece.

At **Havsa** the N6 enters the E5 (north). It is now only another 15km back to **Edirne** and to the end of this tour of the European part of Turkey.

Lake Bafa

Euromos — the Temple of Zeus

Uçhisar in the Göreme Valley

3 ROUTE TWO: ISTANBUL TO CENTRAL ANATOLIA

Istanbul • Sile • Kandira • Adapazari (210km) • Düzce • Bolu • Gerede • Ankara (520km) • Polatli • Eskisehir • Bursa (910km) • Yalova • Izmit • Istanbul (1160km)

The route leaves **Istanbul** and crosses into Asia Minor. Cars and buses may cross over the famous Europa Bridge, while railway passengers may use the Kabatas ferry and join the train at Üsküdar. The road leaves the town in an easterly direction, and then turns north-eastwards.

It meets the Black Sea coast not far from Sile. This small holiday town has a marvellous sandy beach. The hot sand is supposed to cure rheumatic ailments. The area is a popular weekend and holiday retreat for people from Istanbul. They come to enjoy the sun, whether at Sile itself or on one of the neighbouring beaches such as Sile Feneri, Kumbaka, Ocak Ada or Aglayan Kaya.

The route turns inland again. 60km further on is the small town of **Kandira**. At this point the road turns south towards the provincial capital of **Adapazari**. Adapazari lies in the broad green valley of the River Sakarya, known in antiquity as the Sangarios. The plains are fertile and productive, and the town's inhabitants live mostly from the associated agricultural trade. It is also a good place for buying cheap leather goods, including clothes and handbags.

The road crosses the river, and continues over a pass into the plains around Düzce. There are fields as far as the eye can see, and the local harvest is considerable. There is nothing worth stopping for in **Düzce** itself, though it is worth mentioning the ruins of the ancient settlement of Dusai to the south of the town.

After Kaynasli there follows an impressively built stretch of road through the heavily-wooded Pontine landscape. The road climbs up the **Bolu Pass**, providing some marvellous views. The

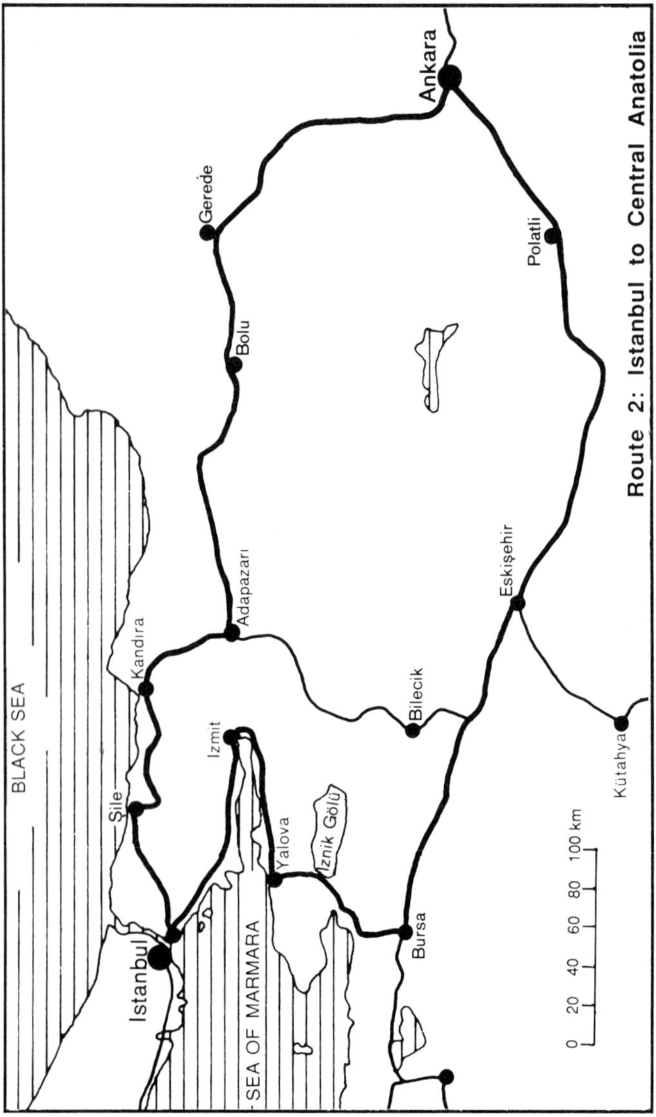

Route 2: Istanbul to Central Anatolia

Sile, on the Black Sea coast

Bolu Pass is 1,000m (3.300ft) above sea level, and forms the boundary of central Anatolia. The scenery here is delightful. The tree-covered mountains and green valleys are a welcome distraction from the scorching heat.

About 6km beyond the pass, there is a turning along a side road for **Lake Abant**. The road runs all the way round the lake (7km), which nestles among green meadows and coniferous forests. There are numerous camping sites and holiday homes in the vicinity.

The main road descends into the valley, passing several hotels and filling stations. The town of **Bolu** lies to the right of the main road, which bypasses it. There has been a settlement here since ancient times, when it provided a stopping point for merchants embarking on the difficult journey through Anatolia to central Asia.

The E5 crosses the plain, and bridges the Büyüksu Irmagi. It then climbs steeply again to 1,000m (3,300ft). The next two places are **Yeniçaga** by Lake Çaga and **Gerede**, whose wooden houses are typical of this heavily forested region. The road goes in a straight line through a mixture of cornfields, meadows and forests. This area of mountains and forests is popular with holidaymakers, and attracts many weekend tourists from Ankara. There is no shortage of camping sites and holiday homes.

The road climbs steeply again to 1,500m (4,900ft), and passes close to a mountain called the Civcan Dagi. It drops down again into the valley of the Kimir Çayi. The scenery is varied, with some wonderful views. On the way down the road passes through a wild and beautiful gorge.

The road goes through the village of **Bulak** and arrives at the small spa town of **Kizilcahamam**, which is to the right of the road. The thermal springs here have a temperature of 50°C (122°F). They were well known to the Greeks, who built the ancient town of Manegordus on this site. The spa waters are very slightly radioactive and contain carbon dioxide. The baths are at the top end of the town. Visitors can either bathe alone or take a dip in the communal baths, which are made of marble. There is a modern hotel about 4km away from the main E5 road. It is in the middle of the nature reserve that adjoins the town.

The road leaves the valley of the Kimir Çayi, where rice and other crops are grown, and continues to **Akdogan**. 60km further on, at the Susuzköy Mocamp, there is modern accommodation available. About 20km before Ankara, the E5 is joined by the N1, which also comes from Istanbul.

The road approaches Ankara along a fast road through a bare, treeless region of hills and dried-up valleys. It enters the Turkish capital via the Istanbul Caddesi, which goes all the way into the city centre. If one goes straight on at the main central square, one comes into the Atatürk Bulvari, the city's main shopping street.

The railway from Istanbul follows a more direct route. However, given the slowness of Turkish trains, it is scarcely faster than the journey by bus or by car. One should allow at least a day for visiting **Ankara***, or preferably even 2 days.

It was Kemal Atatürk, father of modern Turkey, who made Ankara the capital of the Turkish republic. He wished to reward its inhabitants for their loyalty during his long struggle for power. He planned a new city on Western lines on the bare steppes of Anatolia. Thus Ankara became the first modern city in Turkey, and is almost the embodiment of twentieth-century Turkey. To foreigners its architecture is disappointingly unimaginative and functional, but the Turks are nonetheless very proud of it. The old town with its citadel seems to lead an entirely separate existence.

The return journey to Istanbul follows the E23/N68 Afyon road, leaving it to join the N2/60 for Eskisehir and Bursa, which is 389km from Ankara. The road is good throughout, and has plenty of fast straight stretches. The rail journey takes 5 hours as far as Eskisehir and a total of 12 hours to Istanbul. The overland bus route takes roughly the same time. The scenery along this route is not particularly interesting, but the hot, arid plateau has an unforgettable atmosphere all of its own.

The road route leaves the centre of Ankara along the Istanbul Caddesi. 2km out of the centre it goes left at a set of traffic lights to join the E5 Adana road. The E5 runs past the hippodrome and crosses the railway. Then after another 5km the route turns right onto the E23/N68.

About 25km out of Ankara, the road passes the green oasis of Dinlenme Parki, which also has a small lake. This is followed by the village of **Temelli** and the small town of **Polatli**. Polatli is an important collection point at harvest time, but the town possesses little of interest. The railway has so far remained close to the road, but it now takes a short cut along a separate route.

About 17km after Polatli, there is a right turn along a side road to the ancient ruins of **Gordium***, which is 12km away from the main road next to the village of **Yassihüyük**. The old Phrygian city of Gordium was the site of a well-known oracle concerning the famous Gordian knot. Whoever could undo the knot was destined to conquer the world. When Alexander the Great came through here during one of his campaigns, he is said to have had no difficulty in cutting the knot open with his sword. He later fulfilled the prophecy by founding a great empire.

The E23/N68 crosses the Sakarya and passes through the picturesque little village of **Oglacki**. The next town is **Sivrihisar**, which is 2km off the main road along a small road to the right. This interesting little town contains a number of old mosques and khans, plus the ruins of a Byzantine castle. It is dominated by a nearby mountain called the Çal Dagi (1,700m (5,576ft)).

About 10km to the south of Sivrihisar, near the village of Ballihisar, is the site of the ancient temple of **Pessimus**. This was once the home of the Magna Mater, patron goddess of Asia Minor. The temple complex was one of the most famous in the whole of the Mediterranean. At the beginning of the third century AD, the Romans removed the statue of the goddess and took it

Typical of Turkey's villages — narrow streets and overhanging houses

back to Rome with them. Though the site is hidden beneath the undergrowth, it is still possible to make out the acropolis, together with the theatre and the cemetery to the south.

The route continues along the N2/60, which runs in a straight line through cornfields and steppe. It passes through very few villages, and the filling stations are at 40km intervals.

Detour to the Phrygian Rock Tombs

Anyone interested in archaeology is recommended to make this detour to see the Phrygian remains in the area around **Çifteler**. To do this, one should turn left off the main N2/60 road along the N29 to the village of **Hamidiye** (2km), where there is a right turn for Seyitgazi (30km).

Overlooking **Seyitgazi** is a fourteenth-century dervish monastery. A holy man called Seyit Gazi is buried here in a 4m (13ft) long sarcophagus. He was accidentally killed by a princess, who afterwards committed suicide and is buried beside him.

40km to the south of Seyitgazi is the village of **Kirka**. The area around here was once the centre of the Phrygian empire (later the province of Galatia). The Phrygians were an Indo-European tribe that settled here in about 2000 BC. They developed a very advanced culture that was later wiped out by the Persian invasions. These rock tombs are virtually all that remains of the Phrygian civilisation. Most of them are scattered among the inaccessible mountains of Yazilikaya between Kirka and Çifteler.

The tombs continue to baffle archaeologists. The inscriptions on them remain largely undeciphered, and the only word to have been recognised is the name 'Midas'. This was found in the oldest and largest tomb, which is appropriately known as the Tomb of Midas. Its enormous gabled entrance has been hewn out of the bare rock, and its walls are covered with geometrical designs. It was built in the sixth century BC, and was apparently a temple to a Phrygian deity whose name is as yet unknown. On the nearby plateau are the remains of a Phrygian city, which is supposed to have been called Midas. The ruins opposite are those of the former castle of Pimiskale.

The valley of the Kumbet also contains several tombs and temples. Yet more are to be found either side of the road that goes south towards Afyon. One of these is the so-called Lion Rock or Arslan Kaya, which contains a statue of the mysterious Phrygian goddess Cybele flanked by lions. Other examples include Arslan Tas, Küçük and Bahsis.

All these sites are inaccessible and difficult to find. Visitors are therefore advised to hire the services of a guide at Seyitgazi or Kirka. The cost should be agreed on beforehand, a reasonable fee being about half what the guide first suggests.

The N2/60 continues towards Eskisehir through a relatively monotonous landscape. 20km further on, near the villages of **Imisehir**, **Tokat** and **Karatepe**, the road passes a series of meerschaum mines on the right. The meerschaum extracted from them is the valuable substance from which clay pipes are made. It is mined to a depth of about 10m (33ft).

The road descends gently to the provincial capital of **Eskisehir***. This large and fairly modern-looking town is an important railway junction, with many industries including cement and sugar. After Eskisehir the landscape remains rather monotonous, but the road is both fast and straight.

25km further on there is a turning along a small unmetalled road to **Sögüt**. This was the ancestral seat of the Ottoman dynasty, and the home of its founding father Ertogul. His tomb is still on view to visitors. On 9 March every year, nomads come

Eskisehir on the River Porsuk

here from all over Turkey to pay homage to him.

The N2 continues across the steppe at a height of about 800m (2,624ft) above sea level. The next village, **Poyra**, is typical of the Anatolian steppes. Just after Poyra there is a left turn along a side road to **Inönü** (13km). Its name was adopted by the former Turkish president (later deposed) because of his victorious battle here against the Greeks in 1921 during the Turkish War of Independence. The village is interesting for its fourteenth-century mosque and the nearby cave dwellings of **Tutluca Tepe**.

Bozüyük is in a beautiful situation in a valley watered by a tributary of the Sakarya. The road crosses the valley to a junction, where the present route goes straight on along the N2. This road climbs up through a narrow valley to the top of a pass, and winds steeply down the other side to Pazaryeri.

The section that follows is all uphill and downhill, with some marvellous views on the way. The road passes through **Bahçesultan**, **Kursunlu** and **Inegöl**. Items of interest include the Ishak Pasa Mosque and a fourteenth-century caravanserai. The road climbs over several spurs of the Uludag (Olympus) mountain range, and finally descends into the Bursa valley.

Bursa* is one of the most delightful cities in Turkey. A whole day at least is needed to see everything. But there is plenty of overnight accommodation. This one-time capital of the Ottoman empire has preserved its old Turkish buildings beautifully intact. Its lovely houses, magnificent mosques and the exotic Muradiye Cemetery are all worth a visit for their own sake.

One can return to Istanbul by air or by road. The bus follows the same route as the car, leaving Bursa in a northerly direction along the road past the *Kumluk Restaurant*. Soon there is a wonderful panorama of the Gulf of Gemlik. **Gemlik** itself was originally founded by Greeks from Miletus, on a site that coincides with the present old town.

The road carries on to **Orhangazi**, which is close to the beautiful Lake Iznik. It is possible to make a detour all the way round the lake. At the opposite end is the picturesque village of **Iznik** — the one-time Greek town of Nicaea.

The main road continues northwards towards the coast. It climbs through a range of coastal mountains and drops down into **Yalova**, which is 70km from Bursa. Yalova is delightfully situated by the coast. Since time immemorial it has been famous for the local thermal springs, which are about 10km away. They are next to the remains of ancient baths, known from the Argonaut legend as Pythia. The modern baths are built next to these ruins.

There are ferries from Yalova that go across past the Princes' Islands to Kartal near Üsküdar. The road, meanwhile, follows a much longer route around the coast of the Gulf of Izmit. About 10km from Yalova, on a peninsula called Hersek, are the remains of the ancient Greek town of Helenopolis. This was the birthplace of Helena, mother of Constantine the Great.

The road continues via **Karamürsel** and **Golcük** to the port of **Izmit**. The only remnant of Izmit's glorious past is the acropolis at the northern end of the town. It was once the Greek city of Nicomedia, and was the residence of the Roman emperors Hadrian and Diocletian.

Near **Hereke** are the ruins of the Byzantine walled city of Ancyrum, which is where Constantine the Great died in AD 337. The road continues for another 20km through a fruit-growing area to **Gebze**, where there are numerous Byzantine remains. The mosque dates from the sixteenth century, and possesses some noteworthy porcelain decorations.

A small side road leads off from Gebze to the ruins of Libyssa, where Hannibal is supposed to have taken poison so as to avoid being captured alive by the Romans. Centuries later, Emperor Septimius Severus built a mausoleum here around the tomb of Rome's greatest enemy. It was plundered on several occasions, and is now completely destroyed.

⌘ Just past Gebze there is a left turn to **Darica**, where there are yet more ancient remains. The nearby ruin of Eskihisar was another Byzantine settlement which was destroyed by the Turks.

Next comes the small town of **Pendik**. This town was heavily fortified in the Byzantine period, and acted as an eastern bulwark for the provincial capital of Chalcedon (now Kadiköy). Chalcedon was where leaders from all over Christendom held their fourth ecumenical council in AD 451. Pendik today is a lovely little seaside resort, with a beach and a nice camping site.

The road continues past **Kartal**, and after another 15km enters the Asian suburbs of Istanbul. There is a fast road through the well-to-do suburb of **Kadiköy** (see above) and past the Great Cemetery to **Üsküdar**. From here one can return to **Istanbul** by ferry. Alternatively, one can bypass the eastern suburbs and cross the Bosporus via the Europa Bridge.

4 ROUTE THREE: THE BLACK SEA COAST ROAD

Ankara • Kastamonu • Inebolu (360km) • Sinop • Samsun • Ordu • Giresun • Trabzon (960km) • Gümüshane • Askale • Erzurum • (1,335km) • Erzincan • Sivas • Yozgat • Bogazkale • Ankara (2,285km)

The route leaves **Ankara** in an easterly direction along the E23 Sivas road, which goes through **Kayas** and **Elmadag**. 20km further on, the route turns left and goes northwards along the N39 to **Kalecik**. From here onwards the road is unmetalled, but is fortunately not too dusty.

The ruined castle near Kalecik was built during the time of the Byzantine empire to protect the route to the Black Sea at the point where it forded the Kizilirmak. There are more castles further along the route, showing how important it was at that time. One of these castles is at the next town, **Çankiri**, which also has an interesting sixteenth-century mosque.

The road begins to climb over the Pontic Mountains that run parallel to the Black Sea coast. It is 50km to the main pass, where the road is extremely twisty as it climbs up to 1,780m (5,838ft). The mountainous terrain makes the route take much longer than the 115km between Çankiri and Kastemonu might suggest. The castle at **Kastamonu** was the seat of the Comnenes dynasty, and the Ismael Bey Mosque is also extremely interesting.

It is only another 2 hours' ride along the N39 to the Black Sea port of **Inebolu**. Inebolu has some beautiful wooden houses, a ruined castle and a marvellous bathing beach. The route turns east here along the N12 coast road, which has a metalled surface.

This coast road is one of the most scenic routes in the whole of Turkey. It passes through seaside towns such as **Abana**, with a camping site and 5km of beach, and **Ayancik**, which has as many as 10km of beach. The coast is bordered by thick forests.

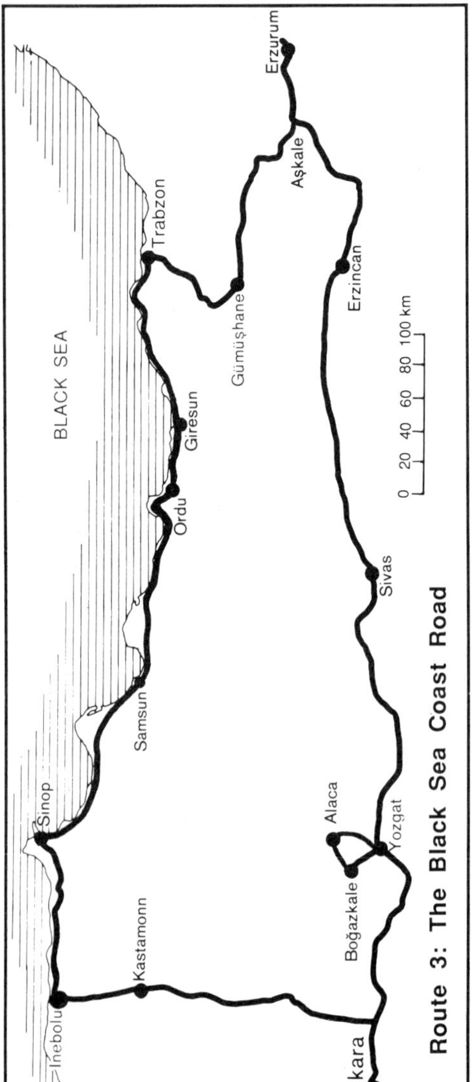

Route 3: The Black Sea Coast Road

The road remains twisty; it turns inland after Ayancik, and eventually returns to the coast near Sinop.

Sinop* is delightfully situated on a volcanic peninsula; it is the most northerly town in Turkey. The route turns southward for a little towards the small port of **Gerze**. The road is now the N20, which is a considerable improvement on previous roads. The next town is **Bafra** .

The area bordering the Gulf of Samsun is mostly planted with tobacco and maize. The town of **Samsun*** is the biggest port along the Black Sea coast. This bustling modern city has a population of over 450,000. There are some beautiful beaches to the east and the west of the town.

The route continues along the N20. The next town is **Çarsamba**, which stretches out along the banks of the Yesilirmak. There follows the insignificant little town of **Terme**, which in ancient times was the legendary city of Themiscyra. This is supposed to have been the home of the Amazons, where Hercules achieved the impossible feat of stealing the girdle of Hippolyta, the Amazon queen. More historically verifiable is the siege of the city by the Romans under Lucullus in 73 BC, during the third of their wars against Mithridates of Pontus.

The stretch of coast which follows is known as the Hazelnut Coast on account of its vast numbers of hazel bushes. The road passes through many small fishing villages, where the hard-bitten fishermen still capture dolphins from rowing boats. The scenery is idyllic, with long, sandy beaches, lined by an impenetrable barrier of hazel scrublands.

The road passes through **Ünye**, picturesquely situated by a bay. There are some magnificent views along the section between **Fatsa** and **Bolaman**. The houses here are supported on stone foundations. The ground is boggy, and the stones are supposed to stop the damp from entering the houses.

Persembe is followed by **Ordu**, where Xenophon is supposed to have embarked with 10,000 soldiers on his way back to Thrace. Ordu is a port of call for ships cruising in the Black Sea. This has resulted in the development of a modest tourist industry, including restaurants and some rather spartan hotels. Ordu is also a major port for the shipment of wood and hazelnuts.

Along the next section via Bulancak to Giresun, the mountains come much nearer to the coast. **Giresun** is perched on the slopes of a rocky peninsula, and is overlooked by the ruins of a once proud fortress. There is a magnificent view from the top. The town's two main attractions are the mausoleums of two Seljuk princes called Seyyidi Vakkas and Osman Aga. To the east of ⌘ Giresun is an island called **Büyük Adasi**, which according to legend was a landing point for Jason and the Argonauts, Hercules and Orpheus. All that now remains are the ruins of a Greek temple and of a Byzantine monastery.

The coast road continues through **Kesap**, **Tirebolu**, with its Byzantine castle, and the picturesque little port of **Görele**, with its ruined castle and monastery. These are followed by **Eynesil** and **Vakfikebir**, which has a camping site. It is now only a short distance to Trabzon. The port of **Trabzon*** (formerly known as **Trebizond**) has a long and illustrious history. Overland trade routes from Persia and Afghanistan used to end here, and ships have docked here for 2,500 years.

Excursion to Hopa near the Soviet Border

Hopa is the last Turkish port along the Black Sea coast, and is only 17km from the Soviet border. The route is scenic, but the road is unmade for part of the way, and much of the Hopa area is a restricted military zone. Potential visitors should therefore check up at the tourist information office in Trabzon, to make sure that the way through is clear.

The small town of **Rize** is about half-way from Trabzon to Hopa, and is surrounded by tea plantations. About 54 million pounds of tea are harvested each year — enough to satisfy Turkey's not inconsiderable home market. After Rize, the mighty silhouette of the Caucasus Mountains appears in the far distance ahead. The road continues through several tunnels.

The rather austere little port of **Hopa** has an approximate population of only 6,000. Though the Soviet border is 17km away, civilians are not allowed near it. The way through to Batumi on the Soviet side is completely closed.

It is 340km from Trabzon to Erzurum along the E100, which is metalled and in a good state of repair. The road follows an old caravan route up the valley of the Degirmen Dere. Xenophon is supposed to have led 10,000 Greek soldiers down this valley under appalling conditions on their return to Thrace.

About 30km from Trabzon is the village of **Maçka**. It is not far from here to the chief attraction between Trabzon and Erzurum: ⌘ the Greek Orthodox monastery of Meryemana at **Sumela**. It is about 12km south-east of Maçka, and is reached via a small side road signposted to Meryemana. The road is unmade and extremely bad, making the monastery almost inaccessible. The buildings are mostly in ruins, but the church is still well preserved. It has been carved out of the bare rock, and is beautifully painted. The site is much more extensive than it looks, and consists of several courtyards surrounded by chapels, workshops and living quarters. Most of the buildings date back only to the nineteenth century, but the monastery itself was founded in the fourteenth century. The Comnene emperor Alexis III was crowned here in 1340. A fire in 1930 destroyed many of the monastery's most valuable treasures, including an icon of St Luke and an extensive library.

The main road continues to climb steeply to the top of the **Zigana Geçidi** or **Zigana Pass** (2,025m (6,642ft)). Here the road passes between the Horos Daglari to the west and the Zigana Daglari in the east, both of which belong to the Pontic Mountains. The road surface is good, but there are some dangerous hairpins. The vegetation in north-eastern Anatolia is markedly different from that on the coast — the woodland retreats replaced by bushes and coarse steppe grass.

The road drops down into the small town of **Gümüshane**, where there are a number of fairly basic restaurants. About 2,000 years ago, Gümüshane became prosperous as a result of silver mines in the vicinity. But 200 years ago the mines were exhausted. Later the town was moved about 200m (656ft) down the valley, and was finally rebuilt in its present location in about 1920.

The road continues towards Erzurum at an average height of about 2,000m (6,560ft) above sea level. There are restaurants and filling stations in the small villages along the route. **Kale** is ⌘
dominated by the massive ruin of a Byzantine castle. It is difficult to imagine how such a well-fortified castle could have been captured. But the Turks managed it about 600 years ago.

Bayburt was once the capital of the Scythians. Its Greek ⌘
name was Gymnias, and Xenophon once stayed within its walls. There is a Byzantine citadel built by Emperor Justinian, and to the left of it a ruined Chaldean fortress.

It is another 125km to Erzurum. The road climbs steeply to the top of the Kopdagi Geçidi, which at 2,400m (7,872ft) is the highest point of the whole route. There is a broad panorama of the bare landscape of eastern Anatolia. To the south-west is the Cosan Daglari (2,960m (9,708ft)). The road descends into the

Ancient minarets, Sivas

valley of the Karasu, which is a tributary of the River Euphrates. The road passes below another castle on the approach to **Askale**, where it joins the E23 from Ankara. The route continues eastwards towards Erzurum through **Kandilli** and **Ilica**, where there are thermal springs.

5km before **Erzurum*** there is a turning for the airport. The road enters the city past the university, which as usual is named after Atatürk. Erzurum is the biggest city in eastern Anatolia. It lies at about 2,000m (6,560ft) above sea level, and the climate is harsh. Erzurum is a melting pot for the many different peoples of Asia Minor. It is also a garrison town and the headquarters of Turkey's eastern border defences. The city itself is full of buildings of historical and cultural interest, and the area around is also very interesting. Travellers should allow at least a day and a half's visiting time. There is plenty of accommodation available.

The route returns westwards along the E23 Ankara road, following the same route back as far as **Askale**. At this point the E23 turns south-westwards. There follows an exciting stretch of road through the mountains, with peaks over 3,000m (9,840ft) visible in the distance. The road climbs up the wild valley of the Degirmen Dere to the little old town of **Tercan**. Tercan was once on the ancient trade route from Persia to Europe. Its twelfth-century buildings are amazingly well preserved.

The next important town is **Erzincan** which developed as an important market and trading town. It is in the centre of a major earthquake zone, and has often been in the headlines as a result.

Visitors who wish to stand on the banks of the Euphrates should make a short detour via **Kemah**. It is not long before the **Euphrates** (in Turkish **Firat**) comes into view. The Euphrates is the longest and most famous river in the Middle and Near East. Alexander the Great and several Roman Emperors bathed in its waters. Herodotus said of it, 'The border between Cilicia and Armenia is formed by a navigable river called the Euphrates. It is a great, rushing river.'

It is about 80km from Erzincan via Kemah to **Refahiye**. The E23 now leaves Armenia, and continues across the mountainous plateau of central Anatolia. The landscape becomes barren and monotonous. After another 100km the road arrives at the town of **Zara**. But rather than stopping here, travellers should press on towards Sivas. If at all possible, one should stay overnight at **Sivas*** so as to leave enough time to have a look at the city.The E23 passes the airport on leaving Sivas, and runs parallel to the trans-Anatolian railway as far as **Yildizeli**. After that it runs in and out of several river valleys, including those of the Kavak, the Germugar and the Gündelen. 190km from Sivas, the E23 arrives at **Yozgat**.

At this point one should ask for exact directions to the ancient

Hittite capital of **Hattusa** (**Hattusas**). The site is by the village of **Bogazkale***, 40km north of Yozgat along a rough road that comes off the E23 just west of the town. These ancient ruins are well worth the effort of getting there. Three to five hours should be spent there to see them properly.

Railway travellers must take a longer route from Sivas via Kayseri. Those wishing to visit Hattusa should get out at Yerköy and take a bus to **Yozgat**. From here one can continue by taxi or *dolmus*, taking care to agree beforehand with the driver on the price for the trip both there and back.

The main road continues from Yozgat towards Ankara via **Yerköy**, **Cerikli** and **Kirikkale**. 15km after Kirikkale, it crosses the great **Kizilirmak** (**Red River**), known in antiquity as the Halys. The Halys became legendary on account of the famous prophecy, 'If you cross the Halys, you will destroy your empire.' Croesus, king of Lydia until 546 BC, bore out this prophecy when he crossed the river in a vain bid to extend his empire, and subsequently fell to the invading Persian armies.

After **Elmadag** the road descends into the Ankara basin. It is only 15km to **Ankara**. Soon the old citadel appears on the horizon, announcing the end of this exciting if rather difficult tour.

5 ROUTE FOUR: THE AEGEAN COAST

Istanbul • Izmit • Bursa • Bandirma • Çanakkale • Troy • Ayvacik • Edremit • Bergama • Izmir (649km) • Manisa • Balikesir • Bursa • Izmit • Istanbul (1,250km)

One should first cross the Bosporus via the Europa Bridge or by ferry to **Üsküdar** or **Kartal**. One can travel on by bus or by car. The route is not suited to rail travel, as there is no railway along the coast of the Aegean. On the other hand, there are plenty of bus connections.

Foot passengers who have already travelled through **Izmit**, **Yalova** and **Bursa** may wish to take a relaxing boat trip across the Sea of Marmara to **Bandirma**. The boat does not, however, take cars, and runs only once or twice a week during the summer.

The route as far as **Bursa** has already been described as part of Route Two. It continues westwards from Bursa along the N2, leaving the Bursa lowlands across a range of hills, to arrive on the north shore of **Lake Ulubat**. This is named after the village of Ulubat on its western shore. It is also known as **Lake Apolyont** after the ancient city of Apollonia, whose ruins can still be seen on its northern shore. The shores were settled as early as 3000 BC, as is attested by the graves that have been found, including the double tomb of a ruler and his wife.

The route continues via **Karabey** to **Bandirma**. Bandirma is in a lovely coastal situation, and has wide streets lined with small second-hand shops. To the west of the town, the peninsula of **Erdek** juts out into the Sea of Marmara. According to a Greek legend, Zeus, the father of the gods, banished his midwives to here in the form of bears.

The N2 turns inland towards **Gönen**. The landscape is wooded again. Just past Gönen and to the right of the road is a large farm called *Tahir Ova* that owes its existence to German development aid. It was built in 1957 as a training institute for Turkish farmers.

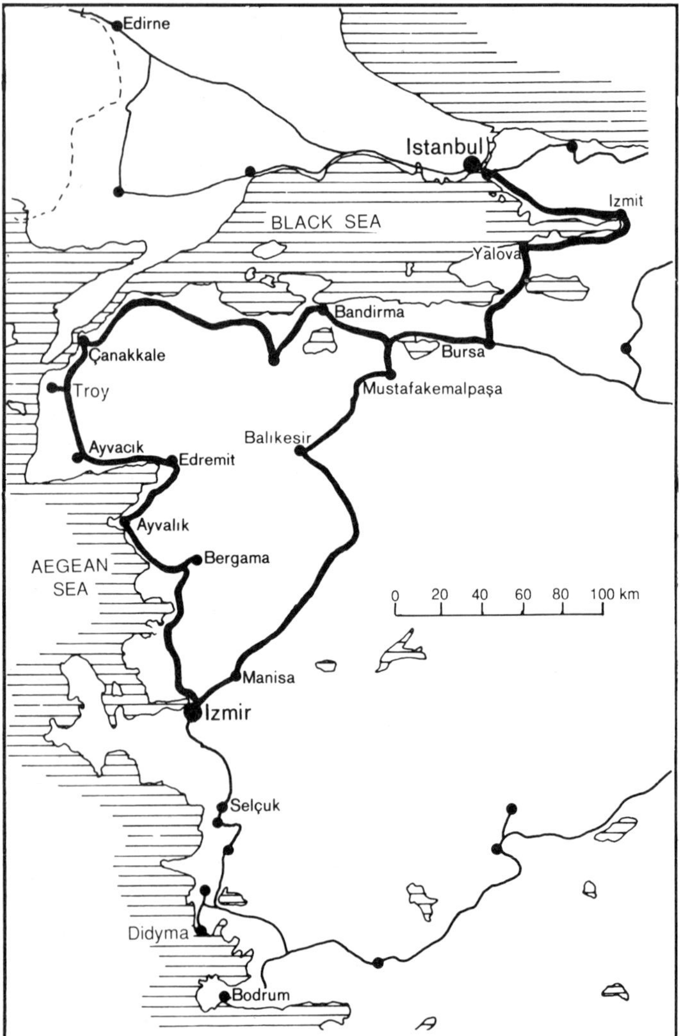

Route 4: The Aegean Coast

The route dogs the tracks of Alexander the Great, who encamped near **Sariköy** after he had routed the Persians by the River Granicus. The road crosses the Granicus shortly after. The villages along the straits of the Dardanelles have a long and illustrious history. In ancient times these quiet little backwaters were thriving Greek colonies that formed the cultural centre of Asia Minor. **Lâpseki** (in Greek Lampsacus) is where Aphrodite is supposed to have given birth to Priapus; Anaxagoras the philosopher died here; Alexander passed through; and Emperor Barbarossa led his fateful crusade from here in 1190.

Later the road bends sharply to the right, and 7km further on enters the port of **Çanakkale*** (population 150,000). Situated at the narrowest point of the Dardanelles, Çanakkale is the largest town along this part of the coast. It is an ideal base for visiting the Dardanelles region, and especially Troy. One good place to stay is the *Hotel Truva*, which is directly next to the harbour promenade. Its windows look out across the strait towards the ferry port on the opposite shore. Equally good is the *Tusan Motel*, which is 15km out of the town and half-way towards Troy (see below).

Along the E24 road towards Intepe, there is a turning for the ancient ruins of **Dardanus**, after which the straits are named. The site is near the shore about 2km from the main road. **Intepe** itself is in a commanding position on a hill. There is a magnificent panorama of the Dardanelles and the European mainland beyond. The village is surrounded by many ancient ruins, most of which have yet to be examined by archaeologists.

At the western entrance to the Dardanelles are the village of **Kumkale** and the nearby ruins of Achillium, neither of which is far from Troy. Two mounds on the plains to the south are supposed be the graves of Achilles and Patrocles. As yet no archaeological evidence has been found to link them with these two Trojan heroes. But great military leaders of the past made a special point of visiting this site to pay tribute to the two legendary warriors. Alexander the Great and Emperor Hadrian were amongst them.

The turning for **Troy*** (in Turkish **Truva**) is well signposted, and it is only 6km from the main E24 road. The best time to visit this or any other ancient site on the Aegean coast is between 8 and 9am or between 6 and 8pm. These sites are best appreciated in an atmosphere of peace and solitude. There is not very much to see at Troy, but the visit leaves an impression which is both vivid and lasting.

Near **Ezine** there is another turning to the right along a tiny road down towards the coast. From **Geyikli** there is a good view of the island of **Bozca Ada** (Tenedus), which has associations with the Trojan War. The Greeks left a wooden horse on the beach, and retreated to hide behind the island. They left soldiers hidden inside the belly of the horse, which the Trojans dragged up inside their city walls. The soldiers came out under cover of darkness, and opened the city gates to their fellow-Greeks, who in the meantime had hurried back from their hiding place. Thus the conquest of Troy was accomplished.

There is a small road going south from Geyikli towards **Odun Iskele**. 3km along this road are the ruins of the famous city of Alexandria Troas, known in Turkish as Eski Istanbul. The city state of Troas was famed throughout the ancient world for its beautiful setting, its culture and its prosperity. Julius Caesar even wanted to make it the capital of the Roman empire. Emperors Augustus and Hadrian had some magificent buildings erected here. Paul the Apostle stayed at Troas frequently, sometimes for a considerable period. The site is very well worth visiting.

About 20km to the north of Geyikli is the small village of **Bunarbasi**. From here it is about forty minutes' walk to the graves of Hector and Priam of Troy. Priam's grave mound is on a hill called Bali Dagi, and is flanked by two smaller mounds on either side. This was also the site of an ancient city, whose name is not known. On a hill across the nearby river (the Küçükmenderes Çayi) is an old Greek fortification.

The E24 Aegean coast road continues southwards through shady coniferous forests. The road is well made, and passes numerous motels and camping sites along the coast.

Ayvacik is a good place from which to visit the ancient city of **Assus**. The village of **Behramkale** has been built over the ruins of this once-famous Greek colony. The scenery is magnificent; one can gaze across the Aegean to the Greek island of Lesbos. Assus has been well-known since the second century BC. Aristotle lived here, and the Stoic philosopher Cleanthes was born here in 331 BC. A significant amount of the city remains, including a 3km long section of the 20m (65ft) high ramparts, the foundation walls of houses and temples, and columns from the temple of Athene at the top end of the site.

The E24 swings round towards the Gulf of Edremit. It crosses a river called Tuzla Dere, climbs up over a spur of the Mount Ida range, and descends towards the Edremit basin. The clearings in the woodland provide glimpses of the Aegean and of the Greek islands that border the Turkish coast.

26km before Edremit, the road passes the village of **Altinoluk** on the left. Amongst the nearby undergrowth are the ruins of the city of Antandrus. It is at the foot of Mount Ida, where the 'judgement of Paris' took place. Paris, son of King Priam of Troy, was asked to judge a kind of beauty competition between the three goddesses Hera, Athene and Aphrodite. He chose Aphrodite, who promised him the most beautiful woman in the world. Encouraged by this, he abducted Helen, wife of King Menelaus of Sparta. The Greek fleet came to Troy to bring Helen back, and thus began the fateful Trojan War.

There are several good beaches along the gulf, of which the most popular is Akçay, 8km before Edremit. **Edremit** itself is the administrative centre of the area, with a bus station, a police station, council offices and several banks and shops. It is surrounded by ancient sites, some of which, such as Thebes and Adramyttium, have yet to be excavated.

As one continues, the woodland is gradually replaced by fruit plantations. The next town is the small but busy industrial port of **Ayvalik**. It is surrounded by salt pans, in which salt is produced from sea water. There are some good beaches and a camping site along the bay nearby.

South of Ayvalik the E24 turns inland. 50km after Ayvalik there is a left turn for **Bergama***, which is 7km off the main road. It is a further 4km to the hill-top site of the ancient city of **Pergamum**. Car drivers can come here direct. Bus travellers must change at Ayvalik and catch a bus that will bring them to Bergama. Alternatively, one can take an overland bus to Izmir, stay there overnight and make a day excursion from there. Many impressive buildings remain of this former Greek capital, making it one of the high points of the tour. At least half a day is needed to see the classical remains of Pergamum and the lovely old town of Bergama, with its ancient basilica.

The road is a very good one as it continues southwards along the fertile coastal plain towards Izmir. There are several ancient sites to the right of the road. Of these, the extensive burial ground at **Myrina** is particularly worth seeing. The ruined city is by the mouth of the Güzelhisar Çayi next to the village of **Kalabak Saray**. Myrina was once a thriving Aeolian port. It is supposed to have been founded by the Amazons, and was renamed Sebastopolis by Emperor Augustus. The present site

Classical remains at Pergamum near Bergama

⌘ includes the remains of the theatre and the castle, and a surprisingly large burial ground. Several thousand graves have been unearthed here, and there are probably another 3,000 still untouched. About 5km from Aliaga are the ruins of Cyme, which was the largest of the Aeolian cities.

⌘ The road approaches **Izmir*** around the end of the Gulf of Izmir. 5km before the centre, in the suburb of Bayrakli, the road passes the original site of the ancient metropolis of **Smyrna**, which is well outside the modern centre. The legendary city of Smyrna was the oldest and largest Greek settlement in Asia Minor, and would have been compared in importance to the modern cities of London, Paris or Rome. It was the birthplace of Homer, author of the *Iliad* and the *Odyssey*. He is supposed to have remained here for many years, and probably wrote parts of the *Iliad* during that period.

The modern city centre is further on, past the rather drab harbour area and along a broad avenue called the Atatürk Caddesi. At least two days is required to visit Izmir and its immediate environs. Yet more time is needed for an excursion along the coast south of here to the ancient sites of Ephesus, Priene, Miletus and Didyma.

Car and bus travellers are recommended to return to Istanbul via Manisa, Balikesir and Bursa. Rail passengers can go by train to Bandirma and continue by ferry across the Sea of Marmara to Istanbul. It is also possible to combine the two by taking a train to Balikesir and continuing by bus for the rest of the way.

The road route leaves Izmir in a north-easterly direction along the N15. It goes through a fertile region of orchards and olive groves. As one travels into Lydia, the landscape becomes more mountainous. After **Bornova** the road climbs a pass called the Sabuncu Beli (750m (2,460ft)). There is a view of the highest mountain in the region, the Manisa Dagi (1,517m (4,975ft)).

The road descends steeply to **Manisa**, where at one time the sultan resided. Manisa is surrounded by beautiful scenery. There are fields full of poppies as far as the eye can see. Until recently the local Turkish farmers made opium from these poppies. Such activities are now illegal, and carry a heavy sentence. But this does not stop a certain amount of black market production.

The next town of **Akhisar** has a long and interesting past. As the city of Thyatira, it is mentioned in the Bible as having a group of early Christians who were especially faithful. However, nothing of historical importance is left. 55km beyond Akhisar, the road climbs the second pass along the route — the Sindirgi Beli (725m (2,378ft). It descends the wooded slopes to **Sindirgi** and continues to **Bigadiç**.

The road carries on from one fertile valley to the next until it arrives at **Balikesir**. The market town of Balikesir has been greatly modernised in recent years, thanks to its favourable position in a thriving agricultural region. Local products include tobacco, poppies, cotton, olives, grapes and figs. The bazaar is a delightful place for tourists, where the lively and fanciful Turkish temperament is shown to the full.

The N15 passes Susurluk, and follows the course of the

Ancient site at Manisa

Simav Çayi. 8km after Susurluk, there is a right turn for the modern town of **Mustafakemalpasa**. From here it is only 60km to **Bursa***. Travellers who have not seen the former sultan's capital of Bursa are recommended to spend at least half a day here.

The return route to Istanbul is the same as the outward one, following the coast road through **Izmit** and **Gebze**. Alternatively, one can take a ferry from **Yalova** to **Kartal**, avoiding the long detour round the Gulf of Izmit.

6 ROUTE FIVE: ANCIENT CITIES OF WESTERN TURKEY

Izmir • Selçuk • Ephesus • Söke • Priene • Miletus • Didyma • Bodrum • Mugla • Denizli (520km) • Dinar • Afyon • Kütahya • Eskisehir • Adapzari • Kandira • Sile • Istanbul (1,290km)

The route leaves **Izmir** in a southerly direction along the E24, which at this point turns inland. The road is a good one, but it is also very busy, especially at harvest time in August and September, when it is full of lorries laden with cotton.

The road passes near a number of important archaeological sites on its way through the ancient province of Ionia. The Ionians were the first Greeks to found colonies in Asia Minor. The towns they built along the coast formed bridgeheads to new and unknown territory. The trade with the hinterland flourished, and the towns soon grew into wealthy cities. The people built magnificent temples to thank the gods for their prosperity. The avenues of columns and broad squares were architecturally the best of their time.

Visitors without a car can hire a taxi from Izmir for the whole day. Using a taxi, one can stop at Ephesus for 3 hours, and also include Magnesia, Didyma, Miletus and Priene. Thus one can do the round of all the important local classical sites within the space of one day. It is important to be firm when bargaining.

Excursion to Colophon

Colophon was once the most important Ionian city apart from Smyrna, and gave its name to a kind of resin called colophony. Its ruins are about 30km from the main road. To reach them, one should turn right about 15km south of Izmir along a road signposted to **Cumaovasi** (5km). The road continues from **Cumaovasi** to the village of **Degirmendere** (25km).

The ancient ruins of **Colophon** are on a hill just to the south of Degirmendere. In about 300 BC the city was defeated in war, and

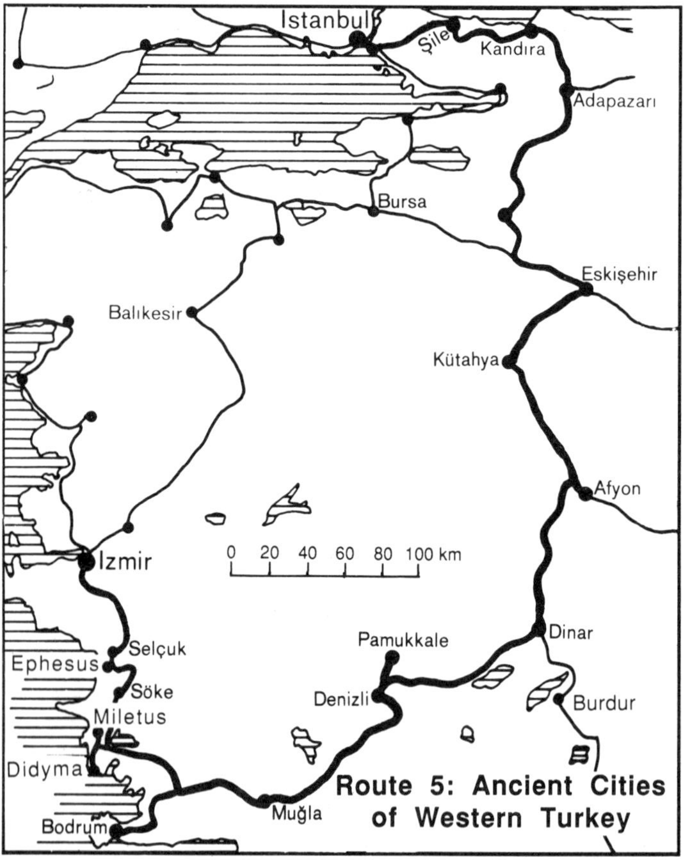

its inhabitants were exiled to Ephesus on the orders of King Lysimachus. But it flourished again under the Romans. It was heavily fortified with 2m (6½ft) thick walls and sixteen towers, the size of which is indicated by the massive foundations that remain. The city had been some distance inland since 2000 BC, and there was a fortified harbour called Notium on the coast some 10km to the south. Its ruins are still to be seen by a small rocky promontory.

2km inland and to the east of Notium is the site of the famous Temple of Apollo at **Clarus**. The steps leading up to the hexagonal temple bear inscriptions made by those consulting the oracle. A flight of steps leads down into the innermost chamber, which being full of water can no longer be entered. The front chamber served as a reception room for prominent visitors to the oracle. The back chamber contains a fountain, where the oracle himself used to meditate. He was usually a priest from Miletus. In the area just to the north of the temple, a marble altar has been unearthed in amazingly good condition.

The road is unfortunately a dead end, so visitors must return to the main road by the same route as they came.

The E24 continues via Torbali to **Selçuk**. This small town on the banks of the Küçük Menderes (Lesser Maeander) is overlooked by an old castle. There are storks' nests on the roofs of the houses. Part of the town is built over the ruins of the ancient city of **Ephesus***, the centre of which is about 3km outside Selçuk. Those arriving by bus should take a taxi from Selçuk .

The route continues along the E24 only as far as the village of **Ortaklar.** At this point it turns right along a more minor road to Söke, which crosses the ancient site of **Magnesia** (in Turkish **Magnizya**). Magnesia once lay on the banks of the famous River Maeander, from which the word meander is derived, but the course of the river has shifted southwards. The Turkish name is the Büyük Menderes (Greater Maeander). According to legend, the city was founded in prehistoric times by a tribe of women called the Amazons. The story is probably connected with the Artemis cult for which the city later became famous. There is in fact no evidence that Magnesia existed before 500 BC. The road passes the ruins of a temple to the north-east of the site. Several more remains are visible to the south of the road, including the smaller Temple of Athene, a market place (agora) and a theatre.

The route continues to **Söke**. The turning for **Priene*** is 15km south of Söke. Travellers are recommended to visit this site in the evening, when the five great Ionic columns are uncannily silhouetted against the setting sun. (Day trippers from Izmir can come here on the way back from Miletus and Didyma.) The chessboard-like street plan of the city is beautifully preserved to an extent hardly equalled elsewhere in Asia Minor. The evening scene at Priene is one of the most overwhelming sights along the whole of the Aegean coast. Gazing across the coastal basin of the Maeander, it is difficult to imagine that in classical times it was covered by the sea. The two main ports on the Gulf of Latmus were Priene to the north and Miletus to the south. They handled goods on their way between the interior of Asia Minor and the Greek homelands across the Aegean. The gulf must have gradually silted up with the deposits brought down by the Maeander. Now all that remains of it is a lagoon called the Bafa Gölü.

The route follows a narrow road signposted to Miletus and Didyma. It runs across the basin and over the Maeander to the village of **Akköy**. One turns north again in the village, and soon one can see the massive columns of the theatre at **Miletus*** (in Turkish **Milet**). The ruins are visible to the left of the road before it has even passed through the next village of **Balat**. To the right is a ruined mosque inhabited by storks.

Not far away is yet another wonder of the ancient world. Visitors should return to **Akköy** and continue southwards towards the Gulf of Mandalya. Next to the village of **Yenihisar** is one of the most famous classical temples in Asia Minor — the Temple of Apollo at **Didyma** (in Turkish **Didim**).

The oracle at Didyma was as important in Asia Minor as the oracle at Delphi was in Greece proper. There had already been a temple here when the Ionic Greeks originally came here. These Greeks took it over, and dedicated it to their own god Apollo. When Darius of Persia destroyed it in 499 BC, the cities of the Ionian federation decided to replace it with a larger and more elaborate construction. It was planned by architects from Ephesus and Miletus, who wished to make the temple of Didyma into the eighth wonder of the world.

The temple was alas never completed, owing to wars and shortage of money. But what remains is a glorious example of Ionian temple construction. Recent excavations have confirmed the reports of crusaders who spoke of it with wonder in the Middle Ages. The temple was 110m (361ft) long and 50m (164ft) wide. The façade consisted of twelve columns 20m (66ft) high and 1.6m (5ft) thick. Behind them was a great portal, and in front of them a flight of thirteen steps. Two of the columns bear recognisable depictions of Zeus and Apollo.

There is a small tourist centre nearby called the Altinkum, providing restaurants and bathing facilities. Visitors who stay longer in the area are also recommended to visit the ancient city of **Heraclia**. It is difficult to find, being on the eastern shore of the Bafa Gölü. One can either take a boat across the lake, or else follow a rough track from the village of **Serçinaus**. But the site is

The Temple of Apollo at Didyma

well worth the effort of getting there. The ruins are spread out along the foot of the mountains. The ancient fortifications are particularly impressive, but the Temple of Athene is equally worth seeing. The hill on which the acropolis once stood became the site for a medieval castle, built by the crusaders as a place for storing supplies.

Since about AD 800, a number of monasteries and hermitages have been set up in the mountains behind. Most of them are a long way from any road. The hermitages are decorated with beautiful cave paintings. The most well-known of the monasteries is that of Stylos or Arabavli, which dates from the tenth century.

The route continues past the southern shore of the Bafa Gölü and through the ancient province of Caria. The road goes via **Selimiye** towards the former Carian capital of Mylasa (now Milas). The region is harsh and mountainous, and has always been thinly populated. The Greek culture never penetrated to the lonely Carian settlements in the mountains of the interior. The people remained 'wild and barbarian', and were later hired by both the Greek and the Roman armies to fight back the attacks of the

Persians and the Seljuks.

The coastal section from Söke to Milas is gentle by comparison, so that one has no inkling of the wildness of the hinterland. There are pine forests and fast mountain streams, with occasional glimpses of the cliffs along the coast, and of attractive coves where one can bathe.

The small town of **Milas** lies in a fertile river basin, which since ancient times has been planted with olives and figs. It is built over the remains of the Carian capital of Mylasa, which was famed for its white marble temples and avenues of columns. A few of these buildings remain: the Güsmüskesen, a mausoleum from the first century BC with Corinthian columns; the former town gate (Baltali Kapi) to the north; and a few remnants of the theatre to the north-east. The remains of an aqueduct just outside the town are surprisingly well preserved. The town also has three mosques from the later Islamic period: The Orhanbey Camii and the Ulu Camii dating from the fourteenth century, and the more richly decorated Fircizbey Camii from the end of the fourteenth century.

Milas is not suitable for staying overnight, as accommodation is poor and limited. But if time allows, one should also make a short excursion to the nearby Carian Temple of Zeus. It is reached via a small side road going north of Milas, turning right after 2km along a small track that is fit for motor vehicles only in dry weather. The track climbs up the hillside to **Labranda**, where the temple once stood. One of its chief attractions to the Greeks of the time was that a pond in front of the temple contained fish decorated with valuable chains and gold rings.

A long, winding road goes south-west from Milas to the small coastal town of **Bodrum*** (70km). Bodrum is beautifully situated above a bay, with its houses built in terraces up the hillside. Out in the bay is the small island of Kara Ada, and beyond it the Greek island of Kos. Bodrum stands on the site of the ancient town of **Halicarnassus**, the remains of which are well worth a visit. And there are some marvellous beaches beyond the ruins.

The route returns along the same twisty road to within 3km of Milas, where it turns right towards Mugla. The road is narrow as it climbs in several tight hairpins onto a high plateau. It passes close to the ancient ruins of Stratonicia. Little of it is left, as most of the stone was taken away for use by local farmers. After **Yatagan** the road improves considerably.

Mugla is a somewhat larger town and travellers will have an opportunity to buy further provisions for the journey. The town has a medieval feel to it, and is overlooked by a fortified castle. All that remain from the Greek period are a few remnants of the ancient acropolis.

The section from Mugla to Denizli is only to be attempted in dry weather. The road is only partially metalled as it crosses the rough mountain landscape of the Carian interior. The route is an exciting one, but great care is required, especially around the dangerous hairpin bends. The only village of any significance is **Kale**, which is 86km from Mugla. So it is important to take extra provisions of food and drink, plus a spare can of fuel. One is also likely to run into a camel procession or a group of nomads. If so, one should remain polite and friendly but not too familiar. And on no account should one leave the vehicle.

Travellers will heave a sigh of relief when they are at last on firm ground again (for 'ground' read 'tarmac'!). From **Tavas** it is only another 50km to the provincial capital of **Denizli***. With a population of over 250,000, Denizli is the largest town for miles around. It spreads out across a broad, fertile plain, and has its quota of hospitals, hotels, police stations, post offices, shops, information bureaux etc.

There is only one local place of interest to tourists: the chalk terraces of **Pamukkale***. These are about 14km from the town, and are well signposted from the station. Bus or rail travellers are recommended to use the regular *dolmus* service that runs past the site. The stops are announced along the route, so it is impossible to get out at the wrong place. The long drawn-out 'Pamukkaleee' of the boys who act as ticket collectors is quite unmistakable. There is also a regular if less frequent local bus service to the chalk terraces.

Pamukkale is an ideal spot for a longer break, especially for travellers who wish to relax for a time amid some of the world's most amazing natural phenomena. Hotel accommodation is plentiful, reasonably priced and usually very good. Some establishments even include villas with swimming pools filled with water from local thermal springs. Guests are strongly recommended to book hotel rooms in advance. They can even make bookings earlier in the journey via hotel receptionists or tourist information offices.

The route continues eastwards along the E24. About 13km after Denizli, there is a right turn for **Honaz**, near to which are the scant remains of the city of **Colossae**, whose citizens were the recipients of the apostle Paul's letter to the Colossians.

The E24 twists and climbs onto the Anatolian plateau, passing several old caravanserais. Shortly after **Çardak**, the glistening white surface of a dried-up salt-lake becomes visible on the right-hand side; the Aci Gölü was even known to Herodotus.

The town of **Dinar** is not particularly interesting in itself, but its immediate environs are fascinating. It is built over the foundations of the ancient town of Celaenae. The source of the River Maeander is immediately in front of the town. To the south are the ruins of the once-prosperous Greek city of Apamea Cibotus. The nearby acropolis was the site of a palace that belonged to King Xerxes.

The route turns northwards along the N25, which runs parallel to the railway across a steppe-like plateau at about 1,000m (3,280ft) above sea level. After about 100km it arrives at **Afyon*** — the opium capital of Turkey. The N25 continues northwards towards Kütahya. It first follows the broad valley of the Akar Çayi, with its fields full of poppies; but then climbs suddenly out of the valley and back onto the unrelenting Anatolian steppes.

The friendly market town of **Kütahya** is about 900m (2,952ft) above sea level. One may wander at leisure through the bazaar, or quench one's thirst at one of the shady *lokantas* along the way. Kütahya is famous as a pottery manufacturing centre, where beautifully decorative plates can be bought quite cheaply. There is a plentiful selection of these at the bazaar.

The town is overlooked by a magnificent castle, where the sultans of Karaman resided in the fourteenth and fifteenth centuries. The town is a melting pot for the different peoples that have settled here and been assimilated over many centuries, including Greeks, Turks, Persians, Magyars and Poles. Of the various mosques, the Ulu Camii and the Yildirun Camii are from the fifteenth century, while the Kale i bala Camii dates back to the end of the fourteenth.

The route continues north-west towards Eskisehir through the fascinating Porsuk Gorge, and runs round a reservoir that was formed by the damming of the Porsuk Çayi.

Eskisehir* was a sleepy little backwater until the end of the nineteenth century. But when the Anatolian Railway was opened, it became an important junction between the lines to Ankara and Konya. It consequently grew into an important industrial centre.

The route. turns west along the N2 towards Bursa (see Route Two). After 56km it turns right along the N25 to **Bilecik**. Bilecik is a small country town in a delightful setting. It nestles at the foot of

Ceramics at Kütahya — famous as a pottery centre

the mighty Ahir Dagi, on whose slopes are the ruins of an unknown city of the past. The lower part of the town contains a monastery that was previously a Byzantine castle. All the mosques in the town were built in the fourteenth century.

3km after the Küplü roadside services (providing food, fuel and camping facilities), the road goes through a magnificent gorge. The scenery becomes mountainous as the road runs down the lovely valley of the Karasu as far as **Osmaneli**. From here it continues northwards via **Pamukova** to Adapazari.

There is a major crossroads just before **Adapazari**, with roads coming in from the left from either side of Lake Sapanca. The road to the right is the E5 for Ankara. Those wishing to travel direct to **Istanbul** should go left along the E5 via **Izmit**. Travellers with more time to spare are recommended to go straight on along the N25 through Adapazari itself and northwards towards the Black Sea coast, continuing westwards to **Sile**. From Sile it is another 70km to **Üsküdar** and **Istanbul** (see Route Two).

7 ROUTE SIX: THE MEDITERRANEAN COAST

Denizli • Dinar • Burdur • Antalya (290km) • Perga • Aspendus • Side • Manavgat • Alanya • Anamur • Silifke • Mersin • Adana (860km) • Pozanti • Ukulisla • Eregli • Karapinar • Konya (1,210km) • Aksehir • Çay • Afyon • Dinar • Denizli (1,660km)

The route leaves **Denizli*** along the E24, and at first follows the same course as Route Five. But just outside **Dinar** it swings south-eastwards as it continues to follow the E24. The road runs in a straight line across a treeless plateau, showing up grey against the colours of the steppe.

Just north of the sulphurous Lake Burdur, the route turns off the E24 towards **Burdur** itself. The town is about 4km from the road. Its history goes back no further than the Middle Ages. There follows a delightful stretch of road over the Çeltikçi Pass (1,230m (4,034ft)). Just after the village of **Çeltikçi** there is a view to the right of the Katranci Dagi (2,340m (7,675ft)). The route comes back into the E24, which runs on past Lake Kestel.

20km further on, there is a turning along an unmetalled road to ⌘ the village of **Korkuteli** (46km), near to which are the remains of the ancient city of **Termessus** (see excursions from **Antalya***). The E24 meanwhile carries on via **Dag** and Dösemealti until the blue waters of the Mediterranean appear shimmering on the horizon. It is not far now to **Antalya***, the main centre of the Turkish Riviera. Antalya is an ideal centre for a longer stay. The old city gates look out across the 10km long beach of **Konya Alti**, which is a paradise for bathers.

The area to the east of Antalya is full of archaeological sites. Investigations over the last 100 years have shown them to rival those of Miletus, Troy and Pergamum on the Aegean coast. The fascinating ruins of Perga, Aspendus and Side can easily be visited in a single day from Antalya, together with the waterfalls at Manavgat, which provide for extra variety. One can either take a

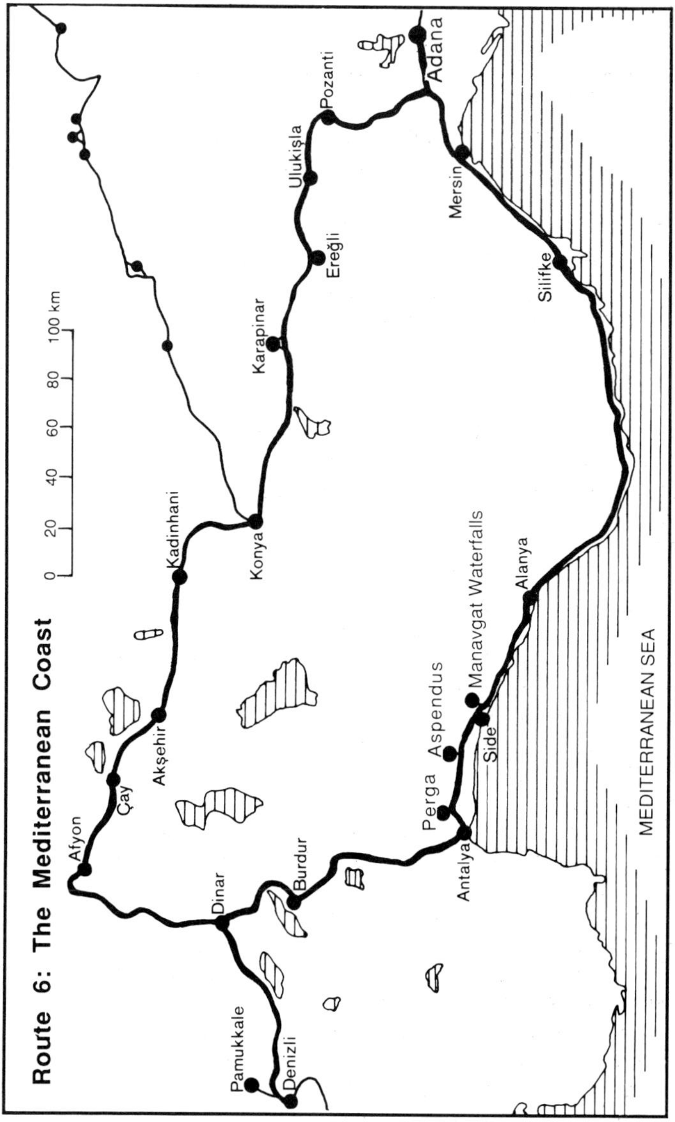
Route 6: The Mediterranean Coast
0 20 40 60 80 100 km
Pamukkale
Denizli
Dinar
Burdur
Afyon
Çay
Akşehir
Kadinhani
Konya
Karapinar
Ereğli
Ulukişla
Pozanti
Adana
Mersin
Silifke
Alanya
Manavgat Waterfalls
Side
Aspendus
Perga
Antalya
MEDITERRANEAN SEA

Lake Salda, near Burdur

car, or else hire a taxi for the day for a reasonable price.

The route leaves Antalya in an easterly direction. About 16km out of the town, just past the village of **Aksu**, there is a left turn for the ancient ruined city of **Perga*** (2km). Archaeological excavations here are at present being extended to new areas as yet uninvestigated.

A short distance further along the main road, after the village of **Serik**, there is yet another left turn, this time for the beautifully preserved theatre of **Aspendus***. Aspendus, like Perga, was centred around a hill overlooking the coastal plain. The ruins are dotted with huts belonging to nomads who have settled here permanently.

The next important Graeco-Roman site is at **Side***, which is signposted sharp right off the E24, about 30km beyond Aspendus. The ancient fortifications are only 2km from the main road. Of particular interest is the theatre in the centre of the site. It usually takes about two hours to visit the ruins themselves, the museum and the nearby holiday village.

Day trippers from Antalya should then arrive at **Manavgat** at about 5pm. To get to the waterfalls, one should return to the E24,

Aspendus Theatre

turn right towards Alanya and take a left turn about 3km further along. The falls are less impressive than postcards might lead one to imagine. The green waters plunge over a rock barrier about 5m (16$^{1}/_{2}$ft) high and about 40m (131ft) wide. The Manavgat Falls are in a beautiful woodland setting. Visitors are invited to sit down at tables beneath the shade of the trees, where they are plied with *çay* (tea) and coca cola. Meanwhile young locals show off to visitors by diving into the falls.

The E24 continues for another 60km along the coast to **Alanya***. The approach to the town is marred by ugly sky-scrapers that obscure the view of the lovely old-fashioned fishing harbour. Alanya is probably the most picturesque of all the towns along the Turkish Mediterranean.

The route leaves the Turkish Riviera as it continues east towards Adana. The road runs along a fertile coastal plain, sandwiched between the Taurus Mountains to the left and the sea to the right. Sometimes the mountains come down to meet the coast, forming cliffs up which the road must climb. This coast was thickly populated in Greek and Roman times. Indeed, the ancient sites are so many that it would be impossible to visit all of them unless one were staying at Alanya for some time. Travellers are usually compelled to limit themselves to the most important sites, passing by the ruins of Syedra, Laertes and Nauli to the left.

As the road approaches the Syrian border, the facilities gradually deteriorate. Hotels and restaurants become more and more basic, while filling stations become increasingly infrequent. It is now essential to carry a large spare can of fuel.

⌘ The village of **Gazipasa** is close to the ancient Phoenician city of **Selinus**. Many of its buildings are still clearly recognisable, including some of the walls and towers of the heavily fortified castle. This is where Emperor Trajan is supposed to have died following a battle against the Parthians.

The road to Anamur was extremely dangerous to drive until recently, when it was at last surfaced and the hairpins were smoothed out. But it still climbs to dizzy heights up the cliffside. Shortly before Anamur the road passes the mouth of the River Kalediran close to the village of the same name.

6km before Anamur, there is a right turn along a side road to ⌘ the ancient city of Anamurium (3km), now known as Eski Anamur. The ruins stand on the southernmost point of Asia Minor. They include the old city walls, two theatres and several aqueducts. Also worth seeing is the enormous graveyard in front of the main site. The modern town of **Anamur** lies on a small coastal plain covered in banana plantations and hemmed in by the Taurus Mountains.

⌘ 7km beyond Anamur, the road passes the Anamur Kalesi on the right. This impressive eleventh-century castle was once used as a place of refuge by both pirates and crusaders. Visitors can walk around the battlements, which are fortified with as many as thirty-six towers. In the nineteenth century the castle was occupied by a Turkish petty prince. Now it is gradually falling into disrepair, with vegetation growing up between the walls.

The route continues along the E24. Near **Bozyazi** there are the ruins of a Greek colonial settlement, the name of which is not known. An island off the coast is similarly covered with ancient ruins. The road passes many more castles and ruins. It leaves the coast for about 35km, and returns along the top of a cliff. It passes the ruins of Melania at Soguksu, and the little port of **Aydincik**, with the Roman site of **Celendiris** nearby. The history of Aydincik goes back to the fifth century AD, since when it has been an important trading post between Cyprus and Asia Minor.

The landscape becomes noticeably harsher, and the many

ruined cities along the route seem strange and ghostly in an area that now is uninhabited. Whether under the Greeks, the Romans or the Turks, they were flourishing centres of commerce and culture. Only 200 years ago, many of the ruined castles were still being used by pirates as shelters.

The cliffs then come to an end at Ovacik, and the road runs along the plain to the town of **Silifke**, which was once the site of an oracle in the country of Cilicia. The Roman ruins are worth visiting, especially the castle of Camardesium. The River Göksu runs close by. It is the river in which Emperor Frederic Barbarossa drowned in 1190 during the Third Crusade.

A paved path leads south from Silifke to **Meriamlik**, which for the first five centuries after Christ was a famous place of pilgrimage. According to legend, St Thecla, a disciple of Paul, lived in a cave under here. The site is covered with the foundation walls of monastery buildings and chapels. Thecla's cave is supposed to have been underneath the largest of the churches.

30km to the north of Silifke are the impressive ruins of the former city of **Olba**, now known as **Ulunzaburç**. The road is unmetalled, but is nonetheless accessible to cars. The temple of Zeus, built in the third century BC, is particularly well preserved, as are also the five-storey tower and the covered street that runs alongside the theatre. About fifty minutes' walk away are the ruins of Ura, which give a vivid impression of the layout of a Roman settlement.

The E24 continues past several lovely sandy beaches; the beach at **Susanoglu** is close to the scant remains of the city of **Corasium**. There are yet more ancient remains to come. The most interesting of these is on a side road down to the sea near **Narli Kuyu**. It is a beautiful mosaic from the fourth century AD.

Just 3km beyond Narli Kuyu are the strange **Corycian Caves**. These two caverns have an uncanny atmosphere about them that is best summed up by their Turkish names Cennet and Cehennem, meaning 'Heaven' and 'Hell'. They are reached via a narrow road that ends in a field covered in ruins. They open off a rocky hollow at the back of the site, and are linked by a 200m (656ft) long chasm. The upper cavern measures 50m (164ft) across, and is called 'Hell'. It is entered via an overhang, so is only accessible to experienced potholers. The lower cavern is about 200m (656ft) long by 100m (328ft) wide, with walls 20m (66ft) high. It is reached via a path that goes down close to the rock. At the end of the cavern are the remains of an Armenian

The fortress of Kizkale, Mersin, on the Mediterranean

cave church. A bottomless vertical shaft opens up by the back wall. Visitors are warned not to venture along the spiral staircase that leads down it. From time immemorial it has been known to be full of poisonous gases. According to legend, a dragon with 100 heads once lived in the bottom. Cerberus, the guard dog of Hades in Greek mythology, is supposed to have been based on this creature.

The next ancient site is near a holiday centre called the *Kizkale Motel*, where the ruins of the Greek city of **Corycus** lie buried beneath the ground. The way into the harbour below was protected by the fortress of **Kizkale**, which can be reached by boat. The sultan who built it is supposed to have been told by an oracle that his daughter would be killed by a snake bite. So he built this island fortress for her, thinking she would be safe from snakes. But when he sent her a basket of fruit, a snake was hidden in the basket. It bit the princess, thus fulfilling the prophecy. Later the castle was notorious as a hideout for pirates.

The next part of the route passes a large number of beautiful beaches. A peninsula dividing two of them is covered with the ancient ruins of Ayas. The road is much improved along the section through Erdemeli and **Mersin**, neither of which is of particular interest. But 3km beyond Mersin, on a hill called Yümüktepe, are the weathered remains of a Hittite fortress built in the fifteenth century BC.

Travellers without a car should note at this point that a rail service operates from Mersin to Tarsus and beyond, but it is slower than the long-distance bus services.

About 12km past Mersin is the site of the ancient city of **Pompeiopolis**, whose tall columns are visible from the road. Originally called Soli, it was several times destroyed by earthquakes, and was rebuilt and renamed by the great Roman leader Pompey. The avenue of columns was originally 30m (98ft) long. All that now remains are twenty-seven Corinthian columns, together with numerous fragments. The site is badly overgrown with grass and bushes. It was destroyed by another earthquake in AD 528, and was never rebuilt. The wrecked buildings were used to provide building stone for the villages around. Visitors are warned that snakes are common in this area, including poisonous vipers.

The E24 continues across the Cilician Plain, which is mostly planted with bananas and cotton. The road is a fast one, and **Tarsus** is only 20 minutes away. Tarsus has nothing of particular interest. But it is famous as the birthplace of the apostle Paul, and was a flourishing port in the Middle Ages. The town has a varied and eventful history going back 3,000 years, the most recent centuries being the least interesting. The best-known events here were the time when Alexander the Great bathed in the river, and the meeting of Mark Anthony and Cleopatra.

The journey to Adana can be exhausting. The Cilician Plain can be unbearably hot, especially in summer. It is essential to carry an ample supply of refreshing drinks, and to avoid using any of the water butts along the way. There is nothing of special interest along the 40km stretch from Tarsus to Adana. Those wishing to continue eastwards from Adana should turn to Route Seven.

Adana* is the fourth-largest city in Turkey. Travellers are recommended to stay overnight so as to be able to see the city at leisure, avoiding the heat of the day. An afternoon bathe is also recommended in the Seyhan Barayi — a 25km long freshwater reservoir that begins just outside the city gates.

The return journey follows the same route back until 3km before Tarsus, where it turns northwards along the E5. The road then begins to climb through the rugged Taurus Mountains, still inhabited by lynxes, eagles and even bears. It follows the same track as the ancient caravan trail. This route was once used by the armies of Alexander the Great, Pompey, Mark Anthony,

Emperor Frederic Barbarossa and the kings of Persia. If the Cilician Gates could only speak...!

The road descends through Pozanti, passing the mighty peak of the Mededsiz (3,585m (11,759ft)) to the left. The small town of **Ulukisla** provides an opportunity to replenish supplies of food, drink and fuel. The next section of the route is monotonous but at the same time fascinating. The road crosses a vast, waterless plateau that extends 350km northwards to within a short distance of Ankara, past the salt lake of Tuz Gölü. These harsh steppe-lands cover the majority of central Anatolia. They are virtually uninhabited apart from the villages that cluster around the oases.

Eregli has little of special interest. Nothing remains on this site of the ancient city of Heraclea. Cicero lived here for a short time as proconsul of Cilicia. There is an ancient Hittite site in the hills nearby, next to the source of the **Ivris** and only a few minutes from the village of Ivris. It includes a stone relief that probably dates back to the eighth century BC, depicting King Warpalawas and the god of fertility. Several cave entrances above it are thought to have led to Hittite dwellings.

The E5 continues from Eregli through the salt wastes of Ak Göl. The many small salt-lakes dry up in the summer, and the steppe is hot and treeless. It is 50km to **Karapinar**, the last town before Konya. There then follows 100km of unrelenting desert. It is vital to take plenty of fuel and drinking water on board before tackling this part of the journey. If the car breaks down, the consequences can be serious.

The Konya oasis forms an island of green amid the shrivelled brown wilderness of the Anatolian steppes. **Konya*** itself is one of the oldest cities in Turkey. It is full of historic buildings from the time of the Seljuks. The city was once the centre of the now prohibited order of the whirling dervishes. Several hours are needed to see the sights, so it is advisable to stay overnight. There is a good modern hotel next to the central bus station, 1km from the centre.

The route continues northwards, leaving Konya via the Istanbul Caddesi. The road follows a straight line across the steppes, passing numerous khans along the way — reminders of a once-prosperous caravan trail. The khans were where the camel drivers and their animals found shelter and lodging along the route. They now follow in close succession: the ruined Dokuzun Derbent Han; the Disçi Mehmet Efendi Han, built in the thirties; the isolated Hafiz Han; and the impressive twelfth-century Kadih

Han, which is still intact.

30km beyond the last of these is the small town of **Ilgin**. Its many items of interest include the Pir Husein Bey Mosque, a khan and the medieval baths. On a hill just outside there are sulphur baths that also date back to the Middle Ages. The Argit Han 20km beyond Ilgin is yet another twelfth-century khan.

The road leaves the salt wastes as it approaches **Aksehir**. Aksehir is known to us from ancient times, when it was called Philomelium. Emperor Frederic Barbarossa was stationed here only days before he drowned in the waters of the Göksü. Cicero held court here, as did sultans and Mongol princes. Aksehir was the birthplace of Nasrudin, the famous Turkish humorist. He also died here, probably in 1285, and his grave is on view to the public. It is easily recognisable, having a dome supported on six pillars. Also worth seeing are the Tas Medrese, built in 1216, the grave of the philosopher Sayid Mahmud, and the fourteenth-century Ulu and Iplikçi mosques.

Being on the edge of the desert, Aksehir was a vital staging post on the caravan trail. The caravans would stop here to make special preparations for the difficult journey across the desert. The same could be said of today's equivalent, the long-distance coach parties, who make an extra-long stop here before setting off for Konya. The town is also an important centre for the Turkish leather clothing industry. Excellent suits, jackets and coats are available at amazingly low prices.

The road passes Lake Aksehir on the right before arriving at the small town of **Sultandagi**. Of particular interest here are the ruined Ishakli Han, built in 1250, and the Ulu Mosque, dating from 1458. The next lake, the Eber Gölü, has practically dried up completely. It is followed by the small town of **Çay**, where items of interest include the river bridge and a thirteenth-century caravanserai.

The route continues to **Afyon***, once the opium capital of Turkey, and still surrounded by poppy fields. For the rest of the journey via **Dinar** to **Denizli***, one should follow the relevant part of Route Five in reverse.

8 ROUTE SEVEN: SOUTHERN TURKEY AND THE ANATOLIAN PLATEAUX

Adana • Ceyhan • Osmaniye • Iskenderun • Antakya (230km) • Kirikhan • Hassa • Maras (495km) • Malatya • Kayseri (1050km) • Ürgüp • Göreme • Nevsehir • Aksaray • Sultanhani • Konya (1340km) • Karapinar • Eregli • Ulukisla • Pozanti • Adana (1690km)

This route goes through a region that is subject to extreme heat from April onwards. But the southernmost corner of Turkey is a fascinating place to visit, and the climate is more bearable if one stays next to the Mediterranean coast. The journey across the plateaux of Anatolia leaves a vivid impression of salt deserts, steppes and bare mountains, not to mention the almost lunar landscape of the valley of Göreme.

The route goes eastward from **Adana** across the hot Cilician Plain. The road is good and fast, and quickly arrives at **Misis**, where it crosses the River Ceyhan. Misis was once an important staging post on the caravan trail between Persia and Europe. All that remain are two ruined caravanserais, dating from the thirteenth and sixteenth centuries respectively. The bridge over the Ceyhan was built by the Romans. Although 1,700 years old, it still carries through traffic. German archaeologists have set up a small museum of fourth-century mosaics. The most impressive of these shows Noah's ark surrounded by four animal figures.

About 10km east of Misis, there are Hittite carvings on a rock face overlooking the River Ceyhan. They date from the reign of King Muwatalli (1315-1282 BC). On the horizon one can just make out the former crusader fortress of **Yilanlikale**.

Ceyhan is the nearest town to the famous Hittite city of **Karatepe***, which means 'black mountain'. The most important find here was a stone bearing parallel texts in Phoenician and Hittite. Discovered in 1947, it enabled experts to decipher the Hittite language for the very first time. An excursion to Karatepe requires at

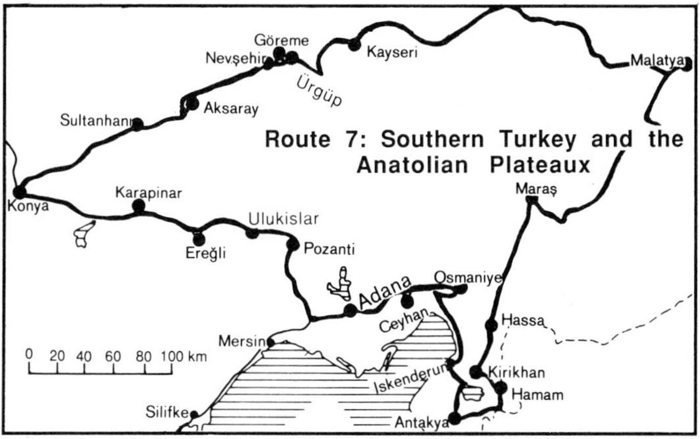

least 6 hours from Ceyhan.

The road passes near to the Toprakkale, a Byzantine castle which the crusaders later extended. This massive edifice of black basalt is in a difficult mountaintop location. The route swings southwards towards the coast, crossing several spurs of the Misis and Amanus mountains. Near **Erzin** are the extensive ruins of the city of Epiphania, which was founded by Cicero. They include an impressive aqueduct. ⌘

The road crosses the Dörtyol plains and comes out onto the coast. It soon approaches the site of the famous battle of Issus. This took place in 333 BC between King Darius III of Persia and Alexander the Great of Macedon, who was in the process of founding a new empire. The two great armies met near the town of Issus, and engaged in a long and bitter struggle. Alexander's victory opened up the way for him across the Middle East. No one knows for sure where the conflict took place, or where Issus actually was. All that is known for certain is that the battle site was bordered on one side by the river, now called the Deli Çayi.

The next town worth visiting is **Payas**, which was a notorious hideout for pirates until as late as the nineteenth century. Items of interest here include the bazaar and the khan next to it, the medieval mosque and the nearby ruins of the Roman baths. The castle was built by the Genoese. ⌘

The road continues over the **Arrian Pass**. This was one of the most dangerous sections of the old caravan trail, with frequent attacks from nomadic robbers. At the top of the pass are

Fishing at Iskenderun

the famous Pillars of Jonah. Much has been said about these, but nothing is known of their origin. Theories have ranged from a triumphal arch to an ordinary city gate. It has even been (quite wrongly) suggested that Alexander the Great was buried here. However, according to legend, it is the place where Jonah came to land when he was spat out by the whale. Not far away are the ruins of the robbers' castle of Calatissia.

About 10km beyond the pass is the town of **Iskenderun**. Iskenderun is second only to Izmir as Turkey's largest and most modern Mediterranean port. It stands on the site of the ancient city of Alexandretta — one of the many cities to have been founded by Alexander the Great during his long journeyings.

The route turns inland through the orange groves. After **Belen** the road begins its steep, twisty climb over the Belen Pass. At the other end of the pass are the ruins of Bagras — a castle built by the crusaders to control the caravan trail over the pass.

The route continues southwards past Lake Amik and via **Bedirge** to **Antakya***, once the ancient city of **Antioch**. Antakya today is the southernmost city in Turkey. It spreads out along the banks of the River Asi.

The route now turns east towards the Syrian city of Aleppo (Haleb). The road leaves Antakya past the ruins of ancient Antioch, crosses the Asi and carries on via **Cilvegözü**. 8km before the Syrian border, at the Yenisehir caravanserai, the route turns left for Reyhanli. It continues northwards via the spa and border town of Hamam, and eventually arrives after another 17km at the small town of **Kirikhan**. Cars must squeeze through the narrow streets of Kirikhan until they come into the N55.

The N55 goes north towards Islâhiye, passing the Amanus Mountains on the left. Along the section before **Güvenç**, it passes the various remains of aqueducts, castles and ancient towns. It continues via Hassa to **Islâhiye**. Islâhiye's main attraction is a ruined castle built in the sixth century BC. The town stands on the site of the city of Nicopolis ('city of victory'), which was founded by Alexander the Great. Until quite recently it belonged to Syria.

About 10km past Islâhiye, there is a badly-signposted turning for the former Hittite settlement of **Sam`al**. The 'road' is no more than a rough track leading to the village of **Zincirli** (4km) and the nearby archaeological site. Sam`al has probably revealed more about the Hittites than any other site. The heavily fortified city flourished between the fourteenth and twelfth centuries BC. In 680 BC it was conquered and burned down by the Assyrians, as is shown by a layer of ashes. But there are still remains of the walls and towers of the city and its castle, together with the castle gate. There are numerous decorative building stones bearing inscriptions and carved figures. However, the best finds have been placed in the Istanbul Museum and the Pergamum Museum in Berlin.

The N55 joins the E99 from Adana, which continues parallel to the railway. The only small town along the 75km section to Maras is **Türkoglu**.

Maras is sometimes shown on maps as Kahraman Maras. Its history is interesting and varied. Originally called Markasi, it was founded by the Hittites in the twelfth century BC. Since then it has passed continually from one set of rulers to another, often within the space of a few decades — Assyrians, Persians, Greeks, Romans, Arabs, Armenians, European crusaders, Seljuks, Mamelukes, Turkmens, Ottomans, Egyptians, British and French. These frequent changes have been associated with war and destruction, with the result that little of historical interest is left. Buildings worth seeing include the castle, two mosques (the

Büyük Camii and Hatuniye Camii) and the Tas Medrese.

The next town is **Pacarcik**, 50km east of Maras and close to an enormous reservoir. The E99 continues north-east from here towards Malatya, staying close to the railway for most of the way. The road is very good, but one must still beware of rockfalls and animals straying onto the road.

Excursion to the Nimrud Dagi

The route to the famous Nimrud Dagi leaves the E99 at **Gölbasi**, and goes eastward along an unmetalled road that can be difficult in bad weather. It is 64km to the isolated township of **Adiyaman**, where overnight accommodation is available. The journey continues eastwards through even wilder scenery for another 40km to **Kâhta**. Kâhta seems almost like a ghost town, but there are hotels here which can be used as a base for an expedition to the Nimrud Dagi. It is yet another 30km to **Eski Kâhta**, which forms the starting point for the last part of the journey. There is a minibus available to take people up the final difficult climb to the top.

The sight that awaits one is well worth the effort. No civilisation apart from the Incas in Peru has produced anything to compare with the **Nimrud Dagi**. Perched on top of the mountain is a group of gigantic statues measuring 10m (33ft) in height. They were placed here in about 50 BC during the reign of King Antiochus I of Commagene, whose tomb stands behind them. The site was discovered in 1881 by a German engineer called Sester. This amazing spectacle is ample compensation for the difficulties of the journey.

The main route crosses the plains of Gölbasi and climbs up beside the River Göksu, penetrating ever deeper into the mountains of southern Anatolia. It carries on over the **Resadiye Pass**, past the village of Dogansehir, and eventually arrives at **Malatya***. Though 1,000m (3,280ft) above sea level, the provincial capital of Malatya has an urban feel to it. It is in the middle of a fertile agricultural area, and the market is very well worth a visit.

The route turns westward from Malatya, and continues across the arid plateau. Rail travellers must change and take the bus for the 327km section from Malatya to Kayseri. The steppe is thinly populated, and for most of the way the road passes no more than a few lonely caravanserais, most of them derelict, and one or two small hamlets. The only exceptions to this are the oasis towns of

Gürün, **Pinarbasi** and **Bünyan**, where oriental carpets are made.

The city of **Kayseri*** is situated in a large oasis, and is overlooked to the south by the snow-capped peak of the Erciyas Dagi (3,916m (12,844ft)). There is much to see in Kayseri, and there are plenty of reasonably-priced hotels. A tour of the city takes about three hours. Car drivers can carry on to Ürgüp and Göreme without returning to Kayseri. But bus travellers will need to make a one-day excursion there, so should plan to stay an extra night.

Car drivers from Kayseri to Ürgüp should first take the E98 Ankara road, then after 14km bear left along a road signposted to Nigde. After 36km this road comes to a crossroads with a filling station. Here one should turn right along a narrow metalled road, which winds through the hills for another 34km until it arrives at Ürgüp. Those arriving by bus or *dolmus* should immediately enquire about the times of the return service in the evening.

The small town of **Ürgüp** is in a beautiful situation. The buildings are clean, and there are numerous craft shops selling items of local interest such as ornaments, clay pipes and carpets. There is a lookout point about a kilometre outside and overlooking the town. From here one can see three rock pyramids capped by pinnacles of harder rock.

The bizarre rock formations of Ürgüp and **Göreme*** are the third great wonder of Asia Minor, surpassed only by the ancient ruins of Ephesus and the limestone terraces of Pamukkale. Indeed, so incredible are these wonders of nature that visitors often make a special day-return flight from Ankara to Kayseri just to see them. They are all the more impressive for the fact that Armenian refugees in the sixth century AD made caves in them to hide from their persecutors. The caves contain painted churches and monasteries, and ordinary dwellings, all of which are now on view to the public.

Only 2km from Ürgüp is the village of **Ortahisar**. The rock formations here are surrounded by lemon plantations that supply Turkey with all its lemons. In the middle of the village is an 80m (262ft) high pinnacle of rock, which was once used as a refuge. It has been carved out into a maze of shafts and passages leading to subterranean chambers. Some of the passages have collapsed, while others have been shored up with walls. More agile visitors can climb up via a series of ladders and shafts to the summit of the rock. From here there is an incredible view of the village and the bizarre landscape that surrounds it.

The 'rock' village of Uçhisar

The strange village of **Uçhisar** is on the road between Göreme and Nevsehir. Most of its inhabitants live in houses inside the strange rock formations. The village lives from lemon- and wine-growing, and also from carpet-weaving. There is a viewing point out among the vineyards and just off the road to Göreme. One need only walk a few yards to have a magnificent view of a whole area peppered with these weird rock formations.

Nevsehir is the nearest town of any size to the valley of Göreme. This typically Anatolian market town clings picturesquely to the hillside, overlooked by a massive citadel. Nevsehir is the best place to stay for visiting the rocks and caves of Göreme. The accommodation is much sparser than in Kayseri, but Nevsehir is very much closer.

Excursion to Yeralti Sehri

The underground city of **Yeralti Sehri** is at **Kaymakli**, 19km south of Nevsehir along the road to Nigde. The site consists of a whole labyrinth of passages, carved out beneath a rock that looks quite unremarkable from the outside. It was created as a refugee hideout during the Byzantine period, and was linked by a series of secret tunnels to the houses of the nearby village. This meant that the people could escape there without coming out into the open. The passages go down to a depth of 40m (131ft), and are arranged in eight layers or 'storeys'.

Though remarkable, the site was not opened to the public until 1964. But now everyone can go down and gain some idea of what it must have been like. The passages and chambers are well lit, but are often very narrow with low headroom. One enters via steep, badly worn staircases that lead down from ground level. The floor is irregular with awkward holes that are difficult to see. Visitors must therefore take care to avoid tripping or falling. Fortunately the caves are dry and not cold.

The underground city contains not only churches and kitchens, but even a burial chamber, where the dead were walled in to prevent epidemics. There is no furniture left, but the layout of the churches amply demonstrates that these caves were inhabited by Christians. The double chapel in particular contains a cross and a font. These people had found a marvellous means of protecting themselves against Moslem persecution.

The route continues south-westwards from Nevsehir along the N73. It passes three derelict caravanserais, of which the last and best-preserved is called the Agzi Karahan. After about 70km the route meets the E5 and turns left into Aksaray.

The green oasis town of **Aksaray** has much to offer the visitor. Its oriental market is well worth visiting. The town's history goes back to AD 800. It was at Aksaray that Henry the Lion is said to have received a generous gift from Sultan Arslan II.

⌘ Buildings of particular interest include the Seljuk castle, the Zimciriye Medrese (1345), the twelfth-century Ibrahim Bey Medrese and the Ulu Camii.

The N73 continues south-west from Aksaray. At this stage the road surface leaves much to be desired. After 30km it arrives at **Ihlara**, famous for its so-called snake churches (Yilani Kilise) — sixth-century Armenian refugee churches consisting of caves with painted walls.

The next stage of the journey is across the arid wastes of the Konya Ovasi. For the next 100km there is nothing but steppe grass and sand, with the occasional shimmering-white salt-lake in the distance. There are one or two small villages along the way. The road is now surfaced and therefore much safer.

The road quickly covers the 40km to **Sultanhani**. Sultanhani is the prototype for all thirteenth-century caravanserais. Those who have seen it can happily pass by other caravanserais, for there is no other to match it. It towers above the horizon, gaunt ⌘ and defiant — a well-fortified castle in the midst of the steppe. Its high walls once protected the caravans, not only from cold and darkness, but from the attacks of marauding nomads. The interior is more friendly, with marble gates leading to courtyards and avenues of columns. There are fountains, baths and a mosque, which once provided both bodily and spiritual refreshment for the hard journey ahead. It is a great shame that the caravanserai is gradually falling into disrepair.

For the rest of the way to Konya, the only human settlement is the village of **Obruk**. The journey leaves an impression that is impossible to describe in words. The heat, the sweat and the thirst make one long for a cool bath. It comes as a great relief to see a green strip on the horizon that gradually becomes larger until one can make out the green palms and minarets of the **Konya*** oasis. The feeling of relief is combined with a wonderful sense of achievement at having crossed the wilderness. After the dry heat of the steppe, the fruit plantations of Konya feel almost like the Garden of Eden.

The rest of the route from Konya to **Adana** follows part of Route Six in reverse.

9 ROUTE EIGHT: THE EASTERN PROVINCES

Malatya • Elâzig • Bingöl • Mus • Tatvan (or Elâzig • Diyarbakir • Bitlis • Tatvan) • Van (565km) • Ercis • Patnos • Agri • Horasan • Erzurum (985km) • Askale • Tunceli • Elâzig • Malatya (1,410km)

Malatya has been chosen as the starting point so as to link with Route Seven. Malatya also has an airport, which means that one can fly here from Ankara or Istanbul to make a bus tour of eastern Turkey. This is the most difficult of all the tours, going through regions where tourism is unknown. In the Van region, for example, children will throw stones at foreigners, while older people will hide. Travellers must learn to do without their customary standards of comfort, hygiene, eating and accommodation. On the other hand, it is an opportunity to see a part of Turkey that few Europeans ever visit, and even many Turks never see it in their lives.

From **Malatya*** the route follows the E99 to Elâzig. After **Kale** it descends into the valley of the Euphrates (Firat). It crosses the river, which at this point rushes angrily through a gorge. At the other end of the bridge is a military control point, where one must show one's passport. There is a derelict caravanserai to the left of the road, and a ruined Seljuk castle on the rock above.

The road climbs again to a height of 900m (2,952ft), and after another 25km arrives at **Elâzig**. This town has changed completely over the last hundred years. High-rise flats seem almost to have grown like mushrooms.

Road travellers have a choice of routes between Elâzig and Tatvan. They can either take the route via Diyarbakir, which is 70km longer, or else follow the N60 via Bingöl and Mus. Rail travellers, however, must follow the Bingöl route.

Elâzig to Tatvan via Diyarbakir

This route follows the N69, rising to a height of 1,200m (3,936ft)

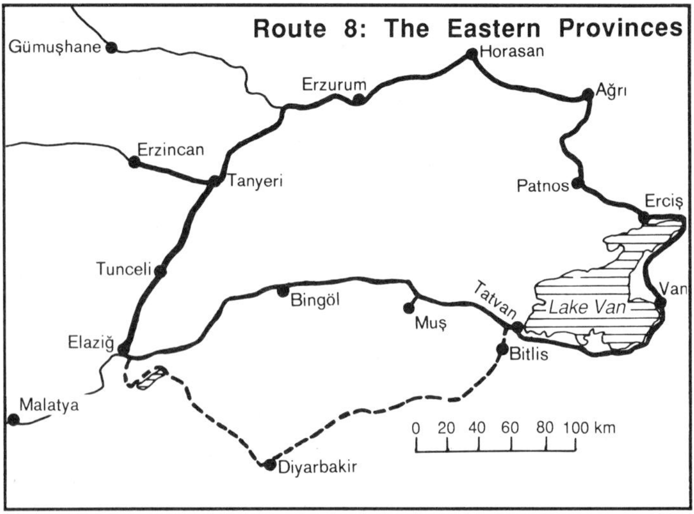

and skirting the northern shore of Lake Hazar. This lake is the source of the **Tigris** (in Turkish **Dicle**), the second-longest river in the Middle East.

The rocks in this area have a reddish tinge. They are full of copper ores, which are extracted by means of underground and opencast mining. The road runs past several copper mines on its way across the mountains. The road surface is often bad along this section. The road passes through the towns of **Maden** and **Ergani**, of which Maden is an important mining and industrial centre.

After Ergani there is 80km of straight road before the walled city of **Diyarbakir***. The town is visible from some distance away. It towers above the River Tigris, surrounded by its imposing many-towered basalt fortifications.

The route turns north-east again, and after another 75km arrives at **Silvan**. This sleepy little town is supposed to have been the site of Tigranocerta, the capital of the Armenian empire. After Silvan the terrain becomes mountainous, and drivers must beware of falling rocks, stray animals and dangerous bends. The road continues via Baykan towards Bitlis. 10km before Bitlis there are two tunnels through the mountainside. The road goes through the lower of them.

The town of **Bitlis** is 1,400m (4,592ft) above sea level. It is a fascinating town, if only for the life in the streets and squares and in front of the *lokantas*. The bazaar is also very good. Of particular interest are the ruined castle and the sixteenth-century Serefiye Mosque and Seref Han.

About 14km beyond Bitlis, the N60 from Elâzig comes in from the left. It is then only another 12km to Tatvan (see below).

Elâzig to Tatvan via Bingöl

The N60 from Elâzig runs in a straight line through the bare undulating steppelands of eastern Anatolia. This route is shorter and easier to drive than the one through Diyarbakir, but is less interesting culturally. The region has an atmosphere of all of its own, with its yellow-grey hills bare of trees, dreamy villages set in lush green oases, and the people that one sees along the way. The railway runs parallel to the road for most of the way.

The road first descends into the Euphrates valley, and then climbs up onto the plateau. There are nomad tents either side of the road. The nomads are generally peaceable, but travellers are advised not to stop. Being Kurds, they can be extremely temperamental. One need only photograph the women, or annoy the men by unwittingly breaking their code of conduct, and they will suddenly flare up, putting the traveller's life at risk.

Bingöl is roughly half-way to Tatvan. It is another 117km to **Mus**, which is about 2km south of the main road. Buses usually stop here for a tea break. The moment one leaves the vehicle, one is besieged by people. They are usually warm and friendly, and insist on shaking hands. To avoid upsetting them it is best simply to play along with them. They do not expect presents, and the men like to be photographed. The town of Mus has seen better days in the past. In the sixth century AD it was called Taron, and was the capital of the kingdom of Armenia. There are several monasteries hidden in the hills around. It is another 83km to Tatvan.

Tatvan is a small town at the western end of **Lake Van**. It has a railway station and a bus station. In the summer there is a weekly ferry service across the lake to Van. The crossing takes between five and seven hours. Car drivers are advised to use the road that runs along the southern shore of the lake. The railway ends here, so rail travellers must continue by boat or by bus.

Lake Van is the largest and most interesting lake in Turkey, covering an area of 3,800sq km. It was originally formed through volcanic activity, when a vast lava flow blocked the rivers that flowed through the area. There are signs of human settlement from as early as the ninth century BC. The lack of a visible outlet and the high summer evaporation mean that its deep-blue waters are extremely salty, with an unusually high concentration of sodium carbonate. But it is nonetheless safe to bathe in. Its maximum depth is not known, but is probably several hundred feet. The lake supports very little life. Some experts say that there are no fish in it, while others say that just one species of whitefish can survive in its alkaline waters. There are three camping sites around the lake; it is dangerous to camp elsewhere.

The road along the southern shore is preferable to that along the west shore. It is metalled and runs close to the much-indented shoreline, with some lovely views across the lake. It passes a number of grey mud huts belonging to semi-nomadic Kurds.

The offshore island of **Ahtamar** is the site of the tenth-century Armenian church of St Cross. The island is difficult to get to. There is a jetty with a motorboat on the shore facing it, but one is best advised to obtain exact information from the tourist office in Van. Probably the most reliable method is the hour-long crossing from **Gevas** at the south-eastern corner of the lake.

The domed church stands amid the ruins of a former monastery. One can still see the friezes on the façade, and representations of the four evangelists under the gables. The frescos inside are equally fascinating. The architecture, sculpture and paintings are typical examples of how Armenian religious art absorbed stylistic elements from the contemporary Islamic culture.

The road turns north along the eastern shore towards **Van***, which is the nearest town to the Iranian border. Van's isolated location has enabled it to develop a unique atmosphere of its own. It is the gateway to the 'Wild East' of Turkey, where the protagonists of Kurdish blood feuds escape from the police by hiding out in the mountains. Political refugees and criminals hide there too. At least three days is needed to see Van and its surroundings.

The route follows the N95 northwards to **Ercis** on the northern shore of the lake. Leaving the lakeshore, the road becomes very dusty and difficult as it crosses the mountains to **Patnos** (50km). The surface does not really improve until the road enters the E23 at **Agri** (another 82km). Agri is the administrative centre of the province of Agri (or **Ararat**). Its economy depends on the agricultural products of the fertile valley of the Murat, one of the two main headwaters of the Euphrates.

Traditional dancing

The route turns westward along the E23 towards Erzurum. 34km further on is the town of **Eleskirt**, where Xenophon camped with 10,000 Greeks. There was probably an Urartian fortress here, as is shown by the remains that have been found — in particular the Stone Tablets of Menuas, king of Urartu in the eighth century BC.

The road is already 1,820m (5,969ft) above sea level, but it climbs yet further up a steep, winding pass to an altitude of 2,391m (7,842ft). There is a magnificent view of the surrounding mountains. To the east is the mighty **Mount Ararat** (**Agri Dagi** — 5,165m (16,941ft)), where Noah's ark is supposed to have landed (though investigations at the peak have failed to bear this out). To the south is Süphan Dagi (4,430m (14,530ft)); Kökse Dagi (3,450m (1,131ft)) is closer at hand, while to the north one can see the jagged outline of the Kars Mountains.

The road drops slightly along a precipitous slope. Then after **Tahir** it climbs again over the **Tahir Pass**, which at 2,475m (8,118ft) is one of the highest passes in Turkey. The road descends steeply and squeezes through a narrow gorge before eventually coming out into a wider valley at **Horasan**.

At this point the E23 goes left through a region that is subject to severe earthquakes. **Pasinler** is overlooked by an impressive fortress — a gloomy edifice perched on top of a rock. Visitors may enter its dungeon-like chambers and examine the casemates. The nearby thermal springs are reputed to have healing powers.

The road leaves the Armenian plateau, and crosses over the Deveboynu Pass to **Erzurum***. From Erzurum the route follows the same course as Route Two until just before Tanyeri, where it turns left along the E99 for Tunceli and Elâzig. 10km further on, the road begins to climb as it crosses the **Pülümür Pass** (1,900m (6,232ft)). There is a marvellous view of the Munzur Silsilesi range to the south-west. The road descends steeply past the salt gardens of **Pülümür**, and continues through the mountains towards Elâzig.

The section which follows includes a number of tunnels and gorges. **Tunceli** is just off the E99, but is worth a short detour for a refreshment break. Then there is the lovely village of **Pertek**, which clings to the mountainside above the course of the Murat. The nearby ruined castle was used by Seljuks and the crusaders to control the river crossing below. The village also has an old caravanserai and a mosque. The route crosses the Murat for the second time (see above), though this time the river is very much wider.

The E99 climbs over the Gülmez Tepe (1,315m (4,313ft)) and drops down to Elâzig. The return journey from Elâzig to **Malatya** follows the same route as before.

10 CITIES, TOWNS AND PLACES TO VISIT

Adana

24m above sea level; population 1,200,000

The city of Adana on the Cilician Plain was founded by the Hittites in the tenth century BC. Adana is the fourth-largest city in Turkey, and its main southern industrial centre. Most of the buildings are modern, with very little remaining from earlier periods.

The **Great Mosque** (**Ulu Camii**), built in 1507, is particularly impressive. It is surrounded by a complex of buildings enclosed by a wall, including a school and a mausoleum. Other interesting mosques include the **Hasan Aga Camii**, the **Yag Camii** and the **Yeni Camii**. ⌘

The **Roman Bridge** is also worth seeing. It was built under Emperor Hadrian in the second century AD. It is 310m (1,017ft) long, and rests on twenty-one columns, fourteen of them original. The **museum** is very informative, and contains a number of interesting exhibits. ⌘

Information: State Tourist Office.
Transport connections: bus, rail and air.

Excursions

1. Karatepe* near Kadirli. The ruined city and fortress are one of the most important Hittite sites to have been discovered so far. Karatepe can be reached via Ceyhan (140km — see Route Seven). The road is in a bad state along the last part of the route. ⌘

2. The Ceyhan Reservoir (8km). A popular bathing and holiday resort.

3. Karatas (50km). A seaside resort on the Mediterranean coast, with some ancient ruins on the nearby headland.

Afyon

1,000m (3,280ft) above sea level; population 250,000

An enormous rock of black basalt casts an ominous shadow over the city. Turkey's opium capital is surrounded on all sides by poppy fields, which provide the raw material for the opium.

Afyon was founded by the Hittites in about the fifteenth century BC. It subsequently came under Phrygian, Persian and Roman rule, and in 1428 was conquered by the Turks. The Greeks occupied the city for a few months in 1921-2.

From time immemorial, Afyon has been an important staging post on the caravan trail. The caravans are no more, but Afyon has since become an important road and railway junction.

The first thing to see is the old **Karahisar** or 'Black Opium' Castle in the centre of the town. The **Ulu Camii** (**Great Mosque**), built in 1272, is typical of the many wooden mosques of that period. Also worth visiting are the **Kuyulu Camii** (**Fountain Mosque**), with its graceful minaret, the **Kubbeli Mesçit**, with its beautiful entrance door, the **Kâbe Mesçit**, with its artistic reliefs, and the **Misrî Camii**, with its lovely mosaics. The fifteenth-century **Imaret Camii** has an associated school and a bathhouse. The **Archaeological Museum** is housed in one of the side-buildings of the **Ahmed Gedik Pasa Camii**. It contains a large collection of items from the prehistoric, Hittite, Phrygian and Hellenistic periods.

Other things to see are the tomb of Sultan Divani, and the war memorial by the park commemorating the victorious battle of Dumlupinar in 1922. The events of the Turkish War of Independence are documented in the **Town Hall Museum**.

Information: town hall (*belediye*).
Transport connections: bus, rail and air.

Excursions

1. The **Phrygian rock tombs** around Göynük, Avdolos and Ligen (40km).

2. The **Iscehisar marble quarries**, where the coloured marble came from that is still found on ancient sites along the Aegean coast.

3. The **thermal springs** (about 25km) — the largest in the whole of Turkey.

Alanya

5m (16ft) above sea level; population 30,850

The town of Alanya is in a picturesque coastal setting 135km east of Antalya along the Mediterranean coast. It enjoys a pleasant Mediterranean climate, and is a popular resort on the so-called Turkish Riviera.

There has been a fortress on the site of the present-day castle ruins since the second century BC. It originally served as a pirate refuge, but was taken over by Pompey when the Romans occupied the coastal plain. In the thirteenth century, after the Turks had taken over, it became the residence of Sultan Ala-Eddin Kaiqobad. The port was extended and fortified, and the ships of the Turkish navy were anchored here.

Time is needed to visit the town's medieval and oriental remains. Down by the harbour is the massive **Kizil Kule** (**Red Tower**), built in 1225. It is 46m (150ft) high and octagonal, and was built to guard both the harbour and the shipyard. The old shipyard is unique, being the only such building to have survived from the Seljuk period. It was erected at the same time as the castle, the Red Tower and the city walls. Turkish warships were built here from timber brought down from the Taurus Mountains. For safety the foundations were hewn out of the rock. It is made up of several boatsheds, each 8m (26ft) wide and 43m (141ft) long, and connected via a series of pointed arches. It is, however, no longer completely intact.

A footpath leads up from the town to the castle ruins, from which there is a marvellous view of Alanya with the Taurus Mountains behind. The courtyard opens out onto a mosque and a lighthouse. The inner chamber on the west side of the castle provides detailed information about how the Turks built their castles. There is also a small church from the Byzantine period. To the north-west of the castle are the **Damlatas Caves**, which were discovered in 1948 during blasting operations at a local marble quarry.

Information: State Tourist Office.
Transport connections: bus only.

Ankara (Ancyra/Angora)

835m (2,739ft) above sea level; population 2,880,000

Ankara became the capital of Turkey in 1923, partly because of its loyal support for Mustafa Kemal Pasa (later Atatürk) in his liberation struggles, and partly because of its central location. At the time it was no more than a small Anatolian town of some 20,000 inhabitants. But within a few years Atatürk transformed it into a vast modern city on Western lines. It is now the second-largest city in Turkey, surpassed only by Istanbul. It is the seat of government and the diplomatic and administrative centre of Turkey.

The History of Ankara

There was probably a Hittite castle on the site of the present old town as many as 5,000 years ago. The Hittites were followed by the Phrygians and later the Lydians until King Cyrus of Persia took the city in 546-545 BC. Alexander the Great also came through here on his way to Gordium, where he severed the famous Gordian knot. The oldest parts of the present citadel were built by the Galatians. The fortifications were then further strengthened by the Romans. Large parts of the structure were subsequently rebuilt and remodelled by Ibrahim Pasa of Egypt.

Most of the ancient monuments one can see today are from the Roman period. For although Ancyra (as it was then called) remained an archbishopric under Byzantine rule, its economic importance diminished considerably. The eighth century saw a further decline, when the town was besieged by both the Persians and the Arabs. In 806 it was sacked on the orders of Harun el Resid, but it was later recaptured by the crusaders and handed back to the Byzantine emperor.

In the mid-twelfth century the town fell into the hands of the Seljuks. It was then taken over by the Ottomans in the fourteenth century, only to be totally destroyed by the Mongols under Tamerlane in 1402. But Tamerlane was forced to withdraw in 1403, and Angora (as it was now called) came back under Ottoman rule. The town became famous in the West for the mohair quality of the fabrics it produced; it also gave its name to the Angora cat.

On 23 April 1920, Mustafa Kemal Pasa held his first Turkish national assembly at Ankara. By then the town's population of 20,000 was only a tenth of what it had been under the Romans. By 1960, however, it had increased to 25 times that amount, and has subsequently quadrupled.

Landscape of 'a thousand hills', Sardis

Turkish carpets at the Bergama bazaar

Hay-making near Çanakkale

Pamukkale

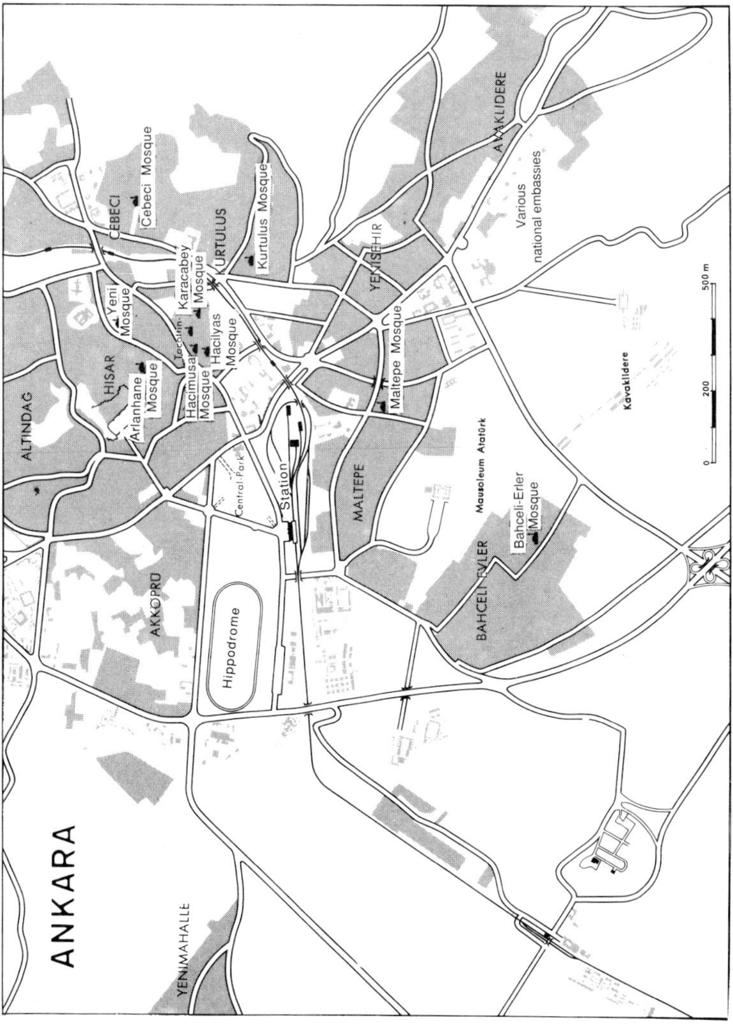

Things to See in Ankara

Hittite Museum (Hittit Müzesi)

⌘ In order to see something of Ankara's past, one should visit the Hittite Museum. One of the most modern museums in the world, it contains the world's richest collection of Hittite treasures. It is housed in the former *bedesten* built by Mahmud Pasa between 1464 and 1471. This massive covered hall has six domes supported on enormous pillars.

The priceless collection includes limestone and basalt friezes from archaeological sites at Kargamis, **Malatya***, **Bogazkale***, **Alacahüyük** (see **Bogazkale***) and Ankara itself.

Immediately to the left of the entrance are friezes found at sites in Ankara depicting lions, horses and other animals. Beyond them is an exhibit from Kargamis showing gods and warriors. To the left at the back are representations of lions, chariots and deer.

Moving to the right-hand side, one can see a frieze from the Alacahüyük site; it depicts groups of soldiers, musicians and guards bringing sacrifices of bulls and a double eagle. Returning along this side, there are hieroglyphs and stone chariots from Kargamis. The frieze immediately to the right of the entrance is from Arslantepe near Malatya; it shows sacrifices being made to the gods, in particular the sun god and moon god.

The middle section includes more lions from Malatya and hieroglyphs from Kargamis, together with winged statues and vases from Bogazkale and further valuable finds from other sites. The glass cabinets contain smaller items made of gold, bronze, iron and clay.

Museum of Ethnology

⌘ The building where this is housed was finished in 1928. Between 1938 and 1953 it was used as a temporary resting place for Kemal Atatürk's body, which was eventually moved permanently to the Atatürk Mausoleum.

The museum is divided into ten sections illustrating various aspects of Turkish life, both past and present. The vast number of exhibits includes items such as carpets, copperwork, pottery, costumes and embroidery. There are also displays showing aspects of Turkish agriculture, fisheries, etc. The courtyard contains a number of old stone sarcophagi from the Seljuk period.

Atatürk Mausoleum

⌘ The mausoleum is situated to the south-west of the city centre on a hill called Rasat Tepe. A broad street leads up to it from the Ulus Meydani. The vast edifice took 9 years to build. It is approached by a 260m (853ft) long mall flanked by long lines of statues, and the ceremonial square is surrounded by long avenues of columns.

Hittite treasure in Ankara's Hittite Museum

The building itself is 72m (236ft) long, 55m (180ft) wide, and 21m (69ft) high. The writing engraved on the façades, both inside and outside, consists of speeches made by Atatürk on the tenth anniversary of the republic. The reliefs either side of the steps depict scenes from the War of Independence.

Atatürk's sarcophagus was placed in the inner chamber on 10 November 1953, the fifteenth anniversary of his death. The main hall is lavishly decorated, while the side halls contain metal wreaths and decorations sent by various foreign representatives at the time of Atatürk's death. Since 1953 Rasat Tepe has been known as Anit Tepe or Memorial Hill.

Citadel

The walls and towers were originally built at the time of Emperor Augustus. But they have so often been altered and rebuilt down the centuries that little of the structure has remained in its original state. The biggest alterations occurred in 1833 at the time of Ibrahim Pasa. The site does, however, contain many statues and other relics that date back to the Roman period. The citadel is a maze of narrow streets that give a vivid impression of what an oriental town must have looked like in the Middle Ages.

⌘ One important building to see here is the **Ala-Eddin Mosque**, built in 1178. The pulpit dates back to the time of the Seljuks. The Ak Kale or White Tower at the highest point of the citadel is unfortunately not open to the public, as it is used for military purposes.

Temple of Augustus

⌘ The ancient imperial temple at the foot of the citadel is only partially intact. The most remarkable item remaining is the Monumentum Ancyranum bearing the last will of Emperor Augustus. It is engraved in stone in both Latin and Greek, and the information contained there has enabled experts to make reconstructions of the temple as it originally was. Archaeological investigations have revealed that it was built on the site of a Galatian temple. Experts have also proved from details given in Augustus's will that Jesus Christ must have been born between 6 and 2 BC.

Other Things to See

Close to the Temple of Augustus is the fifteenth-century **Haci** ⌘ **Bayram Mosque**. Also worth visiting is the **Arslanhan Mosque**, built in the thirteenth century under the Seljuks; the ceilings, the columns and the pulpit are especially worth seeing. Then there is the **Ahi Elvan Mosque**, built in 1423 during the reign of Murad II, which has a beautifully-carved wooden pulpit. Finally there is the **Ahi Serafeddin Türbe**; this once contained a fine sarcophagus, which is now housed in the Museum of Ethnology (see above).

⌘ Next to the Ulus Meydani is the fourth-century **Column of Julian**, also known as Belki's Minaret. The column is smooth and bears no inscriptions. Finally worth mentioning are the third-century **Roman baths**. They were only recently excavated, and have provided much information about how such baths were constructed.

Information: State Tourist Office, Yenisehir, Mithat Pasa Caddesi 20
Traffic connections: bus, rail and air.

Excursions

⌘ **1.** The special Turkish farm at **Gazi** (8km) was built by Kemal Atatürk as an example to the agricultural industry. The fields and meadows are bordered by lovely parks with pleasantly sited refreshment facilities.

Ankara, overlooked by its citadel

2. The **Çubuk Reservoir** is 10km north of Ankara near the road to Çankiri. It provides superb bathing facilities in the middle of the Anatolian steppes.

Antakya (Antioch)

90m (295ft) above sea level; population 450,000

The ancient city of Antioch was a flourishing centre of commerce, but little of it remains today. Antakya nowadays is primarily a garrison town. It is situated 50km from the Syrian border in the southernmost corner of modern Turkey. It is typical of the Near East — a quiet backwater surrounded by olive groves. Lake Amik only 30km away is a popular holiday resort.

Antioch was founded in the fourth century BC by Seleucus, one of the successors of Alexander the Great. The apostle Paul visited Antioch on many occasions, and often stayed here for long periods (see the *Acts of the Apostles* in the Bible). It was at

Roman Mosaic, the Archaeological Musem, Antakya

Antioch that the term 'Christian' was first used to describe the followers of Christ. Emperor Diocletian persecuted the Christians, putting as many as he could behind bars. But Christianity flourished here, and when Constantine the Great made it the official religion, Antioch became the seat of one of the patriarchs. For 150 years it was one of the most important centres in the Christian world, and as many as ten councils were held here. Antioch's importance in the Graeco-Roman world is best illustrated by its population, which was half a million — second only to that of Rome itself. The Games of Apollo were world-famous. The city was full of theatres, baths, canals and markets, and even had street lighting.

In the eleventh century the city was occupied by the Turks, who fiercely defended it against the attacks of the crusaders. The crusaders eventually destroyed it and took it over in the twelfth century. They ruled it for 170 years, but lost it to the Mamelukes in the thirteenth century. From then onwards the city declined into insignificance. In 1918 it was occupied by the French. At a referendum in 1939, the people of Antakya chose to remain in Turkey. The Syrians have always disputed this, and still lay claim to the whole area around Antakya. This is the reason for the strong military presence in the town.

⌘ The first place of interest is the ruined **citadel**, which stands on a rocky shelf to the south of the town. It was built in the eleventh century at the end of the Byzantine period. The river is crossed by a Roman bridge, built under Emperor Diocletian in the third century AD. Next to the city hospital are the remains of an aqueduct from the time of Emperor Trajan.

A short distance away is the **Habib Neccar Camii**. This mosque was originally a Byzantine church, and many of the Christian tombs have remained undisturbed. The minaret was not added until the seventeenth century. The **Archaeological Museum** in the Gündüz Caddesi contains items mainly from the Hittite and Roman periods. Of particular interest are mosaics from Roman villas in the city. Finally there is the bazaar, which is one of the most typically oriental of any in Turkey.

Information: Tourist Information Office, Kanatli Mah. Vali Ülgen Meydani.
Transport connections: bus only.

Excursions

1. St Peter's Grotto (4km) is just off the road to Reyhanli, and is easiest to get to by taxi. The apostle Peter is said to have preached in the church, where early Christians once met in secret. The cave chapel was extended to its present form in the thirteenth century. The trickle of water behind the altar comes from a spring that is said to have healing properties. A small path leads over the rocks to an eighth-century frieze, the subject of which is obscure.

2. The **Temple of Daphne** (8km) is at **Harbiye**, south of Antakya on the road to the Syrian border. 8km further on is the impressive ruined castle of **Kürsat**.

3. Samandag (30km) is a relaxing beach resort on the nearby Mediterranean coast. One can return via the ancient site of **Seleucia**, once the port for the city of Antioch.

4. The **Alalakh** site, 25km to the east of Antakya, was the capital of the Mukish empire in the third century BC. As at Troy, several layers of foundations have been revealed. This would suggest that it was rebuilt several times following destruction by war or earthquakes. There are also the sparse remains of Hittite temples and houses.

Antalya (Attalia)

40m (131ft) above sea level; population 400,000

Antalya is the main tourist centre of the Turkish Riviera. It overlooks a broad bay, and is close to the famous 10km long beach of Konya Alti. The view inland is dominated by the snowy peaks of the Taurus Mountains. The town itself is picturesquely situated above red cliffs that plunge vertically into the sea.

There is everything here that the sun-seeking tourist could possibly want — holiday apartments, big hotels, promenades and restaurants serving international food. The 10km long shingle beach at Konya Alti is not to everyone's taste. The buildings are ugly, and it is lacking in both cleanliness and comfort. Fortunately there are plenty of cleaner, quieter, sandier beaches along the coast in both directions.

The city was founded in the second century BC under King Attalus II of Pergamum, and was called Attalia after him. The Greek rulers were later followed by the Romans, the crusaders and finally the Turks. Attalia was the port where the apostles Paul, Barnabas and Mark landed on their first missionary journey through Asia Minor.

⌘ The main landmark in the centre of Antalya is a thirteenth-century minaret called the **Yivle Minare**. It is built partly of brick and stands next to the Cumhuriyet Meydani. The associated mosque has a ground plan that is normally only found in Christian churches. The mosque complex includes a number of other buildings of interest. The library, for example, contains some beautiful manuscripts, while the art gallery is well worth a visit. It was founded by the painter Esen Emekçil. In July and August it is turned into an enormous art studio, where everyone can paint their own pictures. Entry is free, and anyone can go in to watch. Esen Emekçil is usually there in person, and can often be seen at work. Also next to the Cumhuriyet Meydani is the old city tower. It is part of the old city walls, remnants of which can be seen by the harbour.

The **Atatürk Caddesi** has an atmosphere all of its own. It has a stream running along a gully in the centre, and is lined by avenues of date palms. One can stroll past restaurants, fruit
⌘ stalls and souvenir shops to the **Ala-Eddin Camii**, once a seventh-century Byzantine church. Immediately below it is **Hadrian's Gate**, which was built in AD 130 when Hadrian

St Nicolas' Church, Demre, near Antalya

visited the city. It performed a dual function as a city gate and as a triumphal arch. The Atatürk Caddesi comes out into the town hall square. The town hall stands next to a large park with some valuable trees, where there are some lovely views of the sea, the town and the harbour.

Antalya has several good hotels, including the *Büyük Oteli* and the *Hotel Bambus*, which is 2km outside on the road to Lara (see below). Antalya is also the location for the Golden Orange Film Festival in September.

Information: State Tourist Office.
Transport connections: bus and air.

Excursions
1. Lara Beach, 12km east of Antalya.

2. The ancient ruins along the coast (75km). First there is **Perga***, with its impressive avenue of columns. Further on is **Aspendus***, which has the best-preserved amphitheatre in Asia Minor. The third site is **Side***. All that one can see of this once-prosperous Greek colony are a few temple remnants, a theatre and an aqueduct. The best finds are kept in the museum on the site. There is also a sandy beach nearby. One can round off the journey with a visit to the waterfalls at **Manavgat**.

3. The ancient city of Termessus, 40km north-west of Antalya on the road to **Korkuteli**. The hill-top site is reached via a footpath going up from the village of **Güllük**. There is a magnificent view of the whole area.

Aspendus

30m (98ft) above sea level

Aspendus was once a flourishing city in the province of Pamphylia, and reached its peak during the period of Roman occupation. But the harbour silted up, and its importance gradually diminished. The city is no more, and most of what remains has become totally overgrown.

Aspendus is well worth a visit from **Antalya*** (50km) because of its remarkable theatre. In contrast to the rest of the site, it is the best-preserved example of its kind in the whole of Asia Minor. It was built in the second century AD, and can seat an audience of 15,000. The acoustics are amazing. A conversation at the back of the stage can be clearly understood from the top row of the auditorium without any amplification whatsoever. The theatre is still used for concerts and plays during the Antalya film festival.

Bergama (Pergamum)

50m (164ft) above sea level; population 60,000

The town of Bergama is 100km north of Izmir on the hot plains adjoining the Aegean coast. This small country town is full of life and colour. But its chief attraction for the thousands of visitors that flock here every year is the ancient site of the ruined city of Pergamum, which extends up the hillside about 4km out of Bergama.

Pergamum was famous in the ancient world as the capital of the Pergamene kingdom. But the acropolis at the top of the hill dates back much earlier than this — to the fifth century BC. The first important event in its history was in the third century BC, when King Lysimachus placed a large amount of looted treasure in the acropolis. He entrusted it to the care of Philetaerus, the steward of the acropolis. When the king died, Philetaerus used the funds from the treasure to found an empire of his own.

The Pergamene kingdom flourished for 150 years. Eumenes II (197-159 BC) was a lover of the arts. He beautified both the acropolis and the city, which expanded considerably during his reign. He also founded a library, which with its collection of 200,000 volumes was second only in the world to the library at Alexandria in Egypt.

The last king of Pergamum was Attalus III (138-133 BC), who was deposed by the Romans when they occupied the city and turned the kingdom into the province of Asia. Under the Romans the city expanded further, spreading out across the plain below the acropolis. It continued to flourish under Byzantine rule, but was eventually laid waste in the fifteenth century at the hands of the Mongols and the Seljuks.

Archaeological excavations began here in 1878. The site was discovered by a German engineer called Humann, who had noticed local peasants using ancient decorated stonework for building material. A team of archaeologists sponsored by the Berlin Museum began a systematic excavation of the acropolis. Their most important discovery was the Altar of Zeus, a reconstruction of which is displayed in the Pergamon Museum in East Berlin. Other parts of the ancient city are still being excavated today.

A tour of the site should preferably start at the top of the hill, which can be reached by car, bus or *dolmus*. The recommended route is marked with blue arrows along the way. The **theatre** is particularly impressive. It must have seated an audience of some 15,000 people, though nothing remains of the row of columns that marked the back of the stage. One can still see how beautifully sited the theatre was. The view of the hill country beyond must have formed a lovely backdrop to the stage for the audiences of the time.

To the right of the theatre (looking down from the top) are the remains of the **Temple of Trajan**, which was destroyed in an ⌘ earthquake. It is now being reconstructed in its original form by a team of archaeologists. In front of the temple are the foundations of the famous library, which was built in 170 BC. The library was linked via a covered walk to the **Temple of Athena**. This was the nearest large building to the city gates, and was built in the third century BC in the Doric style.

Looking down from the temple towards Bergama, one can see a rectangular raised platform surrounded by steps. To the left of it are two pine trees, which were planted by the archaeologists Conze and Humann to mark the point where they first discovered the famous **Altar of Zeus**. This was built in 180 BC during the reign of Eumenes II — a period when the city was expanding. The open space below the temple complex was once the **upper agora** or **market place**. The northern wall of the acropolis remains in a good state of repair. It was pulled down and rebuilt several times during the Greek, Roman and Byzantine periods.

Leaving the acropolis area, one may continue downhill on foot through the ruins of the ancient city towards Bergama. Everything is well labelled for the benefit of visitors. The first part of the route runs along an ancient street past the **Temple of Demeter.** This was built in the third century BC, and is the oldest-known building in Pergamum. The sanctuary is surrounded by a square in which mystery plays were performed; this in turn is enclosed by columns and a row of steps where the audience would have sat. The next building is the **Temple of Hera**, which once contained a lovely mosaic. This is followed by the baths, where several statues were found, and the gymnasium. The school area is laid out in three terraces and is again surrounded by columns.

The present ruins end at the **lower agora**. This was built in the second century BC when Eumenes II was expanding the city. It was surrounded by columned arches like those at a bazaar, where traders would have displayed their wares. The Byzantines later built a church on the site, but none of this remains. The car park at the bottom marks the end of the middle sector of Pergamum. The lower city was nearly all built during the Roman and Byzantine periods, but is now mostly covered by the modern town of Bergama.

The exception to this is the site of the ancient **Asclepium**, which is about 1km from the town centre. Although well outside the original acropolis site, it dates back to the fourth century BC. This temple complex was dedicated to the cult of Asclepius, the Greek god of healing. It is supposed to have been founded by a wealthy citizen of Pergamum as a thanks offering to the gods. The leaders of the Asclepium were a group of physicians and priests. The cult of Asclepius involved a combination of mysticism, mystery and medical knowledge that was unique in the ancient world.

The Asclepium was patronised throughout the year by the rich and the powerful seeking cures for bodily and spiritual ills. City governors, kings and emperors were amongst their number. The

The Asclepium, Pergamum

therapy involved bathing, massage, training in auto-suggestion and instruction in philosophy. The Asclepium at Pergamum reached its climax in the second century AD, when Galenus was practising here. Galenus was one of the two most famous physicians of the ancient world, the other one being Hippocrates. According to tradition, the patients treated here included the Roman emperors Caracalla, Hadrian and Marcus Aurelius.

One enters the site via an avenue of columns. This once led to the **propylaea** or entrance hall, of which alas nothing remains. However, the remnants of a column with a carved snake coiled round it help to give an idea of what it might originally have looked like. The temple site was enclosed on three sides by a row of twenty Ionic columns more than 10m (33ft) high. To the right of the propylaea was the library, where one can still see the niches in which statues once stood. To the left of it was the **Temple of Asclepius** — a 20m (66ft) high round structure that was later replaced by a Byzantine church.

To the south of the site is the **Temple of Telephorus**, in the basement of which were the baths and massage rooms. There is a perfectly-preserved tunnel leading from here to the **holy spring**.

The stone lion that stood above it has long since disappeared, but the water bubbles up just as it did 2,000 years ago. The small theatre nearby has now been restored. One item of special interest is the public toilet building on the south-western boundary of the site. This has provided information about the sanitation of the time, which must have been remarkably similar to our own.

Much of Pergamum still remains to be excavated. For archaeologists believe that many more interesting finds lie hidden beneath the kilometre of hard ground that stretches between the present site and the modern town of Bergama. This area was mostly built on during the period of Roman expansion. Two theatres, a stadium and a temple have already been uncovered.

⌘ The main item of interest in the town is the so-called **Red Hall**. Now ruined, it was originally built as a temple during the reign of Emperor Hadrian, and was later converted into a Byzantine church. The **Archaeological Museum** is fascinating. It was built here after the Turkish government had banned the further export of archaeological finds. The **Museum of Ethnology** contains some interesting exhibits of local folklore and traditions. Also worth seeing are the **Seljuk Minaret** and the **Ulu Camii**, both of which were built in the fourteenth century. Finally, the Bergama bazaar is small but very interesting.

Bodrum (Halicarnassus)

50m above sea level; population 15,000

The small port of Bodrum is arranged in terraces up the hillside above a bay of the Aegean. Its whitewashed fishermen's cottages stand on the foundations of the ancient Greek city of Halicarnassus. Halicarnassus was founded by Dorian Greeks in the fifth century BC, and was one of the first Greek colonies in Asia Minor. Its most famous citizen was the historian Herodotus in the fifth century AD.

This beautifully-sited port has been fiercely fought over down the centuries. All the great leaders of Asia Minor laid siege to Halicarnassus at some stage in their careers — Alexander the Great, Ptolemy, Lysimachus, Seleucus, Xerxes, Mithridates, Croesus and Cicero. The city passed from the Greeks to the Persians and eventually to the Romans. From AD 395 it was part of the Byzantine empire. In 1523 it finally fell to the Turks.

Halicarnassus reached its greatest prosperity during the reign of King Mausolus. After his death, his widow had an enormous tomb built for him, which became *the* original **Mausoleum**. It was completed in 351 BC, and was counted as one of the seven wonders of the world. It stood in the centre of Halicarnassus, not far from the present-day site of St Peter's Castle. The ground plan measured 66m (216ft) by 77m (252ft), and the building was enclosed by thirty-six columns. The king's body was entombed in a pyramid 46m (151ft) high. The building also contained some magnificent friezes and life-size statues by the best sculptors of the time. Some of these sculptures are preserved in the British Museum in London.

The enormous structure seems to have remained intact until the twelfth century, when it was presumably damaged by earthquakes. Then in 1415 Franconian crusaders began dismantling it to provide building stone for the nearby St Peter's Castle (see below). The last stones were removed in the sixteenth century.

The **Gümüsli Gate** stands by the broad street that once went past the mausoleum. Not far from this are the remains of the ancient amphitheatre. There is also an old graveyard to the north, and a ruined temple to the right of the theatre. The old Greek walls form the outer boundary of ancient Halicarnassus.

St Peter's Castle (**Bodrum Kalesi**) is by far the most impressive building in present-day Bodrum. It was built by crusaders in the fifteenth century on an island that is now part of the mainland. It is still in good repair, and is open to the public. It stands on the site of a former acropolis, which had been built as a bridgehead by the original Dorian colonists. It was the last Christian stronghold to survive on the mainland of southern Asia Minor. The Christians were eventually forced to retreat to the island of Rhodes. The castle is built in the Franconian style, and the Turks treasure it as the best example in the east of central European castle architecture. There are numerous coats of arms and animal friezes. When the Turks took over, they turned the castle chapel into a mosque. The castle itself later became a notorious prison.

Little else is left of the great city of Halicarnassus. Much more is known from historical records and tradition than from the few odd remnants of the palace of Mausolus, the ancient agora, where a great statue of Ares is supposed to have stood, and the castle of Salmacis to the west of the town.

The entrance to the harbour is hazardous on account of the

shallows of Yassi Ada. Many ancient ships came to grief here, and fishermen are continually catching fragments of classical pottery, sculpture and shipping tackle in their nets. Underwater archaeologists have managed to locate more than a dozen separate wrecks. One of them is supposed to have been King Mausolus's treasure ship, which was attempting to bring in a heavy load of valuables for the purposes of decorating the great family tomb.

Information: Tourist Information Office.
Transport connections: bus and ship.

Bogazkale/Bogazköy (Hattusa/Hattusas)

940m (3,083ft) above sea level

The village of Bogazkale is about 210km east of Ankara. Though insignificant in itself, it is close to the three most important archaeological sites from the time of the ancient Hittites: Hattusas, Yazilikaya and Alacahüyük (see Excursions below).

⌘ Much of the Hittite capital of **Hattusa** still lies buried beneath the ground to the south-east of Bogazkale. The city of Hattusa (in Turkish Hattusas) was on a plateau overlooking what is now the village of Bogazkale. This furrowed plateau has revealed evidence of settlements going back to the third millennium BC, 1,000 years before the Hittites arrived. The Hittites were an ancient race of Indo-Europeans, who probably invaded from central Asia via the Caucasus.

The Hittites built a fortress on Büyük Kale and formed a settlement around it. Hattusa rapidly developed into a trading centre and became the capital of the Hittite empire. From 1460 to 1200 BC, the Hittites ruled the greater part of Asia Minor. Much about them remains obscure, because their written language has yet to be fully deciphered. But it is generally accepted that their culture was extraordinarily advanced for the time. The cities and fortresses that they built, and the works of art that they created, reveal an amazingly high level of sophistication.

The ruins are scattered over a wide area. So visitors are advised to hire a jeep, and preferably a guide as well, on arrival in Bogazkale or in nearby **Sungurlu**. The plateau is bare of trees, and is subject to the full glare of the sun. It is therefore advisable to go early in the morning so as to avoid the heat of the day.

The two stone sphinxes guarding the Hittite site of Alacahüyük

Leaving Bogazkale one first enters the so-called lower city. A little further on to the left is the **Great Temple**, which was probably the largest building in the whole of the Hittite capital. The entire temple complex measured 160m (525ft) by 135m (443ft). It is presumed that the royal treasure was kept in the innermost chamber of the temple. The route continues through the living quarters, where the houses were supplied with running water, baths and flush toilets. ⌘

A steep path leads up to the **fortress**, which was originally built as early as 3000 BC. The Hittites took it over, and in about 1400 BC they strengthened and extended it. Thousands of burnt clay tablets were found along the walls. These must have constituted a library or an archive. The content of the tablets has been partly deciphered, and reveals much about the political state of affairs at the time. The walls of the fortress were built of enormous ashlar stones. No mortar was used, and the stones fit absolutely exactly. Experts are still puzzled as to how the Hittites managed to build with such accuracy, given the primitive tools that they appear to have had. ⌘

The fortress was surrounded by government buildings, reception halls, temples and storage areas. The top of the hill was probably the site of the royal residence, the foundations of which must have been hacked out of the bare rock.

About 400m to the south-west is another former Hittite fortification on a rock called the **Nisan Tepe**. At the foot of the rock is a 9m (29ft) high frieze engraved with Hittite writing that has yet to be deciphered. Another 500m to the south-east is the famous **Royal Gate**. It is fairly well-preserved, and was 6m (20ft) high. The associated city wall is as much as 5m (16ft) thick in places.

The route continues south-westwards past the foundations of four temples. It keeps on climbing until it reaches the highest point of the whole site (1,240m (4,067ft)). This is where the **Yerkapi** stands — a gate that was once flanked by two sphinx-like statues. An underground passage leads from here to the outermost ring of walls. It is 70m (230ft) long and 2½m (8ft) high by 3m (10ft) wide. It was probably used as an escape route or as a means of attacking besieging armies from behind.

If one follows these walls in a north-westerly direction, one arrives after 700m at the **Lion Gate**. The enormous archway has collapsed, but the gate is still guarded on either side by two great stone lions.

The route returns to the Büyük Kale, passing another rocky outcrop on the way. Called the Sari Kale, it was once the site of yet another royal fortress. The return route from Büyük Kale down to the village of Bogazkale is the same as the way up.

Transport connections: bus only.

Excursions

1.Yazilikaya (3km). The Hittite temple at Yazilikaya is easily reached from Bogazkale. It is high up on a rocky hillside, and is centred around a 10m (33ft) long chamber carved out of the rock. This is thought to have been used as a kind of crematorium, and contains some interesting friezes depicting processions. The frieze in the next-door chamber shows twelve male deities with a single human figure among them. It is King Tuthalya IV, who is normally pictured next to his patron, the god Sarruma.

2. Alacahüyük (36km). The third important Hittite site can be reached by going north from Bogazkale for 15km before turning right towards Alaca. The site can be recognised from a distance by a group of tall poplar trees. Like Hattusa it was burned down and destroyed in about 1200 BC. The ruins themselves are less interesting than those at Bogazkale. However, the sphinx gate at the entrance to the site is similar to the lion gate at Hattusa, and is guarded by two stone sphinxes. The museum on the site is fascinating. It contains numerous Bronze Age objects, including beautifully-engraved pottery with animal designs. It also provides some valuable insights into the artistic and cultural development of the area, with displays of local handiwork produced by local farmers.

Bursa

150m (492ft) above sea level; population 850,000

Bursa is one of the most fascinating cities in Turkey. It was the seat of the sultanate before the fall of Constantinople, and has managed to preserve many of its older Turkish buildings. The maze of narrow streets in the old town hides magnificent mosques, elaborate tombs and a colourful bazaar. There is an atmosphere of eastern promise that is even more marked than that of Istanbul. The city is beautifully situated at the foot of the mighty Ulu Dagi (2,543m (8,341ft)), Asia Minor's Mount Olympus. From the edge of the city there is a marvellous view of the whole of Bursa and the fertile valley beyond.

It is not known for sure when Bursa was founded. Hannibal is said to have been its founder, though this has yet to be proved. But a city has certainly existed here since the beginning of the Christian era. The oldest parts of the city are a few remnants of the ancient acropolis. The Romans developed Bursa considerably. They made use of the nearby thermal springs, and built baths and a library. During the course of the next thousand years, the city repeatedly changed hands between the Arabs, the Byzantines and the Turks. Sultan Osman kept the city besieged for 10 years until it was eventually forced to surrender. A magnificent sultan's palace was built here, and Bursa became the favourite residence of the Ottoman rulers. In the nineteenth century much of the old city was destroyed, either in the great fire of 1801 or in the earthquake of 1855. The Greeks occupied Bursa for 2 years during the Turkish War of Independence.

The largest mosque in the city is the **Ulu Camii** next to the Ulu Meydani. It was founded in 1379, but not finished until 1414. The main prayer chamber is almost square with sides measuring nearly 100m (328ft) in length. It is roofed by twenty flattened domes resting on rows of columns. The prayer chamber is cooled

View of Bursa; Sultan Mehmed I's mausoleum in the foreground

by a fountain in the centre. The light entering through windows around the domes serves to illuminate the numerous Arabic quotations from the Koran. The beautiful cedarwood pulpit bears the date AH 802, which is the Moslem equivalent of AD 1400.

The Atatürk Caddesi runs through the main commercial centre of Bursa, where all the main shops are to be found. It also contains the town hall and main post office, and the bank and police headquarters. To the east of the Ulu Camii is the **Orhan Camii**, which was built in 1417. Then there is the Cumhuriyet Meydani, which has a statue of Kemal Atatürk.

⌘ The **Archaeological Museum** (**Arkeologi Müzesi**) is very much worth a visit. It is housed next to the Yesil Camii in the Yesil Caddesi. It possesses a large number of exhibits from the Greek, Roman and Byzantine periods, together with a comprehensive coin collection and items of traditional handicraft.

⌘ The **Yesil Camii** or **Green Mosque** was built for Sultan Mehmed I in the 8 years from 1413 to 1421. The tile decorations are probably the most imaginative of any in Turkey, and the Green Mosque itself is thought to be the most beautiful in the country. The prayer niches are particularly lovely, especially the one above the entrance, which is decorated with plant-like ornamentation. There are also some beautiful statues in the windows. The main prayer hall is divided into two chambers, each with several domes.

There are two small prayer niches either side of the entrance to the mosque. Above these are the rooms that were occupied by the sultan and his wives. The sultan's gallery has rich tile decorations. There is a fountain in the ante-chamber. Either side of the fountain is an entrance leading to the first of the domed halls, which was once occupied by the pupils from the Koran school. It has a T-shaped ground plan. The friezes below the domes are richly decorated with paint and gold leaf.

Three steps lead into the second domed chamber, which has a prayer niche and a pulpit. The geometric tile designs round the walls form a lovely contrast to the varied flower designs around the prayer niche. These were created by craftsmen from Nicaea (Iznik), and were famous in their time. Many different kinds of marble were used in the building of the mosque.

Across the road from the Yesil Camii is the **Yesil Türbe**. This is the mausoleum of Sultan Mehmed I, who died in 1421. It is an octagonal structure with a single large dome and a long flight of steps leading from the road. The simple blue tile decorations on the front are part of the nineteenth-century restorations. The interior of the building is richly decorated with luminous tiles and stained glass windows. The sultan's coffin is mounted on a lovely pedestal inlaid with tiles and inscriptions. At the head of the coffin is a white silk turban surrounded by large candlesticks.

The square in front of the Yesil Camii provides a nice view of the city and of the hills around. One of the hills to the east of the town is the site of the mighty **Yildirim Camii** — the mosque of Sultan Beyazid. It was originally built in 1400, and its ground plan became the standard for most of the other mosques in Bursa. The ante-chamber is particularly good from an artistic point of view. The main hall has two domes, with two small covered chambers opening off on either side. Apart from the lovely marble statues, little of the mosque is original, as it was destroyed in the earthquake of 1855. The columned structure which stands opposite the mosque is the mausoleum of Sultan Beyazid.

On a hill to the west of the town is the **Muradiye Camii** — the

Mausoleum of Sultan Cem, brother of Prince Mustafa

mosque of Sultan Murad II. It was built in 1447 and has two minarets. The beautifully-designed doors and windows are its most noteworthy features.

⌘ Under the old trees by the mosque is the **Sultans' Cemetery**. This is supposed to be one of the most beautiful cemeteries in Turkey. The biggest and most extravagant tomb is undoubtedly the mausoleum of Murad I, who was killed in the battle of Kosovo in 1389. The building has a dome, but it is open to let the rain fall through onto the tomb, following the wishes of the sultan himself. The tombs of his four sons are in an adjoining chamber.

Behind Murad's mausoleum is that of Prince Mustafa, the youngest son of Mehmed II (who conquered Constantinople). The red-and-green tile decorations must have been beautiful once, though little is left of them today. Next to it is the mausoleum of Mustafa's brother Cem, who was buried here after having been poisoned in Naples. There is a lovely marble fountain next to a plane tree. To the left of it is the mausoleum of Prince Musa, who was strangled by his brother Mehmed I in 1413.

In order to get some idea of the early history of Bursa, visitors ⌘ are recommended to go to the upper town. The **citadel** was built on the site of the old Roman and Byzantine fortifications. Only parts of the citadel remain; it originally included four gates. The upper town also gives a good view of the city and the surrounding lowlands, overlooked by the peak of the Ulu Dagi.

The park on the north side of the hill by the clock tower contains two more mausoleums: those of Osman, the founder of the Ottoman dynasty, who died in 1326; and of Orhan, his son and successor, who died in 1360. Neither of these structures is original, as both were rebuilt by Sultan Abdülaziz.

Bursa has been famous since ancient times for the healing properties of its thermal springs. Their temperature varies between 40°C (104°F) and 80°C (176°F). They are iron- and sulphur-bearing, and are supposed to cure rheumatism, sciatica and skin ailments. The associated Turkish baths are popular with visitors from both home and abroad.

The **Old Baths** (**Eski Kaplica**) are out in the suburb of **Çekirge**. There has been a building here since the Byzantine period, though the Turks made considerable changes to it in the fourteenth century. The iron-bearing spring water has a temperature of 38°C (100°F).

The **New Baths** (**Yeni Kaplica**) are along a road that comes off the Çekirge Caddesi by the *Çelik Palas Hotel.* They were built in their present form in the sixteenth century. The building looks rather modest from the outside, but the interior is richly decorated with marble and tiles. The spring water is almost boiling as it comes out of the ground, but cools to 82°C (179°F). The whole process of a Turkish bath is so fascinating to a Westerner that one should try it at least once during a holiday in Turkey. And where better than the historic baths at Bursa?

Information: Tourist Information Office, Atatürk Caddesi;
Turkish Airlines/Türk Hava Yollari, Atatürk Caddesi.
Transport connections: bus and air.

Excursion to Ulu Dagi

With a height of 2,543m (8,341ft), Ulu Dagi is the tallest peak in western Asia Minor. It was known to the ancients as the Bythinian Mount Olympus or home of the gods. It is a popular destination at all times of the year, whether for the wonderful view or for its snow-covered slopes in the winter. It takes 12 hours to climb on foot, so climbers must bivouac at some point on the way. Most visitors will prefer to take the cable car. A tiny road goes to a hotel part way up (35km), which can be reached by bus, taxi or car. There is

Ulu Dagi near Bursa is a well-known ski resort

more to see at every bend on the route, while the woods and green meadows are ideal for picnics. The road ends in front of the *Büyük Ulu Dagi Oteli.* From here it is a 3-hour climb to the top of the west peak. A radar station 5km from the hotel looks down onto the city far below.

Çanakkale

5m (16ft) above sea level; population 150,000

The port of Çanakkale lies at the narrowest point of the Dardanelles, where they are only 1.2km wide. For the rest of their length (61km), the straits are anything up to 7km wide. The deepest point of the Dardanelles has been measured at 103m (338ft).

There are fortifications on both sides of the straits, and there has been a castle at Çanakkale since as early as AD 856. The **Kale Sultaniye** to the north of the town was built in its present form under Mehmed II in 1462. It is now owned by the military, so is not open to the public. Craftsmen, tradesmen and farmers formed a settlement around the castle, which later became a

Dardanelles Memorial at Çanakkale, for the Turkish dead at Gallipoli

centre for the pottery industry. An earthquake in 1912 destroyed large parts of Çanakkale.

The **museum** contains archaeological finds from the Greek and Roman period that have been discovered in the Dardanelles region. Çanakkale is a good place for visitors to Troy (see below) to stay at. Car drivers are recommended to stay at the *Hotel Truva*, which is half-way to Troy and directly by the straits. ⌘

Information: State Tourist Office, Iskele Karsisi (near harbour).
Transport connections: bus and ferry.

Excursions

1. Nara (8km). Once the narrowest point of the straits, it is the place where the armies of Xerxes, Alexander the Great and Emperor Barbarossa crossed the Dardanelles. To the east are the ruins of the ancient city of **Abydus**. This was the original location for the legend of Hero and Leander, which was later transplanted to other places such as Istanbul. Leander lived in Abydos, while Hero was priestess at the temple of Aphrodite across the strait at Sestus. Leander would swim across the strait under cover of ⌘

night to visit his beloved Hero, who would light a beacon to guide him. One night a storm blew the beacon out, and Leander drowned. When Hero found out, she jumped into the sea in despair. Lord Byron the romantic poet was so inspired by this tale that he swam the straits just to prove it could have happened.

⌘ **2. Troy*** (30km). Visitors without a car are advised to take a taxi. The road is metalled all the way, and is clearly signposted off the main E24 road, 25km south of Çanakkale. It ends directly by the site.

Denizli

415m (1,361ft) above sea level; population 250,000

This provincial capital lies in the middle of a broad valley. It is a pleasant town with broad streets, colourfully-painted houses, parks and avenues. The surrounding area is heavily cultivated with fruit trees, pulses, poppies and cotton. Thus the market near the station offers a plentiful choice of goods. The town is amply provided with essential services such as shops, offices, post offices, police, banks, hospitals and tourist information.

Entrance to the castle at the ancient town of Hierapolis, Denizli

Denizli's chief interest from the tourist's point of view is its proximity to Pamukkale (see below). Visitors who prefer not to stay in Pamukkale itself have a wide range of hotels in Denizli to choose from, such as the *Egemen Palas Oteli* or the *Özkardes Oteli*. But if at all possible, one should stay in one of the more comfortable hotels in Pamukkale.

Information: State Tourist Office (near the station).
Transport connections: bus and rail.

Excursion to Pamukkale* (14km)
Pamukkale is famous for its incredible limestone formations. Immediately next to it is the ancient town of **Hierapolis**, much of which still remains to be excavated.

Diyarbakir

648m (2,125ft) above sea level; population 500,000

The ancient town of Diyarbakir stands dark and imposing on a rocky shelf above the Tigris in the south-eastern corner of Turkey. The city wall that surrounds it is an enormous 12m (39ft) high structure made of black basalt. Built in the fourth century AD, it is 5½km in circumference and up to 5m (16ft) thick. It is further strengthened with as many as seventy-two massive towers, only four of which have gates allowing access into the town. The result is a unique combination of Turkish and Byzantine fortification methods.

The **citadel** is to the north-east of the town. It has been rebuilt several times, but was probably first built in the fourth century AD. It is divided from the town by a surrounding wall with three gates. Inside the citadel is a mosque that was founded in AD 555.

Also worth seeing is the **Ulu Camii**, built in the eleventh century. Next to it is the **Zincirli Medrese**, which is now a museum, and the rather larger **Masudiye Medrese**. Also nearby is an old tenth-century caravanserai called the **Hasan Pasa Hani**. A second caravanserai, the sixteenth-century **Deliler Hani**, is next to the Mardin Gate. The five other mosques are less interesting — the Behram Pasa Camii (1572), the Melak Ahmed Camii (1591), the Kasim Padisah Camii (1512), the Fatih Pasa

Diyarbakir fortifications

Camii (1522) and the Safa Camii (1532).

Almost all the houses are built of basalt, creating a gloomy atmosphere in the narrow little streets of the old town. One can easily imagine why so many of the bloody Kurdish rebellions started in Diyarbakir until as late as 1925.

The **River Tigris** is only half an hour's walk from the town. There is an ancient bridge over it that was built by the Romans. Finally, the town has good bus, rail and air connections, but overnight accommodation is very limited.

Information: State Tourist Office.
Transport connections: bus, rail and air.

Edirne (Adrianople)

40m (131ft) above sea level; population 200,000

Edirne lies close to the Greek and Bulgarian borders. Though the second-largest town in European Turkey, Edirne has suffered badly from depopulation. The Turkish government is now trying to stem the tide by the injection of new industry into the area.

The city was founded by Emperor Hadrian in AD 125, and was originally called Adrianople. Two important battles were fought here: in AD 323 Constantine the Great defeated the eastern Roman emperor Licinus to become emperor of the whole Roman empire; then in 378 Emperor Valens fell during a battle against the Goths at Adrianople. The city fell to the Turks in 1365, and the sultans resided here until the eventual fall of Constantinople in 1453.The most important thing to see is the **Selimiye Camii**. ⌘ This vast structure was built between 1567 and 1575, and is the crowning glory of the famous architect Sinan. The dome is 45m (147ft) high, while the four adjoining minarets are over 80m (262ft) high. The interior has rich tile decorations. Some of the columns have been removed from classical buildings. For example, the sixteen columns in the forecourt are from the Temple of Dionysus in Athens.

The oldest part of the town is known as **Kale**, in the middle of which is the **Ali Pasa covered bazaar**. To the north-east is the **Yeni Muradiye Camii** (1430). To the east of the old town is a smaller bazaar called the **Bedesten Hani**. ⌘ Next to it is the **Eski Camii** or **Old Mosque**, built in 1403, which can be recognised from its numerous domes. Also worth visiting is the **Üç Serefeli Camii** (1438), which has interesting tile decorations and a prayer niche.

To the north-west across the River Tunca is the suburb of **Yeldirun**, which is the site of the **Beyazid Camii**, built in 1484. ⌘ This mosque was the prototype for later mosque complexes equipped with kitchens, schools and baths.

Information: State Tourist Office, Hürriyet Meydani.
Transport connections: bus and rail.

Ephesus (Efes)

10m (33ft) above sea level

About 80km south of Izmir and just outside Selçuk is the largest ⌘ and most impressive classical site in the whole of Asia Minor. It is Ephesus, known in Turkish as Efes.

The area was settled as early as 4,000 years ago. It was first colonised by the Phoenicians and then by the Greeks. In 190 BC the port of Ephesus was annexed to the kingdom of Pergamum, and by 133 BC it was already under Roman control. During the

Gates of St John's Basilica, Selçuk

first and second centuries, the city grew into a flourishing commercial and cultural centre. It was the capital of the Roman province of Asia.

Ephesus has suffered numerous disasters, both natural and otherwise. A severe earthquake in AD 29 flattened half the residential area. In AD 263 the Goths overran the city, destroying one of the seven great wonders of the world — the Temple of Artemis. In the fifteenth century the city was overrun by Seljuks, Mongols and Ottomans.

In spite of such disasters, Ephesus was one of the most prestigious cities in the world over a period of several centuries. Many prominent personalities either lived here or paid visits here, and several important congresses were held here. Ephesus was the home of the philosopher Heraclitus. It was at Ephesus that King Mithridates announced his intention to kill every Roman in Asia Minor. The apostle Paul preached in the theatre and was imprisoned in the acropolis; the Bible contains an epistle that he later wrote to the church at Ephesus. The apostle John is said to have died here, and Mary the mother of Jesus is supposed to have been buried here. The third ecumenical council was held at Ephesus in 431.

The city began to decline as the port became silted up. The material brought down by the river eventually blocked the harbour completely. Repeated destruction at the hands of the Seljuks and Ottomans caused the people to abandon the city. The buildings fell into ruin, and Ephesus became no more than a convenient source of building material.

The first archaeological investigations were carried out in 1866 by an Englishman called Wood. The work was continued mostly by Austrian archaeologists, and is still going on today.

The nearby town of **Selçuk** is built over some of the ruins of ancient Ephesus. Of particular interest here are the seventh-century Byzantine gate and the sixth-century **St John's Basilica**, which is supposed to have been built over the tomb of the apostle John. Emperor Justinian and his wife Theodora had a 110m (361ft) long Byzantine church built on the site. The Turks converted it into a mosque and later into a market hall. It was subsequently damaged by an earthquake, and has only recently been partly restored. The massive **citadel** towers above the rest of the town, and is a useful landmark. It was probably built in the sixth century, partly out of stones from the ruins of Ephesus.

Car drivers can drive the 3km from Selçuk to the entrance to the site. Visitors without cars should take a taxi. At least 3 hours is required here to see the site properly.

Leaving Selçuk, one passes a marshy area on the right, which was the site of the famous **Temple of Artemis**. This was so enormous that it became known as one of the seven great wonders of the world. It was 109m (357ft) long and 55m (180ft) wide. The massive roof was supported on 127 columns, with a band of beautiful friezes. The temple was destroyed twice, first by arson and secondly by the Goths in AD 263. It was never rebuilt after that, and the ruins were gradually taken away to provide stone for later Byzantine and Turkish buildings. The columns, for example, were used for the Hagia Sophia in Istanbul. Nothing is left of the original structure.

It is another 2km to the site entrance. The road passes two ruins on the way: the **Gymnasium of Vedius**, built in the second century AD; and the **Stadium**, which was built during the reign of Nero (AD 54-68). The site entrance is surrounded by a small 'colony' of souvenir and refreshment kiosks.

A marble road once led up to the **Coressus Gate**. The route continues past the Byzantine baths and the **council church**, where the Christian leaders met for the council of Ephesus in AD

431. It had three naves and a bishop's residence attached. In the seventh century a dome was added.

The next buildings are the theatre gymnasium and the **Great Theatre** itself. Parts of the theatre are well preserved, especially the orchestra and stage. It once had a capacity of 25,000. The apostle Paul preached here, and the silversmiths of Ephesus staged a demonstration against him because he condemned them as blasphemous for selling model shrines to Diana (Artemis). Paul was subsequently taken into custody, and held prisoner in a tower on a hill top overlooking the harbour.

To the west of the theatre are the **harbour gymnasium** and the second-century **harbour baths**, which have been only partly uncovered. The baths used to adjoin the harbour itself, which has since become dry land. A beautiful avenue of columns once led back from the harbour to the city centre. It was built in about AD 400, and was known as the **Arcadiane**.

To the south-west of the theatre is the **agora** or **market place**, which formed the centre of the city. It was 116m (380ft) long, and was surrounded by rows of columns. A further avenue of columns once led off to the west. Nothing alas remains of the beautiful arches at each end of it. To the south of this avenue was the **Serapium**, a temple to the Egyptian god Serapis. It was barely 30m (98ft) long and enclosed by 15m (49ft) high columns.

Also nearby was the **Celsus Library**, built in AD 135 by Tiberius Julius Aquila in memory of his father Celsus, governor of the Roman province of Asia. The library had three storeys, and was richly decorated in marble. The parchment rolls were stored in niches in the walls. Celsus himself was buried beneath the apse.

Another road leads uphill from the agora. To the right of it is a house by a well called the **Nymphaeum**, and behind it the **Octagon**. Both were probably built as mausoleums. In this area archaeologists have uncovered the foundations of several six-storey apartment blocks. Along a small side road opposite were the ancient public toilets. These could even be used today, were it not for their status as an ancient monument (only modern toilet facilities may be used!).

Back on the main street opposite the well is the ancient city brothel. If one searches the ruins, one can find a small well with a pump, from which water can still be extracted today Further up the hill is the graceful and decorative **Temple of Hadrian**, and next to it the **Scholastica Baths**, named after a rich Christian woman who had them restored in the fourth century.

Library of Celsus, Ephesus

Water storage dome, Datça

The theatre at Cnidus

Waterfront, Marmaris

The **prytanium** or town hall is followed by the **odeon** — a small theatre seating about 1,500, which was built in the second century AD. To the west of this is the **Temple of Domitian**, which was built by the provincial governor in AD 90 for the emperor of that name. A little further on, there is a fountain. **St Luke's Chapel** is a round structure that was built in the Byzantine period over what was believed to be the grave of St Luke the evangelist — though this theory has never been proved.

The road passes several more bathhouses, and eventually comes to the line of the ancient walls. It ends at the **Magnesian Gate**, from which a road went to the nearby city of Magnesia. Just outside the line of the old Greek walls is an old cemetery, where many hundreds of coffins lie buried. Just to the north of the Magnesian Gate is the **east gymnasium**, which is thought to have been a girls' school. It contains a number of large rooms, including a small theatre with a stage and a raked auditorium.

The ruins are spread around the foot of a hill known today as the Panayir Dagi. Visitors are recommended to climb to the top, from which the layout of the city can be seen. The Byzantine wall runs along the top of the hill. Further along this wall is the **Chapel of the Seven Sleepers**. According to legend, seven young Christian men took refuge in a cave beneath here during persecutions in the second century. They were accidentally walled in, and fell into a deep sleep. Over 200 years later, during the reign of Theodosius II, they are supposed to have woken again and to have died shortly afterwards. Theodosius had a church built over the place where the miracle occurred. In actual fact a whole labyrinth of tombs was found beneath here. But directly beneath the chapel was a chamber with ten tombs, inside which there were inscriptions in several languages asking for God's help.

The older Greek fortifications ran along the crest of a hill to the south-west which protected the harbour. Once called **Coressus**, it is now called the **Bülbül Dagi**. A ruined watch tower on one of the highest points is supposed to be where Paul was imprisoned.

It is also worth mentioning the **Archaeological Museum**. This contains a large number of valuable items that have been discovered during the course of the excavations. They include a larger than life-size statue of Artemis that was found on the site of the prytanium (see above).

Visitors to Ephesus are recommended to go an extra 5km to **St Mary's Chapel**, which is supposed to be the last resting place of Mary the mother of Jesus. It is high up on the slopes of the Ala Dagi, and can reached by following a small road sign-posted *'Meryem ana evine gider'*. It is in a beautiful setting surrounded by forest. The building dates back to the first century AD, but was not discovered until many centuries later. Katharina Emmerich (1774-1824) had a vision one night in which she was given exact directions to the place where Mary lived. The directions led to this chapel, which was part of a monastery. The chapel was restored, and has become world-famous as a place of pilgrimage. Its location fits the early church tradition well. For Jesus is said to have entrusted his mother Mary to the care of his disciple John. John was later sent out to Asia Minor, and his grave was traced to Ephesus (see above). This suggests that Mary may well have come with John to Asia Minor and lived near him at Ephesus.

Erzurum

1,950m (6,396ft) above sea level; population 400,000

The largest town in eastern Turkey, Erzurum lies on two important trade routes: the east-west route between Ankara and Persia, and the route between Lake Van and Trabzon on the Black Sea coast. It is high up and surrounded by bare mountains over 3,000m (9,840ft) high. The climate is harsh, with cold winters and hot summers.

There are records of Erzurum going back to the fourth century AD. The town and the castle were built here to defend the Byzantine empire against its Persian neighbours in the east. This border garrison was called Theodosiopolis after the emperor of the time. The town was later conquered by the Arabs and the Seljuks. All the surviving historic buildings in the town are from the Seljuk and Turkish periods.

⌘ The **citadel** is by far the most impressive structure in Erzurum, being situated in an inaccessible position on the steep hill overlooking the town. It was built under Emperor Theodosius at the beginning of the fifth century as part of the eastern bulwark of the Byzantine empire. The massive walls and overhanging battlements are very much in keeping with the harsh atmosphere of Erzurum and its mountainous surroundings.

Below the citadel in the old town is the **Çifte Minare**

The Çifte Minare Medrese, Erzurum

Medrese (1253), a traditional Koran school. It is particularly interesting for its enormous entrance arch and the twin minarets either side of it. Nearby is the **Ulu Camii** (1197), which is in a visible state of disrepair. The university is further west in the more modern part of the town. Also of interest is the **Lala Mustafa Pasa Camii** (1563) next to the municipal park. ⌘

Information: police stations and town hall (*belediye*).
Transport connections: bus, rail and air.

Excursions

1. The imposing fortress at **Tortum**, 57km to the north. ⌘

2. An old caravanserai near **Askale**, 53km west of Erzurum.

Waterfall at Tortum, near Erzurum

Eskisehir

795m (2,607ft) above sea level; population 400,000

The modern city of Eskisehir is on the route from Ankara to Bursa or Istanbul, and spreads along the banks of the Porsuk Çayi. It is not particularly interesting for tourists, being primarily an industrial city specialising in textiles, cement, sugar and machinery.

The town is of no special interest historically, as there are no ancient sites in the present metropolitan area. Places that may be ⌘ of interest include the **Ala-Eddin Camii**, the **Kursunlu Camii** and a **dervish monastery**, all of which date back to the fifteenth and sixteenth centuries.

Information: police stations and town hall (*belediye*).
Transport connections: bus and rail.

Excursions

⌘ **1.** The **meerschaum mines** of **Tokat**, **Imisehir** and **Kara-**

tepe (30km). Meerschaum is a stone from which tobacco pipes are made.

2. The **Phrygian rock tombs** in the areas around **Kirka** and **Çifteler** (120km). ⌘

Fethiye

0-60m (197ft) above sea level; population 22,000

The seaside resort of Fethiye is on the coast of southern Turkey, 200km south-east of Mugla. Like most such resorts, it has developed from an inconspicuous little fishing village. It is overlooked by a massive crusader fortress, and the harbour contains a variety of colourful yachts and fishing boats.

The nearby coast is peppered with sandy beaches of all shapes and sizes. There is also plenty of opportunity for visiting

Ölü Deniz bay at the sea side resort of Fethiye

the nearby islands, either by hiring a boat or by joining an organised trip. This can all be arranged from the hotel. The nearby bay of Ölü Deniz is particularly popular, with its shady beach and crystal-clear waters.

⌘ Not far from Fethiye is the ancient site of **Telmesus**, with its fascinating rock tombs. They are hewn out of a vertical cliff, and have decorated façades. The most impressive of them is the fourth-century **Tomb of Amyntas**. Its façade looks like a Greek temple, with two Ionic columns supporting a decorative pediment. The tomb itself was sealed off by means of an enormous flagstone, making it almost impossible to get into.

Information: Tourist Office, Iskele Karsisi.

⌘ **Excursion to Xanthus** (45km)
The ancient city of Xanthus flourished as early as 1000 BC. Archaeological excavations have uncovered a Roman market place and a theatre. The nearby cemetery contains numerous sarcophagi covered with decorations and inscriptions.

Gordium

690m (2,263ft) above sea level

The ancient site of Gordium is about 100km south-west of Ankara near the village of **Yassihüyük**. Gordium was the capital of the Phrygian empire from about 1200 BC. It became world-famous on account of its oracle, and in particular the prophecy concerning the so-called Gordian knot, which tethered the chariot of King Gordius. The person who could undo this knot would become the ruler of Asia Minor. According to legend, Alexander the Great cut the knot through with his sword at the beginning of his campaign of conquest, and so the prophecy was fulfilled. The other main event associated with Gordium was the suicide of King Midas of Phrygia when his armies had been unable to stave off the repeated attacks of Cimmerian invaders in the east.

The city gate is relatively well preserved, considering that it dates back to the eighth century BC. The parts of it that remain are about 10m (33ft) high. Also worth seeing are two mosaics and ⌘ **King Gordius' Tomb**, which is one of the biggest in Asia Minor. The burial mound is 55m (180ft) high and 250m (820ft) wide. The burial chamber is 40m (131ft) below the surface of the mound, and can be reached via a long passage. According to experts, the tomb dates back to the seventh century BC, which would suggest that it is not that of King Gordius. Indeed, the body that was found in it is thought to be that of King Midas.

Göreme

1,120m (3,673ft) above sea level

The valley of Göreme is the centre of a unique and remarkable natural phenomenon. The whole area consists of a beautiful, almost lunar landscape that is impossible to describe adequately in words. One need only wander about for a short time to feel transported onto another planet. Nowhere else in the world is there such a vast profusion of these strange pyramids of yellow tuff and ivory-coloured pumice with razor-sharp edges.

Equally amazing are the caves that the Armenian Christians hollowed out of the rocks, creating houses, churches and monasteries within them. This man-made phenomenon is just as remarkable as the landscape itself.

The landscape was formed mostly through volcanic activity. It consists mostly of tuff which was spewed out of a volcano called Erciyas Dagi near Kayseri. Being soft, it was quickly eroded. But there were harder lumps of granite and basalt within it. These resisted erosion, causing the tuff to wear away into pyramid-like forms with small crests of harder material.

Göreme is 90km south-west of **Kayseri**. The rock pyramids are mostly confined to a triangular area, the corners of which coincide roughly with the villages of **Ürgüp**, **Nevsehir** and **Avanos**. The **Göreme Valley** is the most fascinating part of the area, because it is where the majority of the most interesting cave dwellings and churches are to be found. It is 6km from Ürgüp, and can be reached by car, taxi or *dolmus*.

The churches and cave dwellings are all well signposted. There are columnar churches over a wide area. They are basically Byzantine in form, but with distinctive Armenian and Syrian features. The cave churches are beautifully painted, mostly in black, white and ochre. Most of the statues of New Testament figures have been badly damaged, because the Turks deliberately destroyed any images they found of so-called infidels. Examples of columnar churches incude the **Elmali**

Rock dwellings in the Göreme Valley

Kilise, the **Karanlik Kilise** and the **Çarikli Kilise**. The last of these stands next to a two-storey monastery with a refectory.

⌘ The largest and most interesting church in the valley of Göreme is the **Tokali Kilise**, which is 200m downhill and to the right of the road, and is enclosed by a high railing. Like most of these churches, it was built in the tenth century. Just above here are **St Theotocus' Chapel** and **St Eustathius' Chapel**. On the opposite side of the car park is a large complex of pyramids full of chapels and dwellings. It is known as the **Kizlar Kalesi** or **Virgin's Castle**, and was probably originally a nunnery.

⌘ There are many more chapels in the Göreme area, some of which are extremely interesting. But they are well hidden and difficult to find without a guide. There is, for example, the **Sakli Kilise**, with its perfectly-preserved thirteenth-century paintings. There are other churches in the valleys of the El Nazar and of the Kiliçlar, home of the **Kiliçlar Kilise**. There are several more on the opposite side of the Göreme valley next to a fenced area. But these have been closed up and turned into dovecotes.

Houses are often built adjoining the rock pyramids, which are

Interior of a cave church, Göreme Valley

then used for animals or storage. Such combinations are commonly found in the villages of **Ürgüp**, **Ortahisar**, **Uçhisar**, **Avcilar** and **Cavusin**. Cavusin is the site of the cave church of John the Baptist. It is typical of these Armenian refugee churches, being high up in a rock face and accessible only by a long flight of steps. The roof of the cave is relatively high, and so the higher parts of the wall paintings are unusually well preserved.

One novel way of seeing Göreme is to ride around on a mule. This can be great fun, and is not difficult to arrange. Anyone can hire a mule in the village of Avcilar, only 2km away.

Izmir (Smyrna)

0-185m (607ft) above sea level; population 1,800,000

Izmir is the third-largest city in Turkey and one of the most modern. Tall buildings line the main shopping and commercial thoroughfare, the Atatürk Caddesi, which runs next to the harbour. All the main hotels, banks, restaurants and trade organisations are to be found along here. The Turkish NATO headquarters are also on the Atatürk Caddesi. Izmir boasts the largest port on Turkey's Aegean and Mediterranean coasts. Thanks to the city's favourable position from the point of view of communication and transport, numerous industries have developed around its fringes.

Izmir is the busiest tourist centre in the whole of Turkey. For although there is much less to see here than in Istanbul, it is the main airport and sea-port for visitors to the classical sites along the coast both to the north and the south.

At least half a day is needed to see the sights of Izmir itself, but time must be added for excursions to the nearby classical sites. Visitors using Izmir as a base should allow at least three extra days for visiting such places as Pergamum to the north and Ephesus and Miletus to the south.

The History of Izmir

Izmir has a history going back more than 5,000 years. The ancient Greek colony of Smyrna was founded on the acropolis site along the bay to the north, now within the modern suburb of **Bayrakli**. It originally belonged to Aeolia and then to Ionia. By 3000 BC it was the most important Greek colony in Asia Minor after Troy. In 1000 BC it is supposed to have been the home of the blind poet Homer, author of the two famous Greek epics known as the *Iliad* and the *Odyssey*.

In 600 BC the Lydians razed Smyrna to the ground. Centuries later, Alexander's generals Lysimachus and Antigonus rebuilt the city further to the south on the slopes of Mount Pagus. Smyrna flourished again in the third and second centuries BC. It was later described by Strabo as the richest and most beautiful city in the whole of the Roman province of Asia. As the harbour at Ephesus silted up, Smyrna replaced it as the foremost port in Asia Minor.

Medieval Smyrna changed hands with the same frequency as

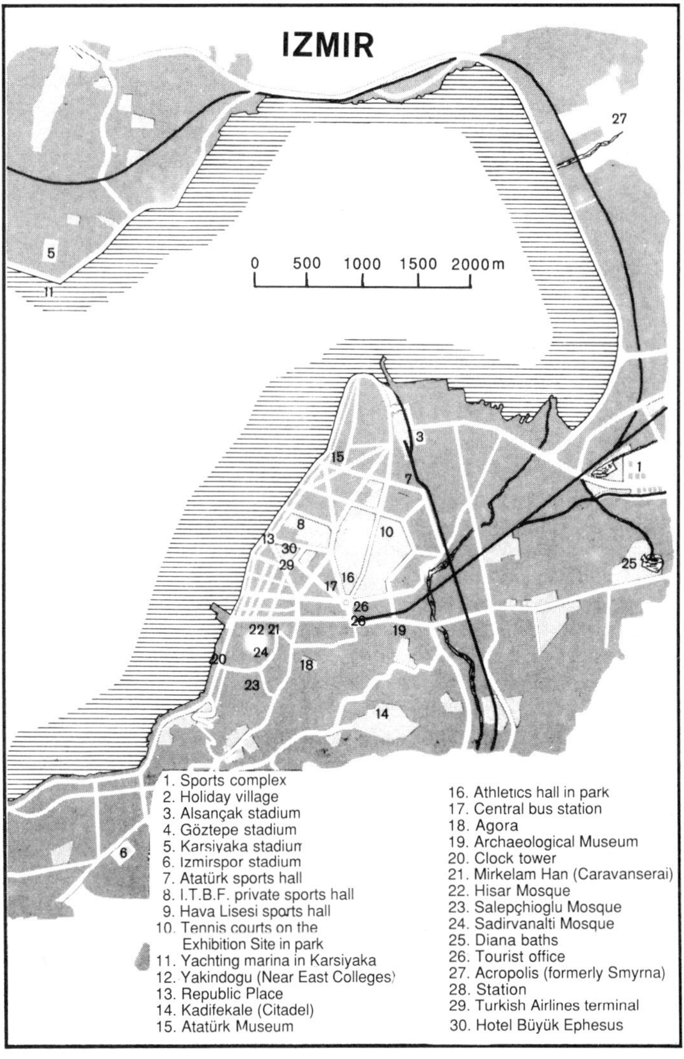

many other cities in Asia Minor. Having passed from Rome to Byzantium, it first came under Turkish domination in 1320. The crusaders managed to take the city, but were unable to keep it. The Mongols wrought havoc on the city before the Turks took over again in 1405. Since then it has remained permanently under Turkish control, apart from in 1919, when it was occupied by the Greeks. But 3 years later it was retaken for good by Kemal Atatürk in the Turkish War of Independence.

Throughout its history, Izmir has suffered repeatedly from fire, disease and earthquakes. The last great fire was in 1922, when more than 30,000 houses burned down. Since then the city has been totally rebuilt on much more spacious lines. Even now the wide streets of Izmir are still able to keep pace with the recent increase in traffic.

Things to See in Izmir

The suggested route begins on the city's main commercial thoroughfare — the 3km long Atatürk Caddesi that runs along the harbour front. About half-way along is the Cumhuriyet Meydani (Square of the Republic), where there is a statue of Kemal Atatürk on horseback.

At the southern end of the Atatürk Caddesi is a busy square called the Konak, which is where the main passenger piers are located. It is easily recognised from the clock tower in the centre and a decorative mosque called the **Konak Camii**. The bazaar quarter is not far away from here. There is no covered market as such, but the passages are covered by canopies.

One should go north along the Atatürk Caddesi and turn right along the Fevzi Pasa Bulvari. There is a further right turn into the Esref Pasa Caddesi. Then the second road on the left comes out into the ancient agora or market place. One can still see parts of the structures that were erected here under the Roman emperor Marcus Aurelius. These include rows of columns, a shopping arcade in several storeys, and many of the elaborate decorations. In one corner there are three statues under an ugly piece of plastic roofing. One is of Poseidon, the second of Demeter, but the subject of the third is not known.

From the agora one can see the **citadel** high above, and to the right of it a mosque with a shining silver dome. To get there one must climb up through the maze of steep alleys and stairways that makes up the old town. The original fortification was built by Lysimachus, but all that can be seen now are remnants of the massive walls and round towers which were built later during the Byzantine period. The main reason for climbing the citadel is the view from the top. There is a wonderful panorama of the whole city

Foça, near Izmir

and of the 30km long inlet that leads out to the Aegean.

There is an enormous park in the city centre, which extends from 9 Eylül Meydani to the Dr Mustafa Enver Bulvari. It covers some of the area that was razed to the ground in the great fire of 1922. The park is used primarily for pleasure and recreation. The great exhibition hall is the site for the Izmir International Fair, which is held here every year from 20 August to 20 September. The **Archaeological Museum** is also located in the park. It ⌘ contains numerous interesting finds from the many ancient sites in the area. One of the most attractive exhibits is a copy of the lovely statue of Artemis from the famous Temple of Artemis at Ephesus*.

Something else worth seeing is the **Kemer Bridge**, which is a ⌘ few hundred yards east of the main railway station along the Gaziler Caddesi. Although most of the present structure is modern, its foundations go back to Greek and Roman times. The bridge was once part of an important ancient caravan route. One can imagine long lines of camels shuffling across it laden with all kinds of oriental treasure. They would often have travelled for

Bridge over the River Meles, near Izmir

months on their way from such cities as Damascus, Baghdad and Tehran.

Information: State Tourist Office, Gazi Osman Pasa Bulvari. Denizcilik Bankasi TAO (Turkish Shipping Co.) Atatürk Caddesi 128. Türk Hava Yollari (Turkish Airlines) Fevzi Pasa Bulvari 17E.
Transport connections: bus, rail, ship and air.

Excursions

⌘ **1. Bayrakli** (4km) and the ancient acropolis of **Tepe Küle**, from the oldest period of Smyrna's history (see above).

2. A tour of the ancient sites to the south of Izmir (200+km), ⌘ including **Colophon**, **Ephesus***, **Magnesia**, **Priene***, **Miletus*** and **Didyma**. They can be managed in a day, but should preferably be spread over at least 2 days. Visitors without cars should go by bus as far as Selçuk and continue by taxi.

3. Inciralti (12km). This beautiful beach to the south-west of Izmir has hotel, restaurant and bathing facilities.

⌘ **4.** The **Agamemnon Ilicalari** (11km) or Baths of Agamemnon are along the same road to the south-west, turning left just after Güzelyari. The waters have a temperature of 40°C (104°F).

5. Çesme (75km). The route continues along the same road beyond Güzelyari via the famous spa town of **Urla**. 4km from Urla is the ancient site of **Clazomenae**, where the philosopher Anaxagoras lived around 500 BC. 4km before Çesme there is a marvellous beach with hotel and restaurant facilities. Çesme itself is a lovely little fishing village with thermal baths and a castle.

6. Seferihisar (50km). The route follows the same road as above, but turns left after 25km. 2km west of Seferihisar is the village of **Sigacik**, and to the south of it the ancient Greek colony of **Teos**.

7. Bergama* (104km). The route follows the E24 north from Izmir for 98km, then turns right for the small country town of Bergama. The ancient Greek city of **Pergamum** extends up the hillside from the edge of the town.

Karatepe

800m (2,624ft) above sea level

The famous Hittite site at Karatepe (which means 'black hill') is about 130km north-east of Adana, and can be reached via Ceyhan and Kadirli. The archaeological remains at Karatepe reveal more about this puzzling civilisation than any other site apart from the one at Bogazkale*. The evidence suggests that the Hittite city of Karatepe flourished between 1000 and 800 BC.

The massive **city gates** are a proud witness to Hittite building skills. An artificial roof has been placed over them to protect them from further erosion. The sculptures and reliefs that were found nearby have provided invaluable evidence about the Hittites' way of life. There are scenes of hunting, wars and feasting, and representations of Hittite gods. Inscriptions found on both gates include parallel texts in Hittite and Phoenician script, and have enabled experts to decipher the Hittite language for the very first time. They consist of a eulogy to the efforts of King Astiwada in securing the safety of the kingdom, and a warning to enemies against attacking the city.

On **Domuztepe**, the hill opposite Karatepe, there are the ruins of a former Roman settlement.

Kayseri

1,060m (3,477ft) above sea level; population 500,000

The city of Kayseri lies in the east of central Anatolia. It is situated below a volcano called the Erciyas Dagi (3,916m (12,844ft)) in the middle of a vast, treeless steppe. It is also an important crossroads between the east-west route from Persia to Europe (via Ankara and Istanbul) and the north-south route from the Black Sea to Adana on the Mediterranean coast. The city is interesting for its remarkable Seljuk buildings, and forms a good base for visiting the strange and wonderful valley of Göreme*.

The original city was built on the slopes to the south-west of the present city centre. It was first called Mazaca, but around 150 BC it was renamed Eusebia and became the capital of the kingdom of Cappadocia. In 77 BC it was destroyed by invading Armenians. The Romans later occupied Cappadocia, and renamed its capital Caesarea Cappadociae. Christianity came quickly to Cappadocia, and spread from here throughout the area that now forms eastern Turkey.

In the fourth century AD a monastery was built on the plains below, which became the new centre for the Byzantine city of Caesarea. Though well fortified, being strategically important, it was frequently ravaged by war during subsequent centuries. Between 600 and 1500 it was plundered by Persians, Arabs, crusaders, Turks and Mongols. In 1468 it was finally taken over by the Ottoman ruler Mehmed II, and since then Kayseri has been permanently Turkish.

⌘ The most impressive structure in Kayseri is the **citadel** in the city centre. Its single fortified entrance opens out onto the Kale Önü Caddesi. The original fortifications were built during the reign of Emperor Justinian in the sixth century AD. They were later extended by the Turks. Visitors may walk along the top of the castle walls, which provide some magnificent views of the old city with the snow-covered volcano in the background. The mosque inside the walls is the fifteenth-century **Fatih Camii**.

The bazaar is to the south-west of the citadel. It is covered partly by canopies and partly by the original vaulting. In front of the bazaar is an old caravanserai called the **Vizir Hani**, which is remarkably well preserved. Its structure is enclosed, but it is still used by fur sellers for displaying their wares.

⌘ **Ulu Camii** (1136) stands just opposite. Its large dome is sup-

Many-domed mosque, Kayseri

ported on four rows of columns. The cleansing fountain to the right of the entrance is particularly interesting. The building next to it is the **Melik Gazi** Koran school. The **Hatuniye Medrese** (1446) is a little further on. The columns for all these buildings came from the ancient ruins nearby.

To the east of the citadel is a complex of buildings called the **Honat Hatun**. It consists of a mosque, a mausoleum and a former Koran school that has been turned into a museum. They were all built in the thirteenth century at the instigation of Sultana Mahperi. The most interesting feature of the mosque is the great entrance door. The museum contains numerous exhibits from the Hittite site at Kültepe (see excursions below), plus some interesting items from the Greek, Roman and Byzantine periods. The sultana's mausoleum is one of the most remarkable in Turkey, both for its architecture and for its decorations. Inside it are the coffins of the sultana herself and of two princesses. The mausoleum is closed on Mondays. ⌘

2½km from the Honat Hatun complex is another mausoleum

called the **Döner Kümbet**, built in 1275 for an unidentified princess. The roof construction creates an optical illusion that makes it appear to revolve — hence the name Döner Kümbet or 'revolving tomb'.

Also worth mentioning is a mosque in the Atatürk Park called the **Kursunlu Camii** (1580), which is supposed to have been built by the famous architect Sinan. It is interesting for its five domes and the beautiful columned hall on the northern side.

The square that opens out in front of the citadel is called the Cumhuriyet Meydani (Square of the Republic). It forms the main hub of the city, and there are several good restaurants along the streets that radiate from it. The old city of Kayseri is a strange mixture of the old and the new, in which centuries-old houses are sandwiched between large modern structures. It will be interesting to see how many of the old medieval buildings will survive the continuing programme of modernisation.

Information: State Tourist Office.
Transport connections: bus, rail and air.

Excursions

1. Ürgüp and the valley of **Göreme*** (90km).

2. Climbing the **Erciyas Dagi** (3,916m (12,844ft)). This volcano was active as late as the nineteenth century. It involves a 10-hour climb from the pass on the road to Develi. Climbers can bivouac overnight in a cave just below the summit.

3. The Hittite site at **Kültepe** (32km). The ancient city of **Kanis** dates back 5,000 years. This was before the arrival of the Hittites, under whom it flourished in about 2000 BC. 800 years later it was destroyed by the Phrygians. But Kanis grew again, and the Assyrian merchants that settled here made it into a great centre of trade and commerce. Its wealth and power was only later eclipsed by the development of the nearby city of Caesarea (Kayseri). Kanis was several times destroyed by fire, earthquake or war, and the inhabitants eventually abandoned it.

Archaeologists began their investigations in 1948, and found evidence of settlement here going back into the Bronze Age. The few fragments of foundation that remain provide evidence of houses, temples and a palace. The most interesting finds are exhibited at the Hittite Museum in Ankara*.

Konya (Iconium)

1,025m (3,362ft) above sea level; population 900,000

Konya was once the home of the whirling dervishes. It is centred around an oasis in the salt wastes on the southern edge of the central Anatolian plateau. The modern town of Konya is fast expanding across the plain. It has little of the atmosphere it once had, and one finds it difficult to imagine that the sultans once resided here before they later advanced north towards the Bosporus.

The oasis was settled by the Hittites as early as 1500 BC. Alexander the Great refreshed himself at the springs of Iconium (as it was then called) at the beginning of his eastern campaign. The apostle Paul also stayed at Iconium during his missionary journeys. When the Seljuks invaded Asia Minor in the ninth century AD, they established themselves here, and Süleyman made the city into the capital of his empire. Konya was taken by Emperor Barbarossa in the crusade of 1190. But following its recapture by the Turks, the city entered a period of great prosperity. Most of the great Seljuk buildings that can be seen here today were built during the thirteenth century.

The acropolis on the western edge of the city is where the earliest signs of settlement have been found. But all that remains is part of an old fortification tower. The acropolis area is now occupied by the Ala-Eddin Park. On the east side of the park is the **Ala-Eddin Camii**, built in 1221. The fifty columns that support the ceiling were taken from the ancient Graeco-Roman site. The mosque contains the tombs of eight Turkish (or rather Seljuk) sultans.

To the north of this mosque is the former **Karatay Camii**, which now contains a museum of decorative wall tiles. The adjoining Koran school was built in 1251. The decorative entrance is particularly beautiful. A side-chamber in the mosque contains the tomb of Emir Karatay, who founded the Koran school. The **Ince Minare Camii**, built in 1258, has similarly been turned into a museum, with a collection of sculptures from several different centuries. The rooms inside the mosque have beautiful wall-tile decorations, and there is some interesting ornamentation around the entrance.

Other mosques worth seeing are the **Iplikçi Camii** (1202), the **Hasan Pasa Camii** and the **Aziziye Camii**. The **Sahip**

Whirling dervishes at Konya

Ata Camii, built in 1258, has a bathhouse and a sultan's tomb adjoining it. The **Archaeological Museum** is nearby, while the **Ethnographical Museum** is to the north of the Mevlâna Monastery (see below).

On the opposite side of the monastery is the **Selimiye Camii**, built in 1566, which can be recognised from its twin minarets. Its most valuable features are the entrance door, the prayer niche and the pulpit. To the right of the mosque is the **Yusuf Aga Library**, which is attached to the monastery. It contains some rare and beautiful handwritten and printed editions of the Koran and of other works.

The **Mevlâna Monastery** is Konya's most celebrated attraction. Once the home of the Turkish order of the whirling dervishes, it has been a museum since 1927, when the order was outlawed by Atatürk. It is built around the mausoleum of Celal-Eddin Rumi, the Moslem philosopher who founded the order. Rumi was born in Afghanistan in 1207, but settled in Konya in 1233. After his death, his followers built a monastery around his mausoleum. Since the whirling dervishes were banned, their order has turned into a kind of secret religious society, which is now becoming increasingly involved in underground political activity. The order got its name from the whirling dance movements that the dervishes employ in their worship.

As one enters the monastery precincts, one comes into a grass court surrounded by the dervishes' residential quarters. **Rumi's mausoleum** is straight ahead, with its distinctive tower consisting of a shiny-green fluted cylinder with a cone-shaped top and resting on a blue-coloured base. This peculiar structure is Konya's best-known landmark. The mausoleum contains the sarcophagi of several important dervishes. But the place of honour is accorded to that of the order's founder, Celal-Eddin Rumi. The other important building is the **Semahane**, where the whirling dervishes used to worship.

The Hükümet Meydani forms the hub of the modern city of Konya. The town hall (*belediye*) information office and the police headquarters are both located here. Most of the sights can be reached from here, either along the main shopping street, the Ala-Eddin Caddesi, or via the Mevlâna Caddesi. The main bus station is about 1km outside the city centre.

Information: Belediye Turizm Bürosu, Ala-Eddin Caddesi.
Transport connections: bus and rail.

Excursions

1. The Temple of Zeus at **Lystra** (35km) can be reached via Hatip and Hatunsaray. This ancient city is recorded in the Bible as the place where the apostle Paul was stoned after healing a sick man. It was also the home town of the apostle Timothy.

2. **St Paul's Monastery**, 4km to the north-west of Konya, is almost completely hewn out of the rock. 4km further on at **Sille** there are cave churches with beautiful frescos.

3. The **Sultanhani** (80km) is the most fascinating medieval caravanserai in the whole of Turkey.

4. The **Binbir Kilise** (**1,001 Churches**) near **Karaman** (145km). The site is well off the beaten track. From Karaman (110km) it is 17km to **Kilbasan** and a further 18km to **Madensehir**. All around Madensehir are the remains of a once-flourishing Christian community, the strength of which is shown by the vast numbers of ruined churches. In the twelfth century

the Turks exterminated all Christians in the area, and looted all their churches. Visitors wishing to see some of these churches should hire the services of a guide, and should be prepared for a 2-hour hike.

Kusadasi

0-150m (492ft) above sea level; population 21,000

Formerly a small fishing village, Kusadasi has developed into one of the best-known bathing resorts on the coast of Asia Minor. This busy little tourist centre is about 90km south of Izmir. The marvellous sandy beach and the clean, unpolluted waters make it an ideal place for a bathing holiday.

The old caravanserai in the town centre has been extended and made into a sumptuous hotel. The camping site is only 6km away, and there are numerous hotels and restaurants. It is a place with atmosphere, and its many little shops are full of oriental colour. The harbour is also very picturesque, and is guarded by a medieval fort.

Medusa's Head, Didyma

Kusadasi is the ideal centre for combining a bathing holiday with visits to places of cultural interest. **Ephesus***, for example, is only 12km away, while **Magnesia**, **Priene***, **Miletus*** and **Didyma** are all within easy reach. The famous Greek island of Samos is just off the coast here.

Information: Tourist Office, Iskele Meydani.

Malatya

1,000m (3,280ft) above sea level; population 325,000

Malatya is in south-eastern Turkey near the southern edge of the Anatolian plateau and not far from the River Euphrates. The original Hittite settlement dates back to 2000 BC. The ancient city of Milid flourished under the Hittites and Assyrians. Malatya has been Turkish since 1168, although it was twice destroyed by the Mongols. In 1835 the old town was razed to the ground by the Egyptians, and the inhabitants were forced to evacuate. The town was then rebuilt on a new site 10km west of the old one.

The modern town of Malatya is rather unattractive, with no buildings of any historical interest. The bazaar, on the other hand, is very much worth visiting, with a wide choice of fruit and salad vegetables.

The site of **Old Malatya** is only 10km away along a rough road that comes off the E99 Elâzig road. The tiny village of **Eski Malatya** lies amid the ruins of the old town, which was evacuated in the nineteenth century (see above). The most interesting remains are those of the **Ulu Camii** (1237), the **Yeni Camii** (1307), the eleventh-century city walls and a seventeenth-century caravanserai.

The Hittite and Assyrian remains are another 4km away at **Arslantepe**, where foundations remain of the original Hittite settlement. The most valuable find here was a larger than life-size statue of the Hittite king of Milid dating from 800 BC. It is now kept in the Hittite Museum at Ankara*.

Information: town hall (*belediye*).
Transport connections: bus, rail and air.

Marmaris

Marmaris

0-40m (131ft) above sea level; population 10,000

Marmaris is 60km south of Mugla on the coast, not far from the Greek island of Rhodes. Once a small fishing village, it has developed into a popular bathing resort. It is situated next to a lovely bay scattered with small islands. The cliffs either side are lined with cool, shady pine forests.

The old fishing harbour is well placed geographically; it has been extended to include a marina, where many boats seek shelter overnight. There are numerous hotels and restaurants providing everything the tourist might require. A special boat taxi service brings guests to the harbour from hotels along the shore. There are also boats for hire so that visitors can get to know the local islands.

Information: Tourist Office, Iskele Meydani.

Excursion to Datça (68km)
For visitors who wish to try another beach, there is the possibility of a bus or *dolmus* excursion to Datça. This former fishing village is situated on a long peninsula to the west of Marmaris. The road along the coast provides some beautiful views of the sea and of the neighbouring islands. Those interested in historical sites are recommended to carry on to the ancient Greek city of **Cnidus**. The remains include two theatres and the Temple of Demeter.

Miletus (Milet)

0-60m (197ft) above sea level

Of the many colonial cities founded by the Dorian and Ionian Greeks, the most important were Troy, Ephesus, Smyrna and Miletus. But Miletus was by far the largest and most powerful of them. The people of Miletus founded as many as twenty-four colonies along the Mediterranean and Black Sea coasts. Miletus was later conquered by the Persians, by the Greeks again under Alexander the Great, and eventually by the Romans.

The city was of great international significance throughout the Graeco-Roman world. The apostle Paul visited Miletus on several occasions, and a strong Christian community grew up here. Other important visitors included statesmen such as Cicero, Julius Caesar and Mark Antony.

In the eleventh century Miletus was conquered by the Turks. The harbour remained intact until the sixteenth century, after which it began to silt up. The city had lost its livelihood, and gradually its inhabitants moved away to settle elsewhere along the coast. This once-powerful city fell into ruins. But Miletus nonetheless remains an impressive sight. The ancient ruins are situated about 150km along the coast south of Izmir.

The **theatre** looks out towards the sea. It is particularly impressive, having once seated an audience of 25,000. The tunnel entrances are still well preserved. The imperial box once stood between the two columns near the front row of the auditorium. There were originally four columns here to support the canopy under which the emperor's family sat.

On the acropolis overlooking the theatre are the remains of a **Byzantine fortress**. From the top there is a panorama of the whole site. The area immediately beyond the acropolis once formed the city's residential quarters. The houses were built close together, and the streets formed a square grid pattern. It is interesting to note that by 500 BC Miletus was organised along the lines of a large modern city. It even had street lighting, flush toilets and underground water pipes. The area is now badly overgrown; all that one can see are a few disconnected walls, with the more substantial ruins further away. The residential area is in the process of further excavation.

Before leaving the acropolis, one should try to imagine where the harbours used to be. The area adjoining the theatre stage was once the theatre harbour. The area to the left of the residential quarter was also an area of harbour, known as the Bay of Lions. Both harbours became silted up with material brought down the River Maeander.

The most important buildings are carefully labelled. Most of them are beyond the residential area and are clustered around the **southern agora** or **market place**. On the north side are the **buleuterium** (**town hall**) and to the right of it **Trajan's Nymphaeum**. Continuing northwards, one comes to the **northern agora** and the **Temple of Apollo**.

On the flat area to the south-west of the theatre is the site of the **Roman stadium**. It was 230m (754ft) long and 74m (243ft) wide. At the western end of it are the **gymnasium** and the **Temple of Athena**. One much later building at the foot of the acropolis is a disused mosque called the **Iliyas Bey Camii**, which was built in 1501.

The Graeco-Roman city numbered several hundreds of thousands of inhabitants, and covered an area that now includes the modern village of **Balat**. There is a small museum to the left of the approach road from the village to the main site. It was built by German archaeologists who were excavating the site. The office and living quarters of the present excavation team are visible on a nearby hill.

The city was protected by strong fortifications, parts of which are still visible. There was a cemetery in front of the walls, and there are still hundreds of sarcophagi scattered all over the area.

The original city of Miletus was out beyond these walls, 2km south of the theatre. It was centred round an acropolis on a hill, now called Kalabak Tepe, and flourished in the seventh and sixth centuries BC. It was destroyed by the Persians, and the inhabitants built a new city on the classical site to the north. For many centuries afterwards, the old city was used as a cemetery.

Pamukkale (Hierapolis)

350m (1,148ft) above sea level

The chalk terraces of Pamukkale are 14km to the north of Denizli, and rise 150m (492ft) above the bottom of the valley. The road leads up through an irregular basin of ivory-white chalk sinter several hundreds of yards wide. The basin is formed into a vast stairway of interlocking cliffs and water pools. Apart from Göreme, there is nothing else in Turkey to match it.

The water that flows down over the terraces comes from thermal springs at the top. The water emerges at a temperature of 33°C (91°F), and has a high concentration of chalk. It deposits 5,500cu yd of chalk sinter each year. Thus the chalk terraces are gradually advancing down the valley. At night the pools of water overflow into each other down the cliffs, adding more chalk to the enormous stalactites that fringe them. During the day the pools evaporate, again leaving chalk behind.

The terraces are peppered with restaurants and luxury hotels.

The chalk terraces of Pamukkale

Some of the hotels have villas and swimming pools attached. At the top of the terraces there is a hotel on the right, and next to it a public swimming bath filled with water from the springs.

The hotels stand amid the ruins of the ancient city of Hierapolis, which was originally founded by Ionian Greeks. The Romans later developed it into a thriving metropolis. They built great bath complexes around the hot springs, which were famous for their healing qualities. An earthquake in AD 17 almost completely destroyed the city, but it was rebuilt on even grander lines than before. The apostle Philip ministered to a Christian community at Hierapolis. He is said to have been martyred here during the later persecution of the Christians. After the Seljuk conquest, Hierapolis declined into obscurity.

As the road climbs the terraces, it first passes a medieval fortress on the left. Its rather fanciful name **Pamukkale** or '**Cotton Castle**' is highly descriptive of the area, and was later extended to include the chalk terraces themselves. To the right of the road are the high walls and arches of the **Roman baths**. The road climbs up past the hotel where the healing springs are found.

It passes through a 1km-long avenue of columns, with a ruined **agora** on the right. Next to it are the remains of a Christian church. The **theatre** above it is fairly well preserved, and once held an audience of 15,000. The site is rather bare apart from a few rather scruffy children selling 'antiques'. For once these may actually be genuine, since the site has yet to be properly excavated. One may, for example, come across some nice fragments of Roman pottery.

From the theatre a path continues uphill to the left. After about twenty minutes' climb, one arrives at a round structure that is thought to have been a mausoleum or memorial chapel for the apostle Philip. Next to it are the remains of a small theatre that is Greek rather than Roman in architecture, and which must therefore belong to the original Ionian colony of Hierapolis.

North of here is an extensive necropolis or cemetery. There are hundreds of opened sarcophagi lying around, some of them very impressive. One can return via the north gate, from which the long avenue of columns (see above) leads back through the old city to the south gate. Beyond the city walls there is another enormous cemetery, including some magnificent family vaults that resemble mausoleums. These two Roman cemeteries outside the old city walls are among the largest and most interesting of their kind.

Perga

10m (33ft) above sea level

The site of the former Greek colony of Perga is 18km north-east of Antakya. The city once stood next to the mouth of the Aksu Çayi. It began with an acropolis on the hill, and gradually expanded across the plain. Perga later suffered the same fate as did Ephesus, Miletus and other thriving Aegean ports: the harbour silted up, and the city lost its livelihood.

The first records of Perga date back to the fourth century BC. The people allied themselves with Alexander the Great, and assisted him in his conquest of Side and Aspendus. Perga was the home of the great geometer Apollonius. In the second century BC the city came under Roman control, and continued to flourish for some time. Visitors to Perga included emperors and governors, and also the apostle Paul. During the Byzantine period the city was gradually abandoned. For it ceased to become viable as the effects of the silting up of the harbour were compounded by earthquakes and piracy.

The ruins of Perga hide a secret that archaeologists have so far failed to uncover: the location of the famous **Sanctuary of Artemis**. During the Roman period it became known about in Rome. For when Verres looted it, Cicero went before the Roman senate to accuse him of violating the gods.

Before entering the 240m (787ft) long enclosure, one passes the **stadium** on the left, where the spectator areas are still clearly visible. On the steep slope to the left of it are the remains of the **theatre**. The semi-circular auditorium and the front of the stage are still well preserved. The theatre had a capacity of about 12,000.

Entering the enclosure, one immediately approaches the city walls and passes through a massive city gate. A long avenue of decorative columns leads from here past the **agora** on the right to the remains of the Greek **acropolis**. A small canal ran across the middle of the avenue, and there were shops between the columns that led off it. Immediately below the acropolis, there is another avenue of columns going in a north-south direction. This is still being excavated.

The ruins at the former Greek colony of Perga

Priene

130m (426ft) above sea level

The ancient port of Priene was the sister town to Miletus. Its importance is shown by the fact that the Temple of Athena was consecrated by Alexander the Great in person. Priene had a ⌘ large, well-sheltered harbour, but was never as powerful as its neighbour across the bay.

Little is known of the town's early history. There is no evidence of settlement here before the foundation of the existing site in the fourth century BC. But Priene is known to date back much earlier. Old Priene was probably built down on the plain of the Maeander; all traces of it must have later been buried under a thick layer of mud at the time when the harbour silted up.

The city of Priene is one of the most impressive among all the ancient ruins of Asia Minor. It was built at the foot of a great cliff. The streets were laid out in a square grid pattern along a series of parallel terraces above the plain of the Maeander.

One enters the residential area through the old city wall. The streets have been completely uncovered. The **agora** is in the centre of the middle terrace. Below it are the **lower gymnasium** and the **stadium**. Immediately above it is a columned **portico**, and above that the **buleuterium** (**town hall**). The rows of seats where the councillors assembled are amazingly well preserved.

Climbing up another street, one comes to the **upper gymnasium**. To the right of it is an **Egyptian temple** that was dedicated to the goddess Isis. The small **theatre** on the top terrace is in almost perfect condition. It has been restored several times since it was built in the third century AD. Next to it is a **Byzantine church**.

Only a few paces away is the famous **Temple of Demeter**. Five of its great Ionic columns have remained standing. Nothing else is left of it apart from several column stumps, a sacrificial trench and the outline of a dais. But the columns are nonetheless impressive, and there is a marvellous view across the plain of the Maeander to the ancient province of Caria. The temple still seems to be haunted by the spirit of the goddess Demeter.

The **Temple of Athena** stood a little further down the hill, but it must have been even more impressive. The foundations include both Greek and Roman features. The temple was built by Pythus, and became a model for all later Ionic temples. The shrine was full of sculptures, the main one being a 7m (23ft) high statue of Athena. There was originally a flight of steps leading up to the high altar.

A precipitous path goes zigzagging up the cliffside to the summit, where there are a few remnants left of the ancient Greek **acropolis**. Early evening is undoubtedly the best time to see Priene. By then the ruins are in shadow, but are beautifully silhouetted against the sunlit plain below.

Samsun

40m (131ft) above sea level; population 450,000

Turkey's principal Black Sea port lies part-way along the coast between Sinop and Trabzon. Samsun was founded as late as the thirteenth century, when the Seljuks extended the harbour here. But the ancient Greek city of Amisus was only 3km along the coast. The city became famous in 1919 as the place from which Kemal Atatürk began his campaign against the Greeks in the

Turkish War of Independence.

Apart from its beaches, Samsun has little of special interest to offer the tourist. Most visitors are merely passing through on a cruise along the Black Sea coast. Two places worth seeing if one does stop here are the **Archaeological Museum** and the **Pazar Camii**. There are good roads linking Samsun with important cities in the Turkish interior such as Ankara, Kayseri, Sivas and Erzurum.

Information: State Tourist Office.
Transport connections: bus, rail and air.

Side

10m (33ft) above sea level

Cleopatra is supposed to have bathed in the sea off Side on the occasion of a secret assignation with Mark Antony. But this is not its only claim to fame. The ancient site of Side is perched on a peninsula, 50km east of Antalya along the Turkish Mediterranean coast.

Little is known of the city's early history, or of the identity of the people whose inscriptions were found on the site. Experts have so far failed to decipher the writing. But the city's founders could possibly have been Phoenician merchants.

Side became the main port for the province of Pamphylia, in spite of the build-up of silt and the dangers that it posed to shipping. Dozens of Greek and Roman ships lie buried beneath the mud off the coast. The port flourished under Roman occupation, and remained prosperous for many more centuries. Between the sixth and tenth centuries, Side was notorious for its slave market.

By the twelfth century, however, the city had already been abandoned. No one knows exactly why this happened. It was not resettled until the beginning of this century, when Greeks from Crete built the village of Selimiye amid the ruins.

Side has now turned into an idyllic Mediterranean resort. It has much to recommend it as a place for a longer stay: ancient ruins, well-run hotels and restaurants, miles of sandy beaches, and the kind hospitality of the people of Selimiye. Cars are banned from the village, and drivers must leave them at the car park opposite the theatre. A sleepy little village has been transformed into a bustling town within the space of 10 years. The long shopping

Theatre at Side, the largest in Asia Minor

streets have a bazaar-like atmosphere, and the beach is lined with hotels as far as the eye can see. Peace and tranquillity are no more, but there is much for the tourist to enjoy.

The approach road enters the ancient site through the great gate in the old fortifications. Nearby is the so-called **nymphaeum**, which was probably a large water tower used for storing the city's water supply. Though it is now only 12m (39ft) high, its original height must have been at least 50m (164ft). ⌘

The road ends at a car park next to an interesting museum. The ancient **theatre** opposite is by far the largest theatre in the whole of Asia Minor. It stands on the narrow neck of land that links the peninsula to the mainland. The terrain is flat, so the auditorium, which would normally nestle in the hillside, towers majestically above the sea. From the dizzy heights of the top row, there is a wide panorama of the ruined city with the open sea beyond. The arena below is scattered with various remains. Archaeologists are trying to reassemble all the beautiful pieces of sculpture that are left from the stage. ⌘

Not far from the stage is an **agora** measuring 65m (213ft) square, and to the south-west of it a 30m (98ft) long building with a columned hall that is partially intact. There are life-size statues standing in the alcoves along the walls. It is not known whether the building was a temple or Roman villa.

Visitors are recommended to walk on to the harbour at the southern end of the peninsula, where there are the sites of three interesting temples. The first is semi-circular and was dedicated to the moon goddess Mene. A Byzantine church stands over the other two temple sites, but they are thought to have been those of Apollo and Athena, patron goddess of Side.

Sinop

30m (98ft) above sea level; population 25,000

Turkey's most northerly town is picturesquely situated in the middle of the Black Sea coast, with the mighty peaks of the Pontic Mountains in the background. Sinop is no longer as important as it once was. As a port it has been overtaken by Samsun, and the town has consequently become a rather quiet little backwater.

Sinop, however, has a long and illustrious history. The colony of Sinope was founded in 800 BC by a band of Greeks from Miletus. It quickly grew into a busy commercial and trading centre. Diogenes came from Sinope, and Xenophon passed through with the remnants of his army on their return to Greece. Many centuries later, the Crimean War began here with a sea battle off Sinop in which the Russians bombarded the town.

Visitors to Sinop should visit its two most interesting mosques: ⌘ the **Seit Bibal Camii** and the **Büyük Camii**. It is also worth taking a walk up the nearby hill, from which there is a marvellous view of the whole area around.

Information: town hall (*belediye*).
Transport connections: bus and ship.

Sivas

1,300m (4,264ft) above sea level; population 322,000

The old merchant city of Sivas is situated on the crossroads of two important caravan routes: the north-south route between the

Black Sea and Mediterranean coasts, and the east-west route from Erzurum via Ankara to Istanbul. It is still an important traffic junction, though the nature of the transport has changed. The caravan trail has been replaced by road and rail. Sivas is an important station on the Trans-Anatolian Railway.

The town of Sebastea (as it was originally called) was founded shortly after the birth of Christ. It has been Turkish since the eleventh century, apart from a short period of Mongol domination in the fourteenth century. The Mongols massacred the Christians here, killing as many as 10,000 of them.

There was originally a fortress on the **Toprak Tepe**, from which there is a good view of the whole city. Buildings worth visiting include the eleventh-century **Ulu Camii** and a seventeenth-century hospital called the **Dar Us Sifa**. Opposite the hospital is the thirteenth-century **Çifte Medrese**, which can be recognised from its two minarets. Only 5 minutes' walk away is the **Muzaffer Barucirdi Medrese**, which was also built in the thirteenth century. The tower-like **mausoleum of Sey Hasan Beg** was built in 1347. **The Gök Medrese** from 1271 is particularly fascinating, and has some beautiful ornamentation. There is a central court surrounded by the school's former classrooms, which are now used as a museum.

Information: town hall (*belediye*).
Transport connections: bus, rail and air.

Trabzon (Trapezus/Trebizond)

40m (131ft) above sea level; population 270,000

The port of Trabzon lies on the most beautiful section of the Turkish Black Sea coast, and is the most easterly port along that coast. The town is spread over three hills.

The colony of Trapezus was founded in the eighth century BC by Greeks from Sinope. It developed into a rich port, where for many centuries caravans from Persia unloaded their goods onto ships. The city was first destroyed in AD 260, and was later plundered by the Ostrogoths on their way from east to west.

In the thirteenth century, following the sack of Constantinople by the crusaders, the sons of the deposed emperor came to Trebizond, which became the capital of the Comnene empire in Asia Minor. The town fell to the Ottomans in 1461, since when

Hagia Sophia Church, Trabzon

Trabzon has remained permanently in Turkish hands.

The port has declined during the last 100 years, thanks to the gradual improvement of the road network and the building of the Trans-Anatolian Railway.

The most impressive structure in Trabzon is the massive city wall, which still forms a complete ring round the old town. A castle once stood on the east side of the wall. Several of the old church buildings of Trebizond have been preserved as mosques. The old-⌘ est is the **Küçük Ayvasil**, built in the eighth century and originally dedicated to St Anne. The **Ortahisar Camii** was built as a church in the fourteenth century. There is a cleansing fountain in front of the entrance.

By far the most interesting building is the thirteenth-century ⌘ **Hagia Sophia Church**, which is about 3km outside the town centre. Though converted into a mosque, it has subsequently been turned into a museum. The ground plan is in the form of a Greek cross with a dome at the centre. There are many beautiful paintings along the walls.

Information: town hall (*belediye*) and State Tourist Office.
Transport connections: bus, air and ship.

Excursions

1. **Boztepe** (3km). This hill just outside the town is famous for the thirteenth-century Byzantine church of **Theoskepastos**. It is hewn out of the rock, and contains some beautiful frescos. ⌘

2. **Meryemana Monastery** at **Sumela** (42km). The route goes along the E100 Erzurum road as far as **Maçka** (30km), and continues south-east along a rough, unmade road. It is another 12km to Sumela, which is a short way beyond **Kopru Kanali**. The monastery was built in the fourteenth century, and clings to the cliff face at the dizziest of heights. The frescos in the church are a masterpiece of Byzantine sacred art. ⌘

Troy (Truva)

25m (82ft) above sea level

Lonely and desolate, Troy must be the quietest of all the ruined cities along the Aegean coast of Asia Minor. And yet none of the others reveals so many remains, and none was as famous as Troy. Troy is certainly a site that brings the past back to life. Here beneath the parched earth that borders the entrance to the Dardanelles lies that jewel among cities that was fought over by famous heroes such as Hector and Priam, Achilles and Agamemnon. The walls stand lonely and abandoned on a bare, uninhabited plain that was once covered by the sea. This was the beach where the Greeks encamped for the 10 long years of the Trojan War, which was immortalised in Homer's *Iliad*. ⌘

Troy is about 30km from Çanakkale and 5km from the main E24 road. The site should be visited as early as possible in the morning. The area looks lovely in the gentle morning sun, with a pleasant breeze coming down from the Dardanelles. The sooner one gets there, the longer one has to appreciate its mystic wonder undisturbed by the noise of other tourists.

According to archaeologists, no less than nine cities have been built here during the history of Troy, each on top of the previous one. The second layer from the bottom was the one that Heinrich Schliemann discovered with the help of Homer's description. The beautiful treasure that he found there was believed by many to be that of King Priam.

Even the most careful excavation has failed to reveal the actual date when Troy was founded, but it no doubt goes well back into the Bronze Age. The second city was built in about 2600 BC, and was larger and more magnificent than the first. The valuable collections of armour and jewellery suggest that Troy II was extremely wealthy. The city guarded the entrance to the Dardanelles, and charged tolls from all the ships that passed through. Heinrich Schliemann among others claimed that Troy II was the city of Homer's *Iliad*. A thick layer of charcoal suggests that it was destroyed by fire.

Layers three to five contain little of special interest. Troy during that period was a small, rather insignificant little town. But Troy VI indicates a period of considerable expansion between 1900 and 1300 BC. The strong fortifications and extensive foundations suggest a city that was both large and wealthy. It was destroyed by an earthquake, but was rebuilt in equal splendour.

This was Troy VII, believed by most recent experts to have been the Troy of Homer's *Iliad*. In about 1200 BC it was destroyed by an unknown attacker. This event is now linked with the legend of the Trojan War. Now Troy was certainly occupied by the Phrygians, who also conquered the Hittites. So it may be that Troy VII was destroyed by the Phrygians.

For the next five centuries, Troy was overrun by people migrating between Europe and Asia. Nothing is known about Troy during this period. Troy VIII must have had some importance again, since it was visited by Alexander the Great in 334 BC. The ninth and final layer was that of the Roman city, which flourished considerably thanks to the patronage of Julius Caesar and Augustus. In AD 267 Troy was plundered by the Goths. But it quickly recovered — so much so that Emperor Constantine considered making it the capital of the eastern Roman empire. In the event he chose Byzantium.

Historians are just as uncertain about the date of Troy's demise as about that of its foundation. All that is known is that the city was abandoned some time soon after the Turkish conquest in the fourteenth century. The site quickly became overgrown; palaces, temples and theatres all fell into ruin and became buried beneath a thick layer of soil.

The buildings that have been uncovered are well signposted

and easy to identify, so only the most important of them need be mentioned here. The **city walls** with their many guard towers were built in the fourteenth century BC, and must therefore have belonged to Troy VI. The **pillared house** was named after the column stumps found inside it, which supported a roof or a second storey. The **columned house** had twelve columns supporting the roof, and also dates back to the fourteenth century BC.

The **Temple of Athena** was the city's main sanctuary, and stood at the top of the hill. All that now remains of it is a number of large stones and column shafts. Of particular interest is the surviving base from the so-called **holy fountain**, which was probably used by the priestesses, including perhaps Helen of Troy herself, in some kind of ceremonial function. The best-preserved building on the site is much later, being the small **Roman temple**.

Before leaving the site, it is important to visit the small **museum**, which contains an interesting collection of finds and facsimiles from the various periods in Troy's history. In front of it is a house-size statue of the famous wooden horse in which the Greek soldiers are supposed to have hidden in the last battle of the Trojan War.

Van

1,750m (5,740ft) above sea level; population 215,000

Van is the last important town before the Iranian border. It is difficult to get to by car or by bus, and there is only one air flight per week. The town is situated 5km from the eastern shore of Lake Van. A military garrison is stationed here, officially for the purposes of 'guarding the Iranian frontier', but probably also because the area has a large Kurdish population. The Kurds have frequently staged rebellions against the Turkish state. They also continue to carry on vendettas, though the practice is now strictly forbidden by the Turkish government.

There is nothing remarkable about the town itself. The broad main street has one or two hotels and restaurants. Men sit on the roadside, drinking *çay* as they wait for a car or a bus. In the evening the streets are patrolled by plain-clothes police, who check the restaurants and prevent crowds from assembling.

Landscape of the 'Wild East' of Turkey

Tourists are few, and are therefore likely to be stared at. Visitors should be extremely careful in their dealings with the local population, and should not, for example, be inveigled into going on outings with them. It is best not to walk through the villages, as the Kurds are often hostile to strangers.

⌘ There is a small **museum** in the main street. A few yards further on is the State Tourist Office, where one can find out about possible excursions to Old Van and to other places of interest in the area. The present town of Van was built as late as 1918. The former site, now known as Eski Van or Old Van, is 5km to the west near the lake shore, and at the foot of a massive rock platform that towers above the surrounding plain.

In about 850 BC this was the capital of the mighty kingdom of Urartu. At that time the rock was crowned by an invincible fortress, much of which remains to this day. Following the demise of Urartu, the Medes conquered it for a short time. But in the fifth century BC they gave way to the Persians. In the tenth and eleventh centuries AD, Van was the capital of the Armenian empire. After that it was overrun by Turks and Mongols. In 1387 it was razed to its foundations by the Mongol leader Tamerlane. In 1534 it became permanently Turkish.

During World War I, Van was so frequently plundered by both the Turks and the Russians that it never recovered. The town was rebuilt on a new site further east. The remains of Old Van became no more than a useful source of building stone for the new town. Nothing remains of Old Van apart from two mosques that have been partially restored and a few fragments of foundations.

Several cave entrances are clearly visible on the cliff face above. They lead to a whole labyrinth of passages and chambers, which are now believed to have been made by Urartians. They must have used them to hide in or to bury their dead. The entrances can only be reached by abseiling from above, so are accessible only to mountaineers and potholers. The labyrinths themselves have yet to be fully explored, so are not without their dangers either.

It is relatively easy to reach the top of the cliff via a path that goes up round the north side. It passes a small abandoned mosque in a cemetery. An enormous square chunk of basalt was found in a small niche under the cliffs here. It measured $1^1/_2$m (5ft) in height, and was engraved all over with cuneiform inscriptions that have so far proved impossible to decipher. According to some archaeologists it was placed here at the time of King Xerxes of Persia. But others believe that it is Urartian in origin and dates back to the reign of King Argistis I around 780 BC. There are one or two isolated caves around this side too, some of them decorated with Urartian inscriptions.

There is a marvellous view from the top of the cliff. To the east are the great mountains along the Iranian border. Across the lake to the north-west is Süphan Dagi (4,434m (14,543ft)), which Turks claim to be the real Mount Ararat where Noah's ark landed (as opposed to Agri Dagi or Ararat itself — see Route Eight). The fortification tower and the gateway were both built during the Ottoman period. A steep path through the gateway leads back down the north cliff to a spring at the bottom of the rock.

Visitors without a car are advised to take a taxi to Old Van and arrange to be picked up again at the spring 3 hours later. Visitors on foot should be wary of being too friendly with the inhabitants of the small nomad settlement next to the dirt road between Van and Old Van. Children will gather round to stare, while women will usually hide. The poorness of the dwellings is in stark contrast to the colourful clothes that the people wear.

Information: State Tourist Office.
Transport connections: bus and air.

Excursions

⌘ 1. **Toprakkale** (5km) is an Urartian site to the north-east of Van. It is not yet known whether it was built primarily as a town, a castle or a temple. But the site is undoubtedly Urartian in origin, dating back to the eighth century BC. The massive fortifications contain numerous foundation walls, including those of a temple dedicated to the god Chaldis. There is also an underground passage leading to a burial chamber.

2. The island of **Ahtamar** (35km) is the site of the famous ⌘ Armenian **church of St Cross**. It lies 4km off the lake shore and to the south-west of Van. The best way to get there is by hiring a boat with a guide from the nearby village of **Gevas**. The church was built in the early tenth century, and was originally part of a castle belonging to King Waspurakan. This was later turned into a monastery, which exerted a considerable influence throughout eastern Anatolia. The monks abandoned it in the mid-thirteenth century, possibly as a result of Seljuk raids. There is a beautiful frieze running all around the outside, showing scenes from the Old Testament such as Adam and Eve, Noah landing on Mount Ararat and Daniel in the lions' den. There are representations of the four evangelists under each of the gables. The lovely frescos on the inside were also painted in the tenth century. This church is probably the world's greatest monument to Armenian culture. For although it shows evidence of Arabic influence, there is no purer example anywhere of medieval Armenian art and architecture.

⌘ 3. **Susans Dagi** (20km). The area to the east of Van contains a large number of ruined monasteries, all of them built by Armenian Christians in the tenth century. The best-preserved of them are **Karmrou**, **Surp Grigor**, **Yedi Kilise** (**Seven Churches**) and **Senekerim Hohwanes**. They contain interesting frescos, and the last of these includes a beautifully-decorated church.

---

11 ADVICE TO TOURISTS

1. Travelling to Turkey

By Air

Most visitors to Turkey are unwilling to undertake a long and often difficult car journey. Air travel saves time and is much more comfortable. The routes are served by many large international companies, and there are charter flights available at considerable reductions. Details can be obtained from travel agents.

By Rail

The rail journey across Europe involves 50 or more hours of travelling on top of the ferry time from, for example, Harwich or Dover in England to Ostend in Belgium. The old Orient Express is no more, but there are still a few through carriages that cover the whole journey from Ostend to Istanbul. The Tauern-Orient Express, for example, goes from Ostend via Aachen, Frankfurt, Munich, Salzburg, Zagreb, Belgrade, Sofia and Edirne. The journey is long and sometimes uncomfortable, and the train is usually full of Turkish 'guest workers' returning home from Germany, Switzerland and Austria.

By Car

The car journey across Europe is no easier, as it is well nigh 3,000km from Ostend to Istanbul. The first part of the route is along fast motorways through Belgium, Germany and Austria: Ostend — Brussels — Liège (Belgium) — Aachen — Cologne — Frankfurt — Nuremberg — Munich (Germany) — Salzburg — Klagenfurt (Austria). The route becomes slower as it leaves the motorway and crosses into Yugoslavia. But the transit roads through Yugoslavia are still fairly good: Ljubljana — Zagreb — Belgrade — Nis. It is worth stopping for a break at the Bulgarian capital of Sofia before tackling the last part of the journey through Bulgaria to Edirne and Istanbul. The whole journey should take about four days, allowing more time for the slower sections through the Balkans.

Travellers with more time may care to extend their journey by another 350km for the sake of some sightseeing in Greece. For this one should drive south from Nis through Skopje and cross the border into Greece near the historic city of Salonica. The route continues along the northern coast of the Aegean through the fascinating town of Alexandroupolis. At least 6 days should be allowed for this option.

An even longer option is to turn off at Ljubljana and follow the beautiful Dalmatian coast to Dubrovnik and Kotor. From here the route turns inland through the gorgeous mountain scenery near the Albanian border (Cetinje — Titograd — Çakor — Tetovo), and joins the previous route at Skopje. 7 days are needed for this third option.

By Coach

Details about coach tours can be obtained from travel agents.

By Sea

One of the most desirable options is a cruise of the Adriatic and Aegean. One route goes from Trieste and Venice in Italy via Athens to Izmir and Istanbul. There are about three ships a week, and the cruise takes between 4 and 6 days. There is a similar option from Genoa. In both cases cars may be loaded on board.

The shortest ferry connection from Italy is from Naples to Izmir and takes 2 days. Some tour operators run cruises from Britain to the Turkish coasts. Details of all these options can be obtained from travel agents.

Inoculation

There are no compulsory inoculations for visitors to Turkey, but some are recommended. Turkey is liable to diseases such as hepatitis, typhoid, typhus, cholera, malaria and rabies, but the situation changes from year to year. Travellers are therefore advised to consult their doctors about what inoculations to have. At all events, travellers should take care to avoid drinking the water or eating unwashed fruit during their stay in Turkey. Health insurance is recommended.

2. Border Formalities

Passports and Visas

British and US visitors to Turkey need a valid passport only (without visa) for a stay of up to 3 months. A transit visa is required for visits to Bulgaria.

Currency Import and Export

1. Unlimited sums of foreign currency may be brought into Turkey from abroad. Sums taken out must be declared if they are more than 3,000 US dollars (£1800, 1 May 1987) or the equivalent in other currencies.

2. Unlimited amounts of Turkish currency may be brought into the country. Amounts taken out should not exceed 1,000 US dollars (£600, 1 May 1987) or equivalent. Turkish currency may be freely exchanged for other currency at a Turkish bank up to a maximum of 100 US dollars. Larger sums require a special exchange voucher from a Turkish bank.

Customs Regulations

A verbal decaration is normally sufficient, and luggage is not normally examined.

Import

An individual may bring the following items into Turkey without paying duty: personal effects; one portable typewriter; cosmetics; sports equipment; not more than one musical instrument; one camera with small attachments and up to ten rolls of film; five video cassettes (unrecorded); one slide projector; one pair of binoculars (with case); one portable radio; one cine-camera and projector up to 8mm; two albums without photos; one hand-held hairdryer; one hand-held massager; ten children's toys, with no more than one of each kind; 400 cigarettes; or 50 cigars; or 200g tobacco and 50 leaves of cigarette papers; 1kg coffee; 1.5kg instant coffee; 1kg tea; 1kg cocoa; 1kg confectionery; five 100cc bottles or seven 70cc bottles of alcoholic drinks (provided that there are not more than three of one sort); eau de cologne, lavender water or equivalent up to 1 litre; five bottles of perfume or scent.

Export

Presents and souvenirs may be taken out of the country up to a value of 15,000TL. Items costing more than 15,000TL must be accompanied by a special exchange voucher from a Turkish bank.

A new carpet requires proof of purchase (receipt). But an old carpet, old copper items and old pistols require an additional authorisation in the form of a certificate from the museum directorate. Otherwise the export of antiques and weapons of any sort is prohibited.

Personal valuables may only be taken out if they have been noted in one's passport on entry into the country or if they have been obtained by means of officially exchanged foreign currency.

Minerals found in the course of a field expedition may only be taken out with the written permission of the management of the Museum of Art and History at the MTA Institute in Ankara.

3. Advice to Motorists

Insurance and Driving Licence

A current national or international driving licence and a green insurance card (or Turkish third party insurance obtainable from any of the insurance agencies at the frontier post) are all that are required for drivers staying not more than 3 months. The car details are entered in the driver's passport on entry into the country.

Traffic Regulations

These are basically similar to those in Western Europe. Safety belts must be worn in all cars which are fitted with them. The maximum speed limits are 50km/h (31mph) in built-up areas and 99km/h (62mph) on other main roads.

Fuel

Filling stations are normally open all the time. Only high-octane fuel is recommended, as low-octane fuel may harm the engine. If only low-octane is available, one should avoid accelerating hard, change gear frequently and keep the engine revs moderate. The following makes of fuel are available in Turkey: BP, Petrol Ofisi, Türk Petrol, Mobil and Shell. Fuel prices are below most European ones.

Car Accidents

The police must be informed under all circumstances. The Turkish insurance authorities are only obliged to pay up on submission of an official police report.

If the vehicle is a complete write-off, the driver should report to the nearest customs office, who will take possession of the vehicle, issue an official receipt and delete the vehicle's endorsement on the driver's passport. This receipt will be required upon leaving the country. Without the deletion it is not possible to leave the country. If you have to leave your vehicle at the Customs it should be made clear that this is temporary. Any vehicle not claimed within 3 months will be considered abandoned.

Members of the AA, RAC or AAA should obtain a special overseas insurance document. In case of accident this can be presented to the Turkish Touring and Automobile Association, who will then bear the whole cost of transporting the damaged vehicle to Customs and to your home.

If you hold a credit cheque from your own motoring organisation, the Turkish Touring and Automobile Association (see Useful Addresses) will carry out the necessary repairs and forward the bill in Swiss Francs to your own country.

4. Accommodation

Turkey has few hotels that match up to the usual Western European standards. There are admittedly a few first-class hotels of the international Hilton variety in the three big cities of Istanbul, Ankara and Izmir, and also in some of the well-known seaside and health resorts. But these are the exception, and most Turkish hotels are somewhat basic in the facilities they offer.

The rooms are always kept clean. But it is not always possible to find rooms with integral bath, shower and toilet facilities. On the other hand, virtually all hotels provide hot and cold running water. Single rooms are uncommon, and guests who want a single room are often forced to pay for a second bed. In a few hotels single guests are even accommodated in dormitories. Sanitation is usually adequate. There are usually bath and shower facilities on every floor. But in central and eastern Turkey, toilets without seats are the norm.

Accommodation prices, whatever the category of hotel, are as variable as anywhere in Europe. The inflation rate is so high that it would be meaningless to suggest an average price. But at a rough estimate, accommodation prices are roughly half those in Western Europe.

Breakfast is usually charged separately, with a 10 per cent service charge. It is important to find out the exact price of a room before occupying it. Prices are normally 'standing', which means they cannot be reduced by haggling.

The Turkish Ministry of Culture and Tourism publishes an annual hotel guide, giving details of all recommended hotel accommodation, classified according to the standard of facilities offered. These hotels are given the name 'touristic'. This is available from all Turkish tourist offices, both inside and outside Turkey.There are other establishments registered with local authorities and these too correspond to a certain standard as regards facilities and services.

Camping

Only a small number of camping sites are listed by the Turkish Ministry of Culture and Tourism (see Useful Addresses). But all of them are close to main roads and/or near towns and holiday centres. They are usually open from April/May to October.

Also listed by the ministry are the camping sites of the so-called Mocamp Kervansaray chain, which are thought of as the modern equivalent of the old medieval caravanserais. They are well-appointed, and often have restaurants, guesthouses and sometimes even private beaches attached. Good facilities can be guaranteed for both campers and caravaners.

Camping on open land is not advisable. But if it proves unavoidable, one should at least camp close to a motel or a filling station. Camping on unofficial sites is inadvisable.

5. Travelling in Turkey

By Bus and Taxi

The towns provide plenty of good and extremely cheap bus services. The more important bus stops are often provided with shelters where the passengers may queue. Tickets can be bought from the driver or at a kiosk next to the bus stop.

Dolmus services are almost as frequent, and faster than buses. A *dolmus* is a kind of large taxi that follows specified routes like a bus and is recognisable by its yellow band. The fares are little more than for buses. Each passenger pays according to the distance travelled.

Taxis that the customer orders for himself charge similar prices to those in Britain and the USA. They are numerous in Turkish cities and are recognisable by their chequered black and yellow bands. Turkish taxi drivers are a law unto themselves, just as in other countries. It is vital to agree on a price beforehand. Hire-taxi fares are similar to those in Western Europe. If the driver has a taxi-meter, one should check that it has been set properly and for the correct tariff. The night tariff is higher. It is left to the driver to decide when the night tariff applies, but lighting-up time is usually the cut-off point.

If a taxi driver turns awkward, the best policy is to get him to stop at some large hotel and ask the doorman for assistance. This is normally more effective than asking a policeman, who will usually have no knowledge of English.

Car Hire

Hire-cars are available from Avis and Hertz, who have representatives in Istanbul, Ankara and Izmir. Their prices are very high by Turkish standards. Turkish car-hire firms are usually much cheaper. The best solution is to ask the hotel reception to recommend a good firm. Addresses can be obtained from tourist information offices or travel agents. An international driving licence is required for hiring a car in Turkey.

By Rail

Those travelling with the Turkish State Railways are advised to use express trains only. It takes days to travel from west to east along the Trans-Anatolian Railway (and back), and even short journeys can last several hours. The trains depart as early as five o'clock in the morning. Carriages are divided into first and second class.

Second-class carriages provide plenty of local colour, and fellow-travellers can be delightful to watch if one ignores the discomfort. Turks often carry items such as live poultry and sleeping blankets — everything bar the kitchen sink. It is not long before they begin to ask questions. And it is amazing what can be achieved using gestures and improvised sign language.

The trains travel slowly and stop frequently. Drinks are available on express trains, but it is better to provide for oneself. A 300km journey usually takes between 6 and 8 hours. But rail is the cheapest form of land transport in Turkey. Travellers from Istanbul to places in Asia Minor must first board the ferry to Üsküdar and walk the short distance to Haydarpasa Station.

By Coach

Long-distance coaches are faster than trains. These 'greyhounds of the Orient' provide services to towns all over Turkey. Travellers are again recommended to set off early in the morning. The coaches then travel throughout the day. The prices are half as much again as rail fares. Water and sweet-smelling oils are provided free of charge during the journey. When planning to travel long distances, one should book a ticket on the day prior to departure at the booking office of the coach firm concerned. Coaches depart from the bus station in large towns and from the centre of the town in smaller towns.

By Sea

Turkey provides a dense network of shipping routes covering the Black Sea, the Aegean, the Bosporus, the Sea of Marmara and the Mediterranean. There are routes linking the various ports with each other and with the neighbouring islands. However, not all of these services run daily, so it is important to find out when they run. The prices are even lower than coach and rail fares.

There is a wide choice of day excursions from Istanbul — to the Princes' Islands, for example. Full details are available from the State Tourist Office in the city.

By Air

Turkey is a large country so those wishing to visit the east of the country are recommended to travel at least part of the way by plane. It is unfortunate that the majority of air routes run in and out of Ankara. This means that travellers to places such as Van, Adana or Erzurum must invariably change planes at Ankara. Istanbul does, however, have direct air links with Ankara, Bursa, Izmir and Antalya. The state airline is called Türk Hava Yollari (THY), and has offices in all towns that are provided with an airport.

Student Travel in Turkey

Students and young people are entitled to certain price reductions on travel in Turkey and should carry proof of identity and age.

Air Travel Reductions

Turkish Airlines (THY) offer reductions of 10 per cent on domestic flights for students and up to 60 per cent on international flights.

Rail and Coach Travel Reductions

The Turkish State Railways (TCDD) offer all students a 10 per cent reduction on single and return fares within Turkey. Some students and young people under 26 are entitled to up to 50 per cent reductions on international rail travel between June and October. There are 10 per cent reductions on coach travel between major European cities.

Ferry Reductions

Turkish Maritime Lines offer students up to 15 per cent reduction on a single ticket and 25 per cent on a return on their international lines and up to 50 per cent reduction on domestic lines.

Museums, Shopping and Cultural Events forStudents

There is a wide choice of events organised specifically for students and young people. Some students are allowed free entry into all Turkish museums, and are entitled up to 50 per cent discounts at the cinema and concerts plus special reductions in certain shops and stores.

6. Food and Drink

The big international hotels offer correspondingly international fare, though even here the food is often cooked in lamb fat. Beef is uncommon, and pork is not served for religious reasons. Goulash is usually made with mutton. Turkish cooking is generally very fatty, which can sometimes lead to digestion problems. One way of avoiding this is by having plenty of white bread and rice with meat or vegetable dishes.

The modest street restaurant is often the best place for sampling Turkish cuisine. Large round pans are kept permanently hot, and are filled with stuffed artichokes, kebabs, shashlik, vegetable trimmings, mutton joints and rolls of meat. The waiters will go out of their way to provide just what the customer wishes. Often the customer will be ushered into the kitchen, where the cook will show off his many creations with generous gesticulations.

Among the typical main dishes are: *sis kebab* — small pieces of meat grilled on a skewer; *döner kebab* — slices of meat cut from a large spit roast; *koyun külbastisi* — grilled mutton; and *güveç* — a meat and vegetable casserole with tomatoes, paprika and rice. Specialities such as *dügün çorbasi* (soup with meatballs) and *iskembe çorcbasi* (tripe soup) taste a lot better than they sound.

The Turks are very fond of sweet desserts. Fruit compôte and fruit salad are very refreshing, and are made with fruit such as strawberries, figs, grapes and peaches. Ice cream should be avoided for health reasons. Safer options include cream slices, water melon, *baklava* (sweet pastry with walnuts, honey and pistachios) and *asure* or 'Noah's pudding'.

The Turks drink *raki* with their meals — a kind of anise spirit which they dilute with soda. Although clear, it turns milky when water is added. Those who cannot cope with *raki* should choose beer, coca cola or lemonade. After dinner a sweet Turkish coffee or *kahve* will settle the stomach. Tea (*çay*) is commoner than coffee, and is drunk out of small glasses throughout the day. *Ayran* is a yoghurt drink with a rather salty taste that is good for quenching the thirst. Wine (*serap*) is not often drunk because it is prohibited to Moslems for religious reasons. Mineral water can be ordered at all restaurants to accompany a meal.

Turkish restaurants represent fairly good value to visitors from abroad, but can be considerably more expensive in areas frequented by foreign tourists. In order to avoid being swindled by unscrupulous hosts, one should always ask for the menu (*yemek listesi*) at larger restaurants. Menus are usually written in both Turkish and English. If no menu is provided, then one should find out the prices before ordering. At all events it is important to check the bill carefully, as the waiter is sometimes rather slapdash about such matters. Tips are expected, and a 10 per cent service charge is added.

7. Tips for Travellers

Maps

Tourist information offices provide a free map of Turkey to the scale 1:1,850,000, plus a map of Istanbul. But car drivers will need more detailed maps for finding their way around the country.

Turkish Time

Turkey uses so-called Eastern European Time. This is 2 hours ahead of Greenwich Mean Time in summer and 3 hours ahead of Greenwich Mean Time in the winter. Summer visitors should put their watches and clocks 2 hours forward on arrival in Turkey. Orientals always have plenty of time. Everything will turn out for the best. Allah will provide. So why be in a hurry? Impatience is generally a subject for ridicule. If one asks for something in a hurry, not the slightest attempt is made to speed matters up. It is best to adjust to the Turkish pace — to trust in Allah, and when in difficulty to rely on Turkish warmth and hospitality.

Opening Hours

Shops are generally open from 9am-1pm and from 2-7pm (closed Sunday). Big stores in the main cities remain open throughout the lunch period. Banks are open from 8.30am-12noon and from 1.30-5pm (closed weekends). The bazaars close one hour before sundown.

Government offices are open from 8.30am to 12.30pm and from 1.30 to 5.30pm (closed at weekends).

Although Friday is the Moslem equivalent of Sunday in the Christian calendar, shops and banks normally remain open on Fridays. The 7-day week with a holiday on Sunday was one of the many 'westernising' reforms that Atatürk introduced. In Aegean and Mediterranean regions of Turkey, government offices and many other establishments are closed during the afternoon during the summer months.

Festivals and Events

In October all devout Moslems begin a month of daytime fasting, commonly known as Ramadan or in Turkish as *Iyi-bayramlar.* Moslems follow a lunar calendar, so the time of Ramadan varies in the Western calendar by as much as 20 days. It can, however, be calculated from the date of Easter. 2 months after the end of Ramadan is the traditional lamb feast. The observation of Ramadan does not affect the tourist in any way.

May and June are the months of the film festival in Antalya, with concerts and plays in the theatre at nearby Aspendus. There is a drama festival at the ancient theatre of Hierapolis near Denizli, in which a number of famous actors appear, and a similar festival at Pergamum. July is the period of flower festivals throughout Turkey. Other interesting events are the water melon festival at Diyarbakir and the sword dances at Brussa, both of which take place in September.

Here is a calendar of other festivals and events (official national holidays are marked by an asterisk):

1 January: New Year's Day *
15-16 January: Camel Wrestling Festival, Selçuk
23 April: National Independence Day, commemorating the founding of the Turkish parliament in 1920; Children's Day, with children's celebrations throughout the country *
1 May: Workers' Day and Spring Festivals *
5-12 May: Ephesus Arts and Culture Festival, Selçuk
19 May: Youth Day *
25-27 May: Pamukkale Fête, Denizli
27 May: Constitution Day *
20 June-15 July: International Istanbul Arts and Culture Festival
1 July: sea festivals in many coastal towns
1-31 July: Black Sea Fair at Samsun
7-31 July: folk festivals at Bursa
1 August: annual celebration of the end of the Turkish War of Independence
7-10 August: drama festival at Troy
17 August: Christian festival of the Assumption
20 August: opening of the Izmir International Festival
30 August: Victory Day, with military parades and processions in major cities *
17-22 September: Hittite Festival, Çorum
29 October: Republic Day, with military parades and processions in major cities *
14-17 December: festivals commemorating the famous philosopher Mevlâna Celal-Eddin Rumi, founder of the order of the whirling dervishes (celebrated primarily at Konya)

The performances of the Turkish State Opera and Turkish State Theatre (both at Ankara) are well known throughout the world. The Ankara and Istanbul Symphony Orchestras also have an international reputation. There are no summer performances. The concert and theatre season ends on 1 June and starts again on 1 October.

Souvenirs

Leather goods are invariably good value, including handbags, coats, jackets and suits. Carpets and handmade clothing such as skirts and blouses are also very reasonable. The copperware is good though expensive, and is still cheaper than goods of equivalent quality elsewhere. For smokers there is a wide choice of beautifully decorated hookahs and clay pipes available, which are again cheaper than one could expect elsewhere. Porcelain goods are also good value, with gorgeously decorated plates and ornamental tiles of all sizes.

Currency and Exchange

The main unit of Turkish currency is the Turkish Lira, which is abbreviated to TL. Exchange rates are changing all the time, thanks to the massive inflation rate in Turkey but at 1 May 1987 the exchange rate stood at £1 = 1294TL, $1 = 776TL.

One Turkish Lira consists of 100 kurus, abbreviated to kr. At the present time there are bank notes to the value of 10,000TL, 5,000TL, 1,000TL, 500TL, 100TL, 50TL, 20TL and 10TL; and coins to the value of 5, 10, 25, 50 and 100TL.

Taking Photographs

Photographs are a sensitive subject in Turkey. Portraits are prohibited in the Moslem faith, and Turks are traditionally hostile to being photographed. Men's reactions tend to vary. Older men normally refuse, though a generous tip can sometimes make them change their minds. Younger men, on the other hand, are often quite insistent on having their photographs taken. It is much more of a problem with women in veils, who usually get extremely annoyed. They dart out of sight with loud, angry protests. If their husband is around, it is advisable to disappear with similar agility! Photography is generally forbidden in mosques, except with special permission from the guards at the entrance.

Mosques

Five times a day, the 'Müezzin' calls the faithful to prayer. Shoes are strictly forbidden here, so visitors should enter barefoot or in stockinged feet. Women must wear scarves, and will not be allowed in wearing short skirts. Men in shorts are similarly excluded. The men pray in the main prayer chamber, while women are limited to the small columned side chambers. But women tourists are generally allowed to see into the main chamber.

Turkish Hospitality

Affluent Westerners are sometimes put off by the Turks, with their dark skin, black hair and fiery gaze. They often seem dusty, unshaven and shabbily dressed. But one must be careful not to apply one's own standards to a country that is relatively poor and has sparse water supplies.

The Turks have two ways of offering friendship: the handshake and the invitation to tea (*çay*). If either is offered, then one can accept without misgiving. The Turks have a well-developed sense of hospitality, and from the moment they offer it, they will go out of their way to satisfy the guest's every need. In such circumstances a tip would be taken as an insult. A better way of returning hospitality is with a glass of tea or a small gift of fruit, cigarettes or the like.

It is not easy to distinguish such friendly favours from services that require a tip. A tip is generally expected for all services that are carried out as part of a person's job, such as that of a waiter or a luggage porter. But if a tourist asks someone the way to somewhere and he takes him all the way, then this is a gesture of hospitality and a tip would be totally out of place. A packet of cigarettes would be more appropriate.

Clothing

Women's Dress

Women should be sensitive to Turkish rules of decency. Long trousers and scarves are an essential part of the holiday luggage. Turkish women show as little of their bodies as possible. In central Turkey baggy trousers are the norm. They are colourfully embroidered and reveal nothing. Miniskirts and hot pants might be just about acceptable in Istanbul, Ankara or Izmir, but elsewhere they are regarded as offensive and provocative. Women should be careful not to look men straight in the eye as this may also be thought of as provocative.

Men's Dress

The hot climate may seem a good reason for wearing shorts, but men may be best advised to leave these at home. Turkish men never show their legs in the street, and shorts are prohibited in mosques. The only exception is on the beach, where swimming trunks are the usual garb.

Shopping and Bargaining

When shopping it is important to be able to distinguish between swindling and honest bargaining. A tourist's lack of knowledge in such matters can often lay him open to being swindled by unscrupulous dealers. A waiter in a restaurant may, for example, put the wrong prices on the bill, add them up wrongly and give the wrong change. One should also beware of taxi and *dolmus* drivers, shoe cleaners and sandwich sellers.

Bargaining, on the other hand, is part and parcel of the business of honest trading, and haggling is a vital part of the buying and selling process. Visitors should never accept the first price offered by a street tradesman or at a bazaar. It is normal for the buyer and the seller to agree on a price somewhere in between the first two bids. So the buyer should reply to the first bid with a lower price than the one he intends to pay.

The seller may sometimes begin by trying to catch the buyer out and see if he knows the market. When this happens it is important to appear confident, and to argue the price down if one can. If this does not work, then one can simply walk away. But a long bargaining process usually ends up in the buyer's favour. The best rule of thumb is to try to knock the price down to about half the initial bid.

Hygiene

Care is essential in a hot, arid country such as Turkey, where sanitation often leaves much to be desired. Serious infectious diseases such as typhoid and polio are much commoner than in the affluent West. Visitors should wash their hands as much as possible, and on no account eat unwashed fruit, which has been shown to be the most potent carrier of disease. Ice cream is to be avoided, and is not particularly nice anyway. Well or tap water should never be drunk without first being boiled, although tap water in large cities is usually safe as it is heavily chlorinated.

8. The Language

Before starting to learn Turkish, it is worth noting that English is spoken in most parts of Turkey nowadays. But a few phrases in Turkish may be useful for understanding signs and instructions. Since Atatürk made the Roman alphabet standard in 1928, the older Arabic script has become confined to monument inscriptions and historic documents.

Turkish is a highly phonetic language — in other words, it is easy to work out how it is pronounced from the way it is written. The consonants **b**, **d**, **f**, **h**, **k**, **l**, **m**, **n**, **p**, **t**, **v** and **z** are not very different from the English. The letter **y** is always a consonant (as in **y**es), except possibly when it comes after a vowel to form a diphthong (**ay** sounds rather like the English pronoun 'I'). The **r** is always pronounced; the **g** is always 'hard' as in 'be**g**in'; the **s** is always as in 'bu**s**', and never as in 'busy'. The **c** is unusual in being pronounced like an English **j**.

Of the consonants with diacritics, **ç** is pronounced like **ch** in '**ch**in', while **s** is like **sh** in '**sh**in'. The **g** never occurs at the beginning of a word; it is almost silent, being a slight breathing at the most, and lengthening the preceding vowel; before an **e** or an **i** there is a very slight **y** sound.

Of the vowels, the **e**, the **u** and the dotted **i** are similar to the short English forms. The **a** is like a short **a** with a Welsh, Scottish or northern accent. The **o** is more rounded than the short **o** in English. The **ö** and the **ü** are pronounced much as they are in German, or similarly to the French **eu** and **u** respectively. The **i** or dotless **i** is pronounced rather like the Russian **y** or the northern Welsh **u**. The nearest English sound is the **er** in 'bitt**er**'. The capital letter is similarly dotted or undotted: **I** corresponds to **i**, while **i** corresponds to **i**.

Numbers

0 = sifir	6 = alti	12 = on iki	70 = yetmis
1 = bir	7 = yedi	20 = yirmi	80 = seksen
2 = iki	8 = sekiz	30 = otuz	90 = doksan
3 = üç	9 = dokuz	40 = kirk	100 = yüz
4 = dört	10 = on	50 = elli	1000 = bin
5 = bes	11 = on bir	60 = altmis	1001 = bin bir

Some Useful Words and Phrases

English — Turkish

yes — evet
no — hayir
hello — merhaba
goodbye (by person leaving) — allah ismarladik
goodbye (by person staying) — güle güle

please — lütfen
thank you very much — çok tesekkür ederim
OK — olur
open — açik
closed — kapali
exit — çikis
take care — dikkat
men's (toilets) — erkeklere
women's (toilets) — kadinlara
restricted zone — yasak bölge
excuse me — özür dilerim
What is the time? — saat kaç?
Where is the tourist office? — Danisma bürosu nerededir?
Have you a room free? — Bir odaniz varmi?
How much does the room cost? — Odamin fiati ne kadar?
I don't know — bilmiyorum
bread — ekmek
wine — sarap
grapes — üzüm
the bill, please — hesap lütfen
How long are we stopping here? — Burada nekadar zaman durac agiz?
Where is there a fuel station? — Bir benzin istasyonu nerededir?
Where is there a service station? — Bir oto tamirevi nerededir?
Please put it right — Bunu tamir edim
How do I get to...? — ...a giden yol hangisidir?
right — sag
left — sol
straight on — dogru
postage stamp — pul
Do you speak English? — Ingliz bilir misiniz?
I don't speak Turkish — Türkçe bilimiyorum
pardon? — efendim?

FURTHER INFORMATION

Museums and Monuments

Turkish museums are generally open every day of the week except Mondays. However, opening times should be checked with the local tourist information office before visiting. Often, in order to be able to take photographs in museums or at ruins, a fee is charged. Permission should always be sought. Admission charges have not been included as they are liable to fluctuation.

Archaeological Museums
At the boundary of the first courtyard of the Topkapi palace.
Istanbul
☎ 520 77 40/520 77 41
Includes the celebrated sarcophagus of Alexander the Great.
Open: daily, 9.30am-5pm, except Mondays.

Atatürk Museum
Halaskar Gazi C.250
Sisli
Istanbul
☎ 140 63 19
Atatürk lived in this three-storey house before the Turkish War of Independence.
Open: daily, except the 15th of each month, 10am-12 noon and 2-4.30pm except weekends.

Ayasofya Museum
Sultanahmet
Istanbul
☎ 522 17 50
Ancient basilica built by Constantine the Great. Fine Byzantine mosaics.
Open: daily, 9.30am-5pm, except Mondays.

Beylerbeyi Palace
Abdullah Aga C.
Beylerbeyi
Istanbul
☎ 333 49 60
Richly ornamented buildings.
Open: daily, 9am-12.30pm, 1.30-5pm, except Mondays and Thursdays.

Carpet Museum
Sultanahmet Camii bahçesi
Istanbul
☎ 522 53 32
Open: daily, 8.30am-5.30pm, except Sundays and Mondays.

Dolmabahçe Palace
Dolmabahçe
Istanbul
☎ 161 02 25
One of the most beautiful palaces in Istanbul; collections, paintings etc.
Open: daily, 9am-5pm, except Mondays and Thursdays.

Fethiye Museum
Katip Muslihittin S.4

Fatih
Istanbul
☎ 522 17 50
Open: only at weekends, 9.30am-5pm.

Istanbul Painting and Sculpture Museum
Besiktas
Istanbul
☎ 161 42 98
Founded 1937. Works of Turkish and foreign sculptors and painters; folk art, ceramics.
Open: daily, 8.30am-5.30pm, except Mondays and Tuesdays.

Kariye Museum
Kariye camii S.28
Edirnekapi
Istanbul
☎ 523 30 09
Byzantine memorial, fourteenth-century frescos and mosaics.
Open: daily, 9.30am-5pm, except Tuesdays.

Küçüksu Summer Palace
Küçüksu C.
Küçüksu
Istanbul
☎ 332 02 37
Open: daily, 9am-5pm, except Mondays and Thursdays.

Military Museum
Harbiye
Istanbul
☎ 148 71 15
Open: daily, 9am-1pm, 2-5pm, except Mondays and Tuesdays.

Municipal Museum
Saraçhanebasi
Istanbul
☎ 521 12 64
Daily life of Istanbul.
Open: daily, 9am-11.45am, 1-5.30pm, except weekends and the 5th of each month.

Museum of the Ancient Orient
Sarayiçi
Sultanahmet
Istanbul
☎ 520 77 42
The art of the ancient civilisations of the Middle East.
Open: daily, 9.30am-12 noon, 1-5pm, except Mondays.

Museum of Turkish Court Poetry
Galip Dede C.15
Tünel
Beyoglu
Istanbul
☎ 145 41 41
Open: daily, 9.30am-5pm, except Mondays.

Naval Museum
Besiktas
Istanbul
☎ 161 00 40
Open: daily, 9am-5pm, except Mondays and Tuesdays.

Topkapi Palace Museum
Sarayiçi
Sultanahmet
Istanbul
☎ 582 04 80
Maze of beautiful treasures in many buildings.
Open: daily, 9am-5pm except Tuesdays.

Yerebatan Palace Museum
(Cistern Basilica)
Yerebatan C.
Sultanahmet
Istanbul
☎ 522 12 59
Byzantine cistern with fine brick vaulting and Corinthian columns.
Open: daily, 9am-5pm, except Tuesdays.

Other places of interest, well worth visiting include:

Agora Ruins
Izmir
☎ 25 53 54

Archaeological Museum
Izmir
☎ 21 70 26

Atatürk Museum
Izmir
☎ 21 70 26

Museum of Anatolian Civilisations
Ankara
☎ 24 31 60

Museum of Ethnography
Ankara
☎ 11 95 56

Roman Baths
Ankara
☎ 10 72 80

Tower of Ankara
Ankara
☎ 11 25 40

Travelling to Turkey

By Air
See page 203. Turkish Airlines (THY) has regular flights in Boeing 707s, 727s, DC-9s Airbus and DC-10s to Ankara, Istanbul, Izmir, Dalaman and Antalya from the principal capitals and important cities of the world.

Most international airlines have daily flights from European cities to Istanbul's Atatürk international airport. Services to Ankara's international airport are slightly less frequent but there are THY connecting flights. There are THY reductions on return tickets for students and groups, for excursions (6 days minimum, 1 month maximum) and for inclusive tours of Turkey organised by travel agents.

By Car
See page 203.

By Coach
See page 204.

By Rail
Apart from the services outlined on page 203, there is a daily train departure for Istanbul from Venice by the 'Istanbul Express' via Trieste, Belgrade and Sofia, arriving at Istanbul in the morning of the third day. Wagon-lit services twice a week. There is also a daily service from Vienna for Istanbul by the 'Istanbul Express' and the 'Balkan Express' via Graz, Zagreb, Belgrade and Sofia.

By Sea
See also page 204. Turkish Maritime Lines have regular passenger ferry services to Turkish ports from Ancona (Italy) and Magosa (Northern Cyprus). The Turkish Maritime Lines car-ferry sails on the Ancona–Izmir–Ancona line every week from the end of May to the end of September.

There are also many ferries between Turkey and Greece linking Çesme and Chios, Kusadasi and Samos; Bodrum and Cos and Marmaris and Rhodes. Reductions are offered by TML on return tickets and cruises and for students, teachers, journalists, families and groups.

Travelling in Turkey

By Air

See page 210. Internal air fares are low and most planes radiate from Istanbul, Ankara and Izmir to all major cities. To obtain details of timetables and prices, contact your local THY office.

By Bus
See page 208

By Car
See page 206 and 209. Turkish road signs conform to the International Protocol on Road Signs. Archaeological and historical sites are indicated by yellow signposts. Traffic circulates on the right and the Turkish Highway Code is similar to those of European countries.

By Dolmus/Taxi
See page 208

By Rail
See page 209

By Sea
See page 210. The coastal services provided by Turkish Maritime Lines provide an excellent opportunity for sight-seeing. All of the services depart from the Eminönu or Karaköy sides of Istanbul or from Istanbul's Galata Bridge.

Advice to Motorists

In addition to the rules and regulations outlined on page 206, motorists should also observe the following:

Motor cars, minibuses, caravans, towed boats, motorbikes and bicycles may be brought into Turkey (for up to 3 months) without a *Carnet de Passage* or *Triptyque* (international pass). The vehicle is simply registered in the owner's passport and this registration is cancelled when the owner leaves the country.

For stays longer than 3 months, it is necessary to apply to the Turkish Touring and Automobile Association (see Useful Addresses) for a *Triptyque*, otherwise the vehicle must leave and re-enter the country at the end of 3 months.

If you wish to visit another country from Turkey without your vehicle you should take the vehicle to the nearest custom's authority (Gümrük Müdürlügü) so that the registration of the vehicle in your passport may be cancelled.

If your vehicle is stolen, it is necessary to obtain a certificate from the governor of the province so that the vehicle's endorsement on your passport may be cancelled before leaving the country.

Tips for Travellers

Animals
Domestic animals and hunting dogs must have a rabies vaccination certificate issued 48 hours before departure and it should be translated into Turkish by a Turkish Embassy or Consulate.

Clothing
On the Mediterranean, Aegean and Marmara, take light cotton clothing

with sweaters or cardigans for evenings. At the Black Sea and in Central and Eastern Anatolia take summer wear and warmer clothing for cool evenings.

Comfortable shoes are necessary for visiting archaeological sites and sun hats and sun glasses are advisable in high summer.

Headscarves should be worn by women when visiting mosques.

Credit Cards

Major credit cards such as American Express and Eurocard are generally accepted.

Currency and Exchange

See pages 205and 215. Exchange slips received for the conversion of foreign currency into Turkish Lira should be retained since you may be required to show them when re-converting Turkish Lira into foreign currency and when taking souvenirs out of the country (to prove that they have been purchased with legally exchanged foreign currency).

Customs Regulations

In addition to the regulations covered on page 205, the following must also be observed:

On Entry

1. Valuable items must be registered in the owner's passport for control upon exit.
2. Sharp instruments (including camping knives) and weapons may not be brought into the country without permission.
3. Bringing into Turkey, trading in or consuming marijuana and other narcotics is strictly forbidden and liable to heavy punishment.
4. Antiques brought into Turkey must be registered in the owner's passport to avoid difficulties on exit.

Electricity

220 volts AC in Asian Turkey; 110 volts AC in European Turkey including the European side of Istanbul.

Post

Turkish post offices are easily recognisable by their yellow 'PTT' sign. Major post offices are open from 8am-12 midnight, Monday to Saturday and from 9am-7pm on Sundays. *Post restante* letters should be addressed. 'Poste-restante' to the central post office ('Merkez Postanesi') in the town of your choice. You must produce identification when collecting your mail.

Telephones

Making an Internal Call

Dial 9. When you hear a continuous tone, dial the city code and telephone number. In a major city, a small sum is paid at a post office for a token which is slotted in the machine as soon as the number answers.

Outside major cities, it is sometimes necessary to request the call at a post office. Calls can be made 'normal', 'acele' (urgent) or 'yildirim' (very urgent).

Reduced rates for internal calls apply on Saturdays, Sundays and on holidays.

Some City Codes

Adana 711

Alanya 3231

Ankara 41
Antakya 891
Antalya 311
Bodrum 6141
Bursa 241
Edirne 1811
Istanbul 1
Izmir 51
Konya 331

Making an International Call
First dial 9 and after a new tone, dial 9 again. Then dial the country code and then the local code. There are no reduced rates for international calls.

International Codes
From Turkey to Britain 44
From Turkey to USA 1
To Turkey from USA 011 90
To Turkey from Britain 010 90

Some British Local Codes from Turkey
Aberdeen 224
Birmingham 421
Bristol 272
Cambridge 548
Cardiff 222
Derby 322
Edinburgh 31
Glasgow 41
Ipswich 473
Leeds 532
Liverpool 51
London 1
Manchester 61
Newcastle 632
Newport 633
Northampton 604
Nottingham 602

Some American Local Codes from Turkey
Atlanta 404
Chicago 617
Cincinnati 513
Cleveland 216
Colorado Springs 303
Dallas 214
Detroit 313
Hawaii 808
Hollywood 213
Houston 713
Kansas City 816
Las Vegas 702
Los Angeles 213
Miami 305
New York City 212
Palm Beach 3045
Philadelphia 215
St Louis 314
San Francisco 415

Useful Numbers
Unknown number information 011
Long distance operator 031
Telegrams by phone 041
Long distance enquiries 061
Long distance quick service operator 091
International operator 528 23 03
International enquiries 528 48 20

Tourist Information Offices

Adana: Atatürk Caddesi 13, ☎ 11323
Adiyaman: Atatürk Bulvari PTT yani, ☎ 1008
Afyon: Ambar Yolu 200, ☎ 3268
Akçakoca: Cumhuriyet Meydani, Santral Sokagi 2, ☎ 1554
Aksaray: Bankalar Caddesi, Belediye is Hani, Kat 1, ☎ 2474
Alanya: Iskele Caddesi 56, ☎ 1240

Anamur: Atatürk Bulvari 24E, ☎ 1677
Ankara: Gazi Mustafa Kemal Bulvari 26, ☎ 292930
Antakya: Vali Ürgen Alani 41, ☎ 12636
Antalya: Cumhuriyet Caddesi 91, ☎ 11747/15271
Avanos: Venassa Oteli Alti, ☎ 360
Aydin: Cine Caddesi 6, Kat 2, ☎ 4145
Ayvalik: Sahil Boyu, Atatürk Caddesi, Yali Apt, ☎ 2122
Balikesir: Gazi Bulvari 27, ☎ 11820/15702
Bandirma: Istiklâl Caddesi 26, ☎ 18444
Bergama: Izmir Caddesi, Asclepium crossroads, ☎ 862
Bodrum: 12 Eylül Meydani, ☎ 1091
Bolu: Stadyum Caddesi, ☎ 3632
Burdur: Cumhuriyet Meydani 4, ☎ 1078
Bursa: Atatürk Caddesi 82, ☎ 12359
Çanakkale: Iskele Meydani 67, ☎ 1187
Çesme: Iskele Meydani 8, ☎ 1653
Çorum: Sehir is Hani 1/5, ☎ 4704
Datça: Belediye Binasi, ☎ 163
Denizli: TCDD Gar Binasi, ☎ 13393
Diyarbakir: Lise Caddesi 24A, ☎ 12173
Edirne: Londra Asfalti 48, ☎ 1490
Edremit: Barbaros Meydani 1, ☎ 113
Egridir: Çarsi içi 15C, ☎ 1388
Elâzig: Istasyon Caddesi 35, ☎ 16572
Erdek: Hükümet Caddesi 6B, ☎ 1169
Erzurum: Cemal Gürsel Caddesi, ☎ 15697
Eskisehir: Iki Eylül Caddesi 175A, ☎ 17233
Fethiye: Iskele Meydani 1, ☎ 1527
Foça: Atatürk Mah, Foça Girisi, ☎ 122
Giresun: Fevzi Pasa Caddesi 18, ☎ 3560
Iskenderun: Atatürk Bulvari 49B, ☎ 11640
Isparta: Yeni Hamam Arkasi 2, ☎ 14438
Istanbul:
Mesrutiyet Caddesi 57B, Galatasaray, ☎ 145 6393/145 6875/ 145 6876/149 2782
Hilton Hotel, Cumhuriyet Caddesi, Beyoglu, ☎ 140 6300
Yolcu Salonu, Karaköy, Galata, ☎ 149 5776
Divanyolu Caddesi (near Blue Mosque) ☎ 522 4903
Yesilklöy Airport, ☎ 573 7399
Izmir:
Akdeniz Caddesi, Sokagi 6/22 ☎ 138910/142699
Cumhuriyet Meydani, Merkez PTT Girisi, ☎ 142147
Izmit: Ankara Asfalti 2, Kocaeli, ☎ 15663
Iznik: Kiliçarslan Caddesi 168, ☎ 433
Kars: Ortakapi Mah, Faikbey Caddesi, ☎ 2724
Kas: Cumhuriyet Meydani 6, ☎ 238

Kayseri: Kagni Pazan 61,
☎ 11190/19295
Kirklareli: Belediye Caddesi,
Kizilay is Hani,
☎ 1662
Kirsehir: Asikpasa Caddesi,
Cumhuriyet Meydani,
☎ 1416
Konya: Mevlâna Caddesi 21,
☎ 20926/11074
Köycegis: Kordon Golpark 1,
☎ 87
Kusadasi: Iskele Meydani,
☎ 1103
Kütahya: Yeni Hükümet Konagi,
☎ 2618
Malatya: Sivas Caddesi 5/1,
☎ 17733
Manavgat: Antalya Caddesi 27B,
☎ 1645
Manisa: Dogu Caddesi,
8 Eylül is Hani,
☎ 2541
Marmaris: Iskele Meydani 39,
☎ 1035
Mersin: Inönü Bulvari Limani
Girisi,
☎ 11265/12710
Mugla: Marmaris Caddesi 7A,
☎ 1261
Nevsehir: Lale Caddesi 22,
☎ 1137
Nigde: Vakif is Hani 1D,
☎ 1261
Ordu: Sahil Caddesi,
Belediye Binas,
☎ 4178
Samsun: Irmak Caddesi,
Özel Idare is Hani,
A-Blok 2,
☎ 11228
Selçuk: Atatürk Mah,
Efes Müzesi Karsisi 35,
☎ 328
Silifke: Gazi Mah,
Atatürk Caddesi 1/2,
☎ 151
Silvan: Gazi Caddesi 90B,
☎ 603
Sinop: Iskele Meydani 2A,
☎ 299
Sivas: Hükümet Binasi,
☎ 12850
Sungurlu: Ankara Caddesi 36,
☎ 752
Tekirdag: Atatürk Bulvari,
Iskele Yani,
☎ 2083
Tasucu: Atatürk Caddesi,
Gümrük Meydani 18A,
☎ 234
Trabzon: Taksim Caddesi 31,
☎ 12722/13827
Urfa: Alfaltyol 3D,
☎ 2467
Ürgüp: Kayseri Caddesi 37,
☎ 59
Van: Cumhuriyet Caddesi 127,
☎ 2018
Yalova: Iskele Meydani 5,
☎ 2108

Useful Addresses

Accommodation

For a comprehensive list of hotels, camp sites and youth hostels, contact the Turkish Tourist Office, travel agents or your local Youth Hostel Association office.

American Youth Hostels, Inc.
1332 'I'Street NW
Washington DC 20005
☎ (202) 783 61 61

YHA (England & Wales)
14 Southampton Street
London WC2E 7HE
☎ (01) 836 8541

Advice and Information

British Consulate
Tepebasi
Mesrutiyet Cad. 34
Istanbul
☎ 144 75 40/144 75 45/9

British Consulate
Mahmut Esat Bozkurt Cad. 49
Izmir
☎ 21 17 95

British Embassy
Sehit Ersan Cad. 46/A
Çankaya
Ankara
☎ 27 43 10

Turkish Consulate General
Rutland Lodge
Rutland Gardens
London SW7
☎ (01) 589 0360

Turkish Consulate General
1990 Post Oak Blvd
Suite 1300
New York
☎ (212) 622 5849
(212) 622 0324

Turkish Embassy
43 Belgrave Square
London SW1X 8PA
☎ (01) 235 5252

Turkish Embassy
1606/23rd St NW
Washington DC 20008
☎ (202) 387 3200

Turkish Tourist Office (GB)
170/173 Piccadilly
London W1V 9DD
☎ (01) 734 8681/2

Turkish Tourist Office (USA)
821 United Nations Plaza
New York
NY 10017
☎ (212) 687 21 94
or
2010 Massachusetts Avenue NW
Washington DC 20026
☎ (202) 833 84 11

United States Consulate
Mesrutiyet Cad. 104
Istanbul
☎ 143 62 00/09

United States Consulate
Atatürk Cad. 386
Izmir
☎ 13 21 35

United States Embassy
Atatürk Bulvari 110
Ankara
☎ 26 54 70

United States Embassy
Atatürk Cad. 92/3
Izmir
☎ 13 21 35

Automobile Organisations

Türkiye Turing ve Otomobile Kurumu
(Turkish Touring and Automobile Association)
Halaskârgazi Cad. 364
Sisli
Istanbul
☎ 146 70 90/521 65 88
or
Adakale Sokagi 4/11
Yenisehir
Ankara
☎ 31 76 48/49
or
Atatürk Bulvari 370
Alsançak
Izmir
☎ 21 71 49

Cultural Associations

British Association
Atatürk Cad. 328/7
Izmir
☎ 21 44 63

British Council
Cumhuriyet Cad. 22-24
Ege Han
Elmadag
Istanbul
☎ 146 30 73

British Cultural Association
Adakale S.27
Yenisehir
Ankara
☎ 31 77 88

Ministry of Culture and Tourism
Gazi Mustafa Kemal Bulvari 33
Ankara

Turkish-American Cultural Institute
Cinnah Cad. 20
Kavaklidere
Ankara
☎ 26 26 44

United States Information Service
Mesrutiyet Cad. 104
Tepebasi
Istanbul
☎ 143 62 00

United States Information Service
Atatürk Cad. 386/6
Izmir
☎ 21 36 44

Travel

British Airways
Selancik Cad. 17/1
Ankara
☎ 34 24 18

British Airways
Cumhuriyet Cad. 10
Elmadag
Istanbul
☎ 148 42 35

British Airways
Sehit Fethibey Cad. 120
Izmir
☎ 14 17 88

Turkish Airlines (THY)
11-12 Hanover Street
London W1
☎ (01) 499 9247/48

Turkish Airlines
Hipodrum Cad.
Car Yani
Ankara
☎ 12 49 00
or
Abide-i Hürriyet Cad.
Vakif Ishani Kat: 21 54-156
Istanbul
☎ 140 23 16
or
Büyuk Efes Oteli Alti
Izmir
☎ 14 12 20

Pan American Airlines
Hilton Hotel Arcade
Elmadag
Istanbul
☎ 147 45 30

Pan American Airlines
Atatürk Bulvari 175/3
Ankara
☎ 18 21 70

Pan American Airlines
Vasif Çinar Bulvari
Izmir
☎ 21 42 62

Turkish Maritime Lines (Türkiye Denizcilik Kurumu TAO)
World Trade Centre

1 St Katherine's Way
London
☎ (01) 265 1731

Turkish Maritime Lines
Ulus Ishani
Ankara
☎ 12 38 18
or
Rihtim Cad.
Karaköy
Istanbul
☎ 144 02 07/149 92 22
or
Yeni Liman Alsançak
Izmir
☎ 21 00 77/94

TWA
Cumhuriyet Cad. 135
Elmadag
Istanbul
☎ 140 41 65

Union of Turkish Travel Agencies (Türsab)
Cumhuriyet Cad. 187
Istanbul
☎ 146 02 32/37
or
Atatürk Bulvari 107/72
Ankara
☎ 18 07 75

Vehicle Hire

Avis
Head Office
Tramvay Cad. 72
Kuruçesme
Istanbul
☎ 168 80 40
or
Yedikuyular Cad. 414
Elmadag
Istanbul
☎ 141 29 17

Hertz
Head Office
Cumhuriyet Cad. 295
Harbiye
Istanbul
☎ 141 53 23

Help in Turkey

Ankara
Ambulance ☎ 31 75 75
Health Emergency ☎ 19 44 46
Police ☎ 11 95 55

Bursa
Ambulance (private service) ☎ 19556
Fire ☎ 11010
Police ☎ 48300

Istanbul
Ambulance (private service) ☎ 145 50 50 & 521 91 50
American Hospital ☎ 148 60 30
Atatürk Airport ☎ 573 35 00 & 573 35 10
Fire ☎ 524 11 24
Health Emergency ☎ 521 15 95
Police ☎ 166 66 66
Tourism Police ☎ 528 53 69

Izmir
Ambulance (day) ☎ 13 99 58
(night) ☎ 25 25 05

Road Rescue
Ankara: ☎ 15 83 38
Edirne: ☎ 1170
Istanbul: ☎ 353 35 11

Emergencies Anywhere in Turkey
Fire ☎ 00
Police ☎ 66 66 66
Ambulance varies by town — number to be found in front of White Pages of directories.

INDEX

Index to Places

A

Abana 75
Abydus 153
Adana 107, 110, 118, 125
Adapazari 65, 99
Adiyaman 114
Adrianople 156
Afyon 98, 109, 126
Agri 122, 123
Ahtamar 122, 202
Akdogan 88
Akhisar 89
Akköy 94
Aksaray 117
Aksehir 109
Aksu 102
Alacahüyük 130, 146
Alalakh 135
Alanya 103, 127
Aliaga 88
Altinoluk 87
Anamur 104
Ankara 68, 75, 82, 128
Antakya (Antioch) 112, 133
Antalya 100, 136, 138
Ararat 122, 123
Arrian Pass 111
Arslantepe 183
Askale 80, 81, 163
Aspendus 102, 137, 138
Assus 86
Avanos 167
Avcilar 169
Ayancik 75
Aydincik 104
Ayvacik 86
Ayvalik 87

B

Bafra 77
Bahçesultan 72
Balat 94, 186
Balikesir 89
Bandirma 83
Bayburt 79
Bayrakli 170, 174
Bedirge 112
Behramkale 86
Belen 112
Bergama 87, 138, 175
Bigadiç 89
Bilecik 98
Bingöl 121
Bitlis 120
Black Sea 49
Bodrum 96, 142
Bogazkale 82, 130, 144
Bolaman 77
Bolu 67
Bolu Pass 65
Bornova 89
Bosporus 49
Bozca Ada 86
Bozüyük 72
Bozyazi 104

Bulak 68
Bunarbasi 86
Bünyan 115
Burdur 100
Bursa 73, 83, 90, 147
Büyük Ada 49
Büyük Adasi 78
Büyükçekmece 63

C
Çanakkale 85, 152
Çankiri 75
Çardak 98
Çarsamba 77
Cavusin 169
Çay 109
Celendiris 104
Çeltikçi 100
Cerikli 82
Çesme 175
Ceyhan 110, 125
Çifteler 70, 165
Cilvegözü 113
Clarus 92
Clazomenae 174
Colophon 91, 174
Colossae 97
Corasium 105
Çorlu 62
Corycian Caves 105
Corycus 106
Cnidus 185
Cumaovasi 91

D
Dag 100
Dardanus 85
Darica 74
Datça 185
Degirmendere 91
Denizli 97, 100, 109, 154
Dide *see* Tigris
Didyma 94, 174, 183
Dinar 98, 100, 109
Diyarbakir 119, 120, 155
Düzce 65

E
Edirne 49, 156
Edremit 87
Elâzig 119, 121
Eleskirt 123
Elmadag 75, 82
Ephesus 93, 157, 174, 183
Ercis 122
Erdek 83
Eregli 108
Ergani 119
Erzin 111
Erzincan 81
Erzurum 81, 124, 162
Eski Kâhta 114
Eski Malatya 183
Eskisehir 71, 98, 164
Euphrates 81
Eynesil 78
Ezine 86

F
Fatsa 77
Fethiye 165

G
Gazi 132
Gazipasa 104
Gebze 73, 90
Gemlik 72
Gerede 67
Gerze 77
Gevas 122, 202
Geyikli 86
Giresun 77
Gölbasi 114
Golcük 73

Gönen 83
Gordium 69, 166
Görele 78
Göreme 115, 167, 178
Güllük 138
Gümüshane 79
Gürün 115
Güvenç 113

H
Halicarnassus 96, 142
Hamidiye 70
Harbiye 135
Hattusa 82, 144
Havsa 64
Heraclia 94
Hereke 73
Hierapolis 155, 187
Honaz 97
Hopa 78
Horasan 123

I
Iconium 179
Ilica 80
Ilgin 109
Ihlara 118
Imisehir 71, 164
Inebolu 75
Inegöl 72
Inönü 72
Intepe 85
Iskenderun 112
Islâhiye 113
Istanbul 28ff, 63, 65, 74, 99
—Ahmed III's Well 33
—Asian Castle 57
—Atik Valide Camii 60
—Beyazit Mosque 47
—Belerbeyi 58
—Beyoglu 28
—Blachernae Palace 53
—Blue Mosque 41
—Bosporus 49
—Büyük Camii 60
—Çinili Camii 60
—city museum 49
—city walls 52
—Constantine's Column 44
—Dolmabahçe Palace 56
—Egyptian Bazaar 47
—Egyptian Obelisk 41
—Europa Bridge 58
—European Castle 56
—Executioner's Well 35
—Eyüp Camii 53
—Fethiye Camii 51
—Galata 33, 55
—Galata Bridge 32
—Galata Tower 33, 55
—Grand Bazaar 44
—Great Cemetery 60
—Hagia Sophia 37
—hippodrome 41
—Kadiköy 60, 74
—Kahriye Mosque 51
—Kaiser Wilhelm's Well 41
—land fortifications 52
—Leander Tower 59
—Maritime Museum 56
—Mihrimah Mosque 51
—Mollazeyrek Mosque 50
—Nuruosmaniye Camii 44
—Ortaköy 58
—Prince's Mosque 48
—Rose Mosque 50
—Serasker Tower 47
—Snake Column 41
—Stambul 28, 33
—St Irene's Church 37
—Süleymaniye Mosque 48
—Sultan Mehmed Mosque 50
—Sultan Selim Mosque 50
—Taksim Gardens 56

—Tekfur Saray 52
—Topkapi 33
—University 48
—Üsküdar 28, 58
—walled column 41
—Yediküle Palace 52
—Yeni Valide Mosque 33, 60
—Yerebatan Cistern 41
Ivriz 108
Izmir 88, 91, 170
Izmit 73, 83, 90, 99
Iznik 73

K
Kadiköy 60, 74
Kâhta 114
Kalabak Saray 87
Kale 79, 97, 119
Kalecik 75
Kandilli 80
Kandira 65
Kanis 178
Karabey 83
Karaman 181
Karamürsel 73
Karapinar 108
Karatas 125
Karatepe 71, 110, 125, 164, 175
Kartal 74, 83, 90
Kastamonu 75
Kayas 75
Kaymakli 117
Kayseri 115, 167, 176
Kemah 81
Kesan 63
Kesap 78
Kilbasan 181
Kirikhan 113
Kirikkale 82
Kirka 70, 165
Kizilcahamam 68
Kizilirmak 82
Kizkale 106
Konya 108, 118, 179
Konya Alti 100
Kopru Kanali 197
Korkuteli 100, 138
Kültepe 178
Kumkale 85
Kursunlu 72
Kusadasi 182
Kütahya 98

L
Labranda 96
Lake Abant 67
Lake Apolyont *see* Lake Ulubat
Lake Ulubat 83
Lake Van 121
Lâpseki 85
Lystra 181

M
Maçka 78,197
Maden 119
Madensehir 181
Magnesia 93, 174, 183
Malatya 114, 119, 124, 130, 183
Malkara 63
Manavgat 102, 138
Manisa 89
Maras 113
Marmaris 184
Melania 104
Meriamlik 105
Mersin 106
Meryemana 78, 197
Milas 96
Miletus 94, 174, 183, 185
Misis 110
Mugla 96

Mus 121
Mustafakemalpasa 90
Myrina 87

N
Nara 153
Narli Kuyu 105
Nevsehir 117, 167
Nimrud Dagi 114

O
Obruk 118
Odun Iskele 86
Olba 105
Oglacki 69
Ordu 77
Orhangazi 73
Ortahisar 115, 169
Ortaklar 93
Osmaneli 99

P
Pacarcik 114
Pamukkale 97, 155, 187
Pamukova 99
Pasinler 123
Patnos 122
Payas 111
Pendik 74
Perga 102, 137, 189
Pergamum 87, 138, 175
Persembe 77
Pertek 124
Pessimus 69
Phrygian rock tombs 70, 126, 165
Pinarbasi 115
Polatli 69
Pompeiopolis 107
Poyra 72
Priene 93, 174, 183, 190
Princes' Islands 49
Pülümür 124

R
Refahiye 81
Resadiye Pass 114
Rize 78

S
Sam`al 113
Samandag 135
Samsun 77, 191
Sariköy 85
Sea of Marmara 49
Seferihisar 174
Selçuk 93, 159
Seleucia 135
Selimiye 95
Selinus 104
Serçinaus 94
Serik 102
Seyitgazi 70
Side 102, 137, 192
Sigacik 174
Sile 65, 99
Silifke 105
Silivri 62
Sille 181
Silvan 120
Sindirgi 89
Sinop 77, 194
Sivas 81, 194
Sivrihisar 69
Smyrna 88, 170
Sögüt 71
Söke 93
Sultandagi 109
Sultanhani 118, 181
Sumela 78, 197
Sungurlu 144
Susanoglu 105
Susans Dagi 202

T
Tahir 123
Tahir Pass 123
Tarsus 107
Tatvan 119, 121
Tavas 97
Tekirdag 63
Telmesus 166
Temelli 69
Tercan 81
Terme 77
Termessus 100, 138
Tigris (River) 119, 156
Tirebolu 78
Tokat 71, 164
Toprakkale 202
Tortum 163
Trabzon (Trebizond) 78, 195
Troy 85, 154, 197
Truva *see* Troy
Tunceli 124
Türkoglu 113
Tutluca Tepe 72

U
Uçhisar 116, 169
Ulu Dagi 151
Ulukisla 108
Ulunzaburç *see* Olba
Ünye 77
Ürgüp 115, 167, 169, 178
Urla 174
Üsküdar 58, 74, 83, 99
Uzunköprü 64

V
Vakfikebir 78
Van 122, 199

X
Xanthus 166

Y
Yalova 73, 83, 90
Yassihüyük 69, 166
Yatagan 96
Yazilikaya 146
Yeniçaga 67
Yenihisar 94
Yeralti Sehri 117
Yerköy 82
Yesilköy 63
Yildizeli 81
Yilanlikale 110
Yozgat 81, 82

Z
Zara 81
Zigana Pass 79
Zincirli 113

Index to Subjects

A
accidents 206
accommodation 207
air travel 203, 210, 222, 223
animals 223
Armenians 22
Atatürk 17

B
bargaining 217
boat travel 204, 210, 222, 223
buses 208
Byzantines 12

C
camping 208
car hire 209
car travel 203, 206, 223
climate 20
clothing 216, 223
coach travel 203, 210
credit cards 224
currency 205, 215, 224
customs 205, 224

D
dolmus 208

E
education 24
electricity 224
exchange rate 215

F
festivals and events 213
flora and fauna 25
food and drink 211
fuel 206

G
geography 8
Greeks 10, 22

H
health 204
help 230
history 9
Hittites 10
hospitality 216
hygiene 217

I
inoculation 204

K
Kurds 22

L
language 217

M
maps 212
Mongols 13
mosques 215
Muhacirs 24
museums 220

O
opening hours 213
Ottomans 13

P
passports 205
people of Turkey 21
Persians 10
photographs 215
post 224
public holidays 214

R
rail travel 203, 209, 222
Romans 11

S
Seljuks 13
shopping 217
souvenirs 214
student travel 210

T
taxis 208
telephones 227
time 213
tourist offices 225
traffic regulations 206

U
Urartu 10
Useful Addresses 227
useful words and phrases 218

V
vegetation 27
visas 205